Psychoanalysis and Psychotherapy in China

T0352606

Volume 1, 2015

PHOENIX
PUBLISHING HOUSE
firing the mind

Psychoanalysis and Psychotherapy in China, Volume 1

British Library Cataloguing in Publication Data

Psychoanalysis and Psychotherapy in China—Volume 1

ISBN: 978-1-912691-47-0
(Print) ISSN 2632-0134
(Online) ISSN 2632-0142

Published and distributed by
Phoenix Publishing House, 62 Bucknell Road, Bicester, Oxfordshire OX26 2DS

Cover image: Autumn Forest pavilion, by Bada Shenren (detail), reproduced by permission of Shanghai Museum.

Address for All Articles and for Books for Review:
David E. Scharff, Editor, *Psychoanalysis and Psychotherapy in China*,
6612 Kennedy Drive, Chevy Chase, Maryland 20815
Fax: +1 301 951-6335
E-mail: davidscharff@theipi.org

Produced by
The Studio Publishing Services Ltd

Printed in Great Britain

www.firingthemind.com

CONTENTS

ANNOUNCEMENT AND
CALL FOR PAPERS

Psychoanalysis and Psychotherapy in China
A new international journal

This peer-reviewed journal proposes to explore the introduction of psychoanalysis, psychoanalytic therapy, and the wider application of psychoanalytic ideas into China. It aims to have articles authored by Chinese and Western contributors, to explore ideas that apply to the Chinese clinical population, cultural issues relevant to the practice of analysis and psychotherapy, and to the cultural interface between Western ideas underpinning psychoanalysis, and the richness of Chinese intellectual and philosophical ideas that analysis must encounter in the process of its introduction.

The journal will be published by Phoenix Publishing House twice yearly, first in English and is also planned to be published in Chinese through a collaboration with a Chinese partner. We will feature theoretical and clinical contributions, philosophical and cultural explorations, applications such as the analytic study of art, cinema and theatre, social aspects of analytic thought, and wider cultural and social issues that set the context for clinical practice.

We are now asking for submissions for the journal.

We welcome contributions that are volunteered as well as those commissioned by the editors. We expect that this journal will become a principal resource for the growth of psychoanalysis and psychotherapy in China.

Editorial Introduction to
Psychoanalysis and Psychotherapy in China

David E. Scharff, Editor-in-Chief

It is a great pleasure that, after two years of preparation, the inaugural issue of *Psychoanalysis and Psychotherapy in China* goes to press. It is the result of the inspiration of Oliver Rathbone, publisher of Karnac Books, who saw from Karnac's publication of the recent first international books on the development of psychoanalytic therapy in China that this rapidly growing field deserved an international journal devoted to it, just as there are important regional journals in Europe, Australia, and North and South America.

I have been joined in this endeavour by an eminent group of members of the editorial board, from China and internationally, who have supported this effort, recruited, contributed, and reviewed papers for this issue. Without them, the effort would not have been possible, but more importantly, their collective experience, judgement, wisdom, and enthusiasm makes the launching of this journal such a significant addition to the project of development of psychoanalysis worldwide.

It is intended that this journal be published both in English and in Chinese, both from London and New York, and from China. As we go to press, the practicalities of publishing in China are still to be worked out, but it is important from the outset to state our intention to publish also in Chinese.

Psychoanalysis took root in many countries around the world in the twentieth century, but China has special significance. It was, of course, the largest country from which analysis was completely excluded. It is well known that psychoanalysis, which had barely begun to spread in the first part of the twentieth century, was then forbidden, along with all things western, from 1949 until the Chinese opening up began in the 1980s. It was not only the banning of psychoanalytic thought that marked China in this period. There was also an absence of an effective mental health system during times of great need in China because of war, famine, industrial collapse, enormous population growth, and changes in social structure. This was followed by the economic opening up since about 1980, with further changes in family structure through the one child policy, new policies of entrepreneurship, economic growth, urbanisation, and the interpenetration of China by the west during the four decades since Mao.

Psychoanalysis and Psychotherapy in China, Volume 1, 2015: pp. viii–xi.

Many of our western colleagues have been eager to help China from early on. The Sino–German and Sino–Norwegian programmes, and, in the past few years, the China–American Psychoanalytic Alliance, the Sino-British programme, and others have produced an array of trainings that have begun the process of producing a real psychotherapeutic presence in China. My own contribution has principally been through a programme begun five years ago in Beijing for training in psychoanalytic couple and family therapy, offered from the International Psychotherapy Institute of Washington, DC. The more recent trainings offered in Beijing and Shanghai by the International Psychoanalytic Association have made formal psychoanalysis, and, to my mind more importantly, rigorous psychoanalytic thought, a resource inside China itself.

These western offerings have been planted in fertile ground. Mental health systems are growing rapidly, using the more advanced technologies of the west. The need for services is enormous as China undergoes radical changes through its rapid economic growth, a change from a rural economy to a manufacturing and service economy, radical change in family structure, and increasing levels of education. Many senior Chinese psychiatrists and psychologists have journeyed to Europe and the USA for training and the exchange of ideas, and many Western mental health workers have travelled to China. Additionally, the rapid expansion of distance communication technology for both treatment and psychotherapy education has begun to change the way psychotherapy education and service delivery occur.

Psychoanalytic trainings and ideas are now among the most popular mental health offerings in China. There are growing numbers of trainees, and, as well, growing interest in academic institutions. While those of us who value this approach can feel satisfaction with the appeal of psychoanalytic therapy to the Chinese, that very appeal brings with it an obligation. While China as a whole is prospering, it is as true there as it is in the west that mental health remains underfunded and less developed than it should be. There is opportunity, but that comes with the need to support our colleagues there who work with limited training resources and great service burdens.

There is another caveat in the encounter between east and west that working with psychoanalysis and analytic therapy in China represents. In the overall history of introducing western ideas and methods into China, things have only worked well when this is done by adapting to the Chinese mind and tradition, to the deep structure of Chinese thought and social organisation. Several recent publications have continued a tradition of comparing the structure of Chinese thought with that of the west, especially with the philosophical and practical structure of psychoanalysis. But now that there is such interest in psychoanalytic thought, and in the application of analytic therapies to the mental health needs of China, what had been a philosophical exercise has developed a certain urgency. There is no doubt in my mind that the introduction of psychoanalytic thought and practice into China will change analysis itself worldwide. That has been true historically with its introduction into the UK, France, the USA, and South America from its origins in German-speaking Europe. So we have to expect a similar evolution in the encounter with China and with Chinese thought and language. But Chinese thought and the Chinese language are vastly more different from the western tradition than are the Americas from Europe. The identification of the Chinese self with loyalty to a hierarchy and to the group is well known, which leads to a culture more influenced by "loss of face" than of guilt in the western sense. So also is the difference between a Confucian–Taoist–Buddhist mentality and that derived from Greco-Roman and Judeo-Christian ethics. But we also must reckon with the Chinese penchant for metaphor, subtlety, and indirection in all spheres of discourse, which contrasts with western (or at least American) preference for directness and plain speaking. When we undertake to introduce our ways of thinking and working to such a large and influential population, to such an industrious and serious group of colleagues, we must be prepared to learn from them equally as we offer an opportunity for them to learn from us.

In this spirit, this journal is conceived as a meeting place of cultures, as a place in which the issues of this important world encounter can be documented and examined. It is intended to be an intercultural journal in which theory and clinical experience can be presented and discussed. At a practical level, the editorial board is composed equally of eminent Chinese and western colleagues who share an interest in the introduction and development of psychoanalysis in China. We plan to have articles from both Chinese and western contributors, and to have them discuss each other's presentations and ideas.

This first issue represents these hopes well. We begin with a scholarly history of the development of psychotherapy in China by a Taiwanese author trained anthropologically in the USA and now working in Australia, followed by clinical papers from western and Chinese authors working in China, a research paper on somatic countertransference in China, and two papers on Jungian approaches in Taiwan and the mainland.

The journal then introduces something I hope will become a hallmark: a paper on traditional Chinese painting and its relevance for psychotherapy is our first contribution from another discipline. It is crucial that psychotherapists be widely informed about cultural issues from other disciplines—demography, politics, law, art, and literature, diplomacy, and business. To this end, the journal plans to include at least one contribution from an outside discipline in each issue.

We also have an autobiographical contribution from Shi Qijia, one of the important leaders in the psychoanalytic movement in China, beginning another tradition the journal hopes to continue.

The last section of articles begins a third tradition: a group of contributions along a theme important to the development of psychoanalysis and analytic therapy in China. This first issue's special section examines the use of evolving Internet technology for the conduct, dissemination, and marketing of high quality psychotherapy and psychoanalysis. To this end, the articles examine the use of Skype and similar platforms for direct clinical treatment, for supervision, and for the wider spread of psychotherapy that also requires a high degree of quality control. No issue is more deserving of our attention in this rapidly evolving world of clinical service.

Finally, I note that under the leadership of José Saporta and Qiu Jianyin, we have a strong beginning to our section of Review of Books and Events. This issue offers reviews of four books and a first person summary of highlights of a conference on the work of object relations theorist Ronald Fairbairn in London, a meeting that the reviewer felt offered much to a Chinese audience.

This inaugural issue has been possible because of the generous support of many people, beginning with the members of the editorial boards. I especially want to thank Alf Gerlach, Tomas Plaenkers, José Saporta and Sverre Varvin for their active support and initiative in recruiting contributors, and Jill Scharff for crucial aid in the editing process and for her warm support through the entire process.

Inaugurating this journal brings with it great opportunity for the many colleagues who share an interest in the development of psychoanalytic therapy in China. I invite you to participate in the life of *Psychoanalysis and Psychotherapy in China* by reading it, by contributing to it, by discussing the ideas it contains with colleagues, and by recruiting colleagues to subscribe, read, and contribute to it as well.

I join with the Board of Editors in welcoming you to the journal. We hope that it will enlighten your work in psychotherapy and psychoanalysis, a vital endeavour in which we all share so much interest.

From Psychotherapy to Psycho-Boom:
A Historical Overview of Psychotherapy in China

Huang Hsuan-Ying

Abstract

This article provides a historical overview of the development of Western psychotherapy in China based on existing scholarship and my own ethnography. I describe a meandering trajectory embedded in the shifting political, social, and economic circumstances: the tentative beginning in the Republican period, the transmutation and destruction in the Maoist period, the relatively slow recovery and progress in the earlier reform period, and the eruption of the psycho-boom in the new millennium. Emphasis is placed on the reform period that began in the late 1970s, but by incorporating the previous periods I intend to show that the long-term process is highly relevant to the current psycho-boom. I further reveal that the development of psychotherapy in China has involved a dual process—both the building of this new profession and the infiltration of related ideas into the broader society—and that this duality is particularly evident in the recent psycho-boom. Finally, I discuss the implications of the new Mental Health Law and the preliminary signs that psychotherapy as a profession is taking root in urban China.

Key words: psychotherapy, psychoanalysis, China, psycho-boom.

INTRODUCTION

Psychological ideas, practices, and institutions have flourished in urban China since the early 2000s. Psychotherapy occupies a central position in this so-called "psycho-boom" (*xinli re*).[1] Activities that were promoted as psychotherapy "training" emerged as a craze among the middle class. Corporations offering these programmes have grown into an industry, and a group of celebrity therapists have become ardent disseminators of psychological knowledge through workshops, popular writings, and media appearances. Private counselling centres and individual private practices have mushroomed, forming a new mental health services sector alongside public psychiatric facilities. All of these mark a drastic shift from a dearth of psychosocial treatments described in the earlier studies (Chang & Kleinman, 2002; N. Chen, 2003; Pearson, 1995; Phillips, 1998, 2000). They also mark a shift from the classic depictions of Chinese patients as

Psychoanalysis and Psychotherapy in China, Volume 1, 2015: pp. 1–30.

being prone to somatic complaints (Kleinman, 1986). Even greater is their departure from the Maoist period, when psychotherapy, academic psychology, and the psychological aspects of experience had been repudiated for political reasons.

Despite being in vogue, psychotherapy has received little attention from Sinologists and historians; virtually all the existing historical accounts come from the participants of the local development. Official narratives, composed by the elites of Chinese psychology and psychiatry, typically search for an alternative origin in the nation's longstanding philosophical and healing traditions while considering psychotherapy as a modern, western invention (e.g., Li et al., 2006; Qian et al., 2002; Zhong, 1995). They also tend to follow the dominant grand narrative: the reform period sees all the progress, the Maoist period in which their disciplines fell victim to political persecution receives a brief summary, and the Republican period is deprived of its significance. Foreign therapists who have brought advanced training to China produce a small strand of histories that, though less bound by this frame, are similarly anchored to psychology and psychiatry (Gerlach, 1995; Kirsner & Snyder, 2009; Varvin & Gerlach, 2011). Outside the institutional spaces of these disciplines, anecdotes about celebrity therapists and monumental events abound, but most of them are fragmentary and not easy to verify. Despite the perception that psychotherapy is a recent arrival, many people are aware of its traumatic past and surmise that this has something to do with its current popularity. Frequently, one hears comments such as "Psychology was a problematic discipline back then", or "It was an era in which humanity, particularly the psychological aspects of it, was repressed".

This article offers a historical overview of the development of psychotherapy in China based on existing scholarship and my own ethnography. Since 2008 I have accumulated twenty-six months of fieldwork in Beijing and Shanghai, including a continuous stay between September 2009 and July 2011. The method of ethnography enables me to access knowledge and experiences that are seldom mentioned in published works. This historical overview places more emphasis on the reform period that began in the late 1970s, but it starts with the Republican period (1912–1949), during which psychotherapy was first introduced into China. By incorporating the previous periods, I seek to elucidate their legacies and the dynamic born out of the long-term process. Overall, I delineate a tortuous trajectory embedded in the shifting political, social, and economic circumstances: the provisional reception in the Republican period, the transmutation and destruction in the Maoist period, the relatively slow recovery and progress in the earlier reform period, and the eruption of the psycho-boom in the new millennium.

Psychotherapy, in the broadest sense, includes all kinds of treatment modalities that exert therapeutic effects through psychological or non-physical means. However, I restrict my scope to the particular genealogy that dates back to the birth of psychoanalysis at the end of the nineteenth century and hinges on a number of professions that include psychiatry, clinical and counselling psychology, and social work (e.g., Cautin, 2011; Cushman, 1995; Frank & Frank, 1991, pp. 1–20). This deliberate choice places China at the receiving end of the transnational transfer and implicitly assumes an association with these professions whose conditions depart considerably from their counterparts in the west (cf., Leung & Lee, 1996; Liu & Leung, 2010; X. Zhao, 2009). My treatment of each period begins with a short description of its social context, followed by a synopsis of the development of academic psychology and psychiatry, which, for a substantial length of time, had been the primary sites of reception.[2] I do not merely focus on these institutional domains, but also examine the permeation of psychotherapy into non-professional or popular spheres. This is particularly evident in, but not confined to, the section on the psycho-boom. As we shall see, psychotherapy and its related ideas have shown great potential to infiltrate the broader social and cultural spheres since its arrival in China. I pay the most attention to psychoanalysis, a bias that reflects the pre-eminence this school enjoys in China, though it needs to be understood in vague and inclusive terms here given the lack of formal training.

THE REPUBLICAN PERIOD (1912–1949)

As the official discourse of the People's Republic portrays, the era of Republican China was beset with tremendous injustice and suffering. Throughout the period, the state remained frail. The fledging republic was quickly torn apart by regional warlords. The Nationalist Party reunited the country in 1928 but soon faced the Communist insurgents and the Japanese encroachments, which escalated into full-scale warfare in 1937. The protracted war was succeeded by the Civil War that ended with the Communist victory in 1949. Amid these constant upheavals, new thoughts, artefacts, and values arrived from the west—a process that began in the late Qing period. In metropolises and treaty ports, a new educated class and a vibrant, cosmopolitan culture transpired, creating an environment for the reception of ideas and, to a lesser extent, practices derived from western psychology.

These ideas or practices were most welcomed in intellectual and literary circles. Although far from systematic, the reception followed the western trends closely and covered a wide spectrum that includes psychoanalysis, sexology, hypnosis, psychic research, and experimental psychology. Scholars such as Shih (2001), Wang (1990, 1991), and Zhang (1992) have demonstrated the profound impacts of psychoanalysis on Chinese modern literature, as eminent writers such as Lu Xun, Shen Congwen, Guo Moruo, and the "New Sensationalists" group (*xin ganjue pai*) in Shanghai drew inspirations from it. Some reform-conscious intellectuals also turned to psychoanalysis and sexology in their criticisms of traditional culture. Yet, the enthusiasm for psychology began to wane after the mid-1930s. As literary critics Liu (2004) and Larson (2009) indicate, intellectuals gave in to a more urgent wish for radical social reform. None the less, these trends left an enduring mark in language; scores of psychological lexicons, many of which were borrowed from Japanese *kanji* (Chinese characters) translations, were assimilated into modern Chinese during this period (e.g. H.-Y. Peng, 2009).

Academic psychology and psychiatry were introduced into China through education reform and missionary medicine, respectively, in the late Qing period. Psychology was first taught in 1903 at the Imperial University of Peking (the forerunner of Peking University); in 1898, John Kerr, an American missionary physician, established the first psychiatric institution in Canton (Guangzhou). In 1917, the first psychology lab was set up at Peking University; three years later, the first psychology department appeared at Nanking Normal College (the forerunner of Nanjing University). Psychology gained considerable ground in higher education over the next two decades. More than twenty departments were founded, and Academia Sinica, the country's most prestigious research institution, established an Institute of Psychology in 1929. A national society and several professional journals also existed. Comparatively, the development of psychiatry was more restricted. It was not until the early 1930s that two training centres emerged: the Neuropsychiatry Department at the Rockefeller-funded Peking Union Medical College (PUMC) in Beijing, which was under the tutelage of Richard S. Lyman, and the other in Shanghai, led by Fanny Halpern. The former was particularly influential as it trained a group of psychiatrists who later established training centres in Changsha, Chengdu, and Nanjing.

Psychology and psychiatry greeted psychotherapy in different ways. During the institutionalisation of psychology, influences from the USA gained dominance. While conceiving of their field as research-orientated, many psychologists were interested in psychoanalysis and were keen on translating or interpreting Freud's works. The most notable among them was Gao Juefu, who translated *Introductory Lectures on Psycho-analysis* and *New Introductory Lectures on Psycho-analysis*. However, their incursions into practice rarely went beyond education and psychological testing, since the clinical branch of psychology had yet to be developed. Unlike psychology, psychiatry as a member of clinical medicine is rooted in practice. Chinese psychiatry in the 1930s was under the sway of Adolf

Meyer, a pre-eminent figure in American psychiatry as well as Lyman's mentor at Johns Hopkins University. His theory of psychobiology, which called for an integration of psychological and biological perspectives, and his involvement with the psychoanalytic movement in the USA created an affinity with deep psychology that was transferred to the Chinese context (see Lumsden, 1992). Also worth noting is that Halpern once studied with the Nobel laureate Julius Wagner-Jauregg and the founder of individual psychology, Alfred Adler, while she was in Vienna (Blowers, 2004, p. 94). The tiny yet outstanding cohort of psychiatrists trained in the 1930s and 1940s thus had a certain familiarity with psychoanalytic ideas and their implications for clinical work.

Recent scholarship has drawn attention to a few pioneers who did delve into psychotherapy practice during this period. The most unusual one is Dai Bingham, a USA-trained sociologist–psychoanalyst who was invited by Lyman to join the PUMC unit in 1936. Building on Blowers' (2004) biographical sketch, Wang (2006) further examines Dai's intellectual backgrounds—the Chicago School of Sociology, Neo-Freudianism, and Confucianism—and how he adapted analytic theories and methods to the local reality. Dai left China in 1939 to flee the Japanese occupation and rejoined Lyman at Duke University after the war (see Rose, 2012). Yet, two of his contemporaries, Ting Tsan and Huang Jiayin, stood out for continuing the therapeutic project in China. Ting was a psychologist trained at the PUMC unit under Dai; later he became a leading figure in psychology and, particularly, the sub-discipline of medical psychology in the Maoist period. Conversely, Huang, a renowned writer–publisher in Shanghai, had never received formal training. Around the time of Liberation, he began psychotherapy practice, and these experiences resulted in several booklets of case studies. Blowers (2014) and Wang (2011) also show that during the 1930s and 1940s, Ting and Huang sought to enlighten the public through their writings on psychology, some of which were directly derived from clinical experiences. These were published in *West Wind Monthly* (*xifeng*), a magazine Huang co-founded with the literary luminary Lin Yutang.

THE MAOIST PERIOD (1949–LATE 1970S)

The Maoist period saw the ambitious efforts to thoroughly transform the politico-economic foundations of the society as well as its culture. Workers and peasants became the dominant classes, yet class struggles continued. Political movements, often summoned by the Party's top echelon, periodically seized the society with violence and terror. The revolutionary fervour reached its heights first in the Great Leap Forward (1958–1960), which resulted in an unprecedented famine, and then in the

Cultural Revolution (1966–1976). Psychology and psychiatry went through a similar course during this period. Both experienced massive changes in institutional structures and intellectual orientations, and many of their members, including some of the most respected ones, suffered from horrendous mistreatments, just as intellectuals in other fields did. The development of psychotherapy was first interrupted, and then resumed in an attempt to transform it into a socialist therapy, before succumbing to an even greater destruction.

Soon after the founding of the People's Republic, the Communist regime severed connections with the west and resolved to "lean on one side"— learning extensively and solely from the Soviet Union. The Pavlovian tradition was extolled as the only paradigm that could bridge ideology and science in psychology and psychiatry. Training programmes were held throughout the 1950s to re-educate the researchers and professionals, seeking to eradicate their western views and education that were characterised as comprising imperialist and bourgeoisie elements. Psychiatry, with merely 50–60 physicians and some 1,000 beds in the vast country, was on a negligible scale around the Liberation. It then experienced an explosive growth: the numbers of physicians and beds multiplied more than tenfold during the first decade of the People's Republic (He, 1958; Wu 1959). However, this remarkable increase in quantity was achieved at the expense of quality (Jia, 2004, pp. 61–94). Many of the new facilities were under the administration of the civil affairs or public security authorities, and could only offer custodial care. Psychologists and social workers, both essential members of the psychiatric team in the PUMC model, were expelled from mental healthcare, a loss that even today has yet to be recovered. During the Cultural Revolution, many professionals were sent into the countryside; hospitals in cities either remained open with drastically reduced capacities or were shut down indefinitely.

In comparison, psychology as an academic discipline had an even more tragic fate (see Brown, 1981; Chin & Chin, 1969; Petzold, 1987). In 1956, the Psychology Department of Nanjing University (originally National Central University) was annexed to the Institute of Psychology (IOP) at the Chinese Academy of Sciences, which derived from the Republican-period Academia Sinica. The merger and the massive restructuring of higher education in 1952 confined psychology to the IOP, a psychology major under the Philosophy Department of Peking University, and a handful of teaching and research units dispersed in other universities. The downsized discipline, as a branch of knowledge that sought to understand mental phenomena, suffered from the inherent tensions between it and the dominant materialist ideology. Under a cloud of the infamous label "bourgeoisie pseudo-science", the field was constantly on the verge of losing its legitimacy. A campaign called "criticising psychology" (*pipan xinlixue*) occurred in 1958, followed by a relatively peaceful period. In 1965, the discipline faced a new round of attacks initiated by an editorial written by the "Gang of Four" member Yao Wenyuan under the pseudonym Ge Mingren (1965), which was homophonous to "revolutionary man". Yao's subsequent essay on the play "Hai Rui dismissed from office" unleashed the Cultural Revolution. In 1970, the IOP was abolished. This marked the destruction of the entire discipline as universities throughout the country had been closed since the Cultural Revolution began in 1966.

Obviously, it was impossible to continue the psychotherapy movement that had its tentative beginning during the Republican period. In fact, Freud and his psychoanalytic theory were repeatedly singled out in the attacks on Western psychology. A notable exception was the "speedy synthetic treatment" (*kuaisu zonghe liaofa*) campaign, which was initiated in 1958 by the IOP's medical psychology section—a new division led by Ting Tsan and Li Xintian, a physician trained at the prestigious Hsiang-Ya (Yale-in-China) Medical College—and the Psychiatry Department of the Beijing Medical College. Echoing the spirit of the Great Leap Forward, this elite group assembled a variety of modalities that included pharmacological treatments, physical therapy (electric stimulation), physical exercises (e.g., *taijiquan*), and the so-called "psychotherapy" to combat neurasthenia (*shenjing shuairuo*), a disease that was particularly prevalent among intellectuals and college students who were engaged in mental labour. These treatments took place in the social milieus in which patients worked or spent most of their time—for example, factories and schools—and were conducted in intermissions so as to minimise the interruption of work or study. The entire course of therapy took about a month. Their version of psychotherapy, allegedly based on Pavlovian theories and Marxist–Leninist–Maoist doctrines, combined different formats of individual and small-group sessions and aimed to instil a correct "recognition" (*renshi*) of the diseased condition among patients and to enhance their "subjective initiatives" (*zhuguan nengdongxing*) (see Li et al., 1959; X. Li, 1960; Li et al., 1980). This therapeutic experiment lasted until the outbreak of the Cultural Revolution; through it, psychotherapy preserved its own nominal existence despite being transformed from within.

This campaign was a telling example of how practitioners drew on the dominant ideology to create psychological techniques that were deemed not only legitimate, but also suitable for the local circumstances. However, this episode was not an isolated endeavour, as mental health workers in the Maoist period made routine efforts to accomplish therapeutic outcomes through words and other non-physical means without using the notion of "psychotherapy". "Thought" (*sixiang*) was seen as the locus of therapeutic action, as a motto of that period revealed: "Psychological problems do not exist. Only thought problems do". During the 1960s and

1970s, quite a few professionals from overseas visited China, and their accounts bore witness to the clinical world under high socialism: the egalitarian atmosphere in which the power differential between medical personnel and patients was erased; the absence of psychologists and social workers; the application of traditional Chinese medicine and acupuncture; the routinised claim that mental illness was rare and no longer a major issue; and the use of "heart-to-heart talk" (*tanxin* or *shuo zhixinhua*) and political sessions, which were often compared to individual or group therapy in the west (e.g., Allodi & Dukszta, 1978; Bermann, 1968; Cerny, 1965; Lazure, 1964; Ratnavale, 1973; Taipale et al., 1973). On the other hand, these scenes did not exclusively belong to the psychiatric hospital, but were ubiquitous in a world transformed by revolutionary fervour—in this sense, the hospital was but a microcosm of the society.

THE EARLIER REFORM PERIOD
(LATE 1970S — EARLY 2000S)

After Deng Xiaoping regained power in the aftermath of the Cultural Revolution, the Chinese state launched the economic reform that aimed to create a market economy under firm political control—an approach later branded as the "socialism with Chinese characteristics". Connections with the west were resumed, and intellectuals, who bore the brunt of state violence during the Maoist period, were rehabilitated. The 1980s saw the resurgence of Western ideas and serious reflections on culture and society. This "age of idealism" ended with the military crackdown on the student movement in 1989. The tragedy confirmed the Communist Party's unchallengeable position and fostered the pragmatic ethos of the ensuing epoch. After Deng's southern tour in 1992, the state accelerated marketisation and integration into the global economy. By the turn of the century, the nation's coastal region had turned into the major manufacturing base of the world, and a relatively well-off stratum had emerged in cities.

Psychology recovered its legitimacy when the IOP was restored in 1977, followed by the establishment of the first Psychology Department at Peking University in 1978. Taking command were the senior scholars who received western-style training during the late Republican or the early Maoist period. Their primary concerns were to rebuild the disciplines from the ruins and to catch up with recent progress in the west. The situation was not favourable. Psychology was a small discipline. In addition to the IOP, in the 1980s there were only five psychology departments in the country, supplemented by about a dozen new ones in the 1990s. Psychiatry, as the most disadvantaged member of clinical medicine, also faltered amid the economic transition. The field maintained its narrow focus on major psychoses and was dependent on institutionalisation and pharmacological treatments. It mainly consisted of public institutions. Thus, when state subsidies dwindled, this crumbled the services delivery system, leaving a substantial portion of patients untreated. The World Bank's Global Burden of Disease study (Murray & Lopez, 1996) estimated that in 1990 only 30% of patients with schizophrenia in China received treatment. The treatment rate of bipolar disorder was estimated at as low as 5%.

Psychology and psychiatry set out to reclaim the field of psychotherapy swiftly. In 1979, the Medical Psychology Division of the Chinese Psychological Society set up a working group on psychotherapy. In 1981, a national conference on psychotherapy for schizophrenia was held in Shanghai, followed by the first national training course in Henan Province. In the ensuing years, a network of scholars and practitioners who were interested in talk therapy emerged. The majority of this group came from psychiatry. During the 1980s, medical psychology entered medical education and gradually became part of the medical establishment under the leadership of Li Xintian, the architect of the speedy synthetic treatment. In the meantime, some psychology departments began teaching counselling or "clinical" (*linchuang*) psychology: these two labels were almost indistinguishable in China, as those who graduated from these programmes were not able to work in medical settings. Instead, they practised in college counselling centres that began to emerge in the mid-1980s. Throughout this period, psychiatry and psychology had a collaborative relationship, as shown by the founding of the interdisciplinary Chinese Association for Mental Health (CAMH) in 1985. Its Committee on Psychological Counselling and Psychotherapy has been the leading professional body in the field of psychotherapy since its inauguration in 1990.

These endeavours were rudimentary compared to what happened later in the psycho-boom. When a group of psychoanalysts visited China in 1988, they found little evidence of anything resembling western-style psychotherapy (Halberstadt-Freud, 1991; Sabbadini, 1990). Talk therapy in general was rather marginal in psychology and psychiatry. Psychology was a research-orientated discipline; its counselling or "clinical" branch was small, disconnected from medical institutions, and confined to college counselling. Psychiatry, once governed by Pavlovian theories, rushed to embrace American psychiatry—the diagnostic shift from neurasthenia to depression among the elite psychiatrists was a tell-tale example (see Lee, 1999). The coterie of pioneers involved with the development of psychotherapy seldom claimed expertise in it. Almost none of them was formally trained, and the training they offered was exceedingly brief, with a sole focus on knowledge transmission. Even so, the 1980s and 1990s did see some notable developments, and their lingering influences are still palpable today.

The first was the coining of the term *xinli zixun,* which soon became the standard translation of psychological counselling, and the initiation of various projects under it. In the early 1980s, outpatient clinics with this title began to appear in psychiatric and general hospitals. Treatments offered in these clinics could include health education, psychological assessments, physical examination, blood tests, and imaging studies (G. Zhao, 1995). This so-called "outpatient model" mostly involved one-time consultations and bore little resemblance to western psychotherapy, but it soon had a place in the mental health services system. In the early 1990s the Ministry of Health ordered hospitals above the county level to set up psychological counselling clinics. These facilities provided the institutional spaces for the development of psychotherapy and broadly defined psychological treatments in clinical medicine. Also, in the 1980s, a number of universities set up student counselling centres, and the same title, *xinli zixun,* was employed. After the 1989 student movement, the State Education Council (the precursor of the Ministry of Education) began to revamp the "political thought work" (*sixiang zhengzhi gongzuo*) system in higher education with the new enterprise of counselling. A transition period ensued, during which former ideological workers filled many counsellor positions (see Leung et al., 2000). Today, most universities still juxtapose their counselling centres to the political thought work units, housed under one roof of the "student affairs" (*xuesheng gongzuo*) offices.

One defining feature of this early stage of development is the keen interest in creating therapeutic modalities that were thought to suit the Chinese people, an endeavour that attracted several of the most esteemed figures. Li Xintian, the leader of medical psychology, revised the socialist project of speedy synthetic treatment into "comprehensive practice therapy" (*wujian liaofa*) with his protégé Guo Nianfeng (X. Li, 1991, pp. 159–160; X. Peng, 2010). Lu Longguang (1989) at the Nanjing Brain Hospital developed a treatment governed by the principle of *shudao* (release and guidance). Zhong Youbin, a psychiatrist who was demoted to the outlying Capital Steel Hospital during the Cultural Revolution, was the most influential of all. His "cognitive insight therapy" (*renshi lingwu liaofa*), touted as the "Chinese psychoanalysis", was an illuminating example of how these pioneers grappled with lingering socialist influences and the new possibilities brought by the reform. He espoused Freud's early ideas, especially the existence of the unconscious, the pathogenic effects of childhood experiences, and the focus on sexuality. Yet, his case histories showed that in clinical practice he sought to instil a "correct" appraisal of the allegedly immature and, thus, reproachable symptom formation in his patients (see Zhong, 1988). His method, as the notion *renshi* (recognition) in its title implied, was reminiscent of the thought-altering techniques of the Maoist period (Seurre, 1997).

As China opened itself to the west, therapists from abroad began to arrive. Tseng Wen-Shing, a renowned cultural psychiatrist who received residency training in Taiwan and the Massachusetts Mental Health Center and was then based at the University of Hawaii, started visiting China in 1981. He established a long-term friendship with the Institute of Mental Health at the Beijing Medical College (now the Medical College of Peking University) and gave many lectures on psychodynamic and family therapy there. His introductory textbook (1987), co-authored with his wife Hsu Jing, was one of the most important texts on psychotherapy prior to the advent of the psycho-boom. In the early- and mid-1990s, Morita therapy, a Zen Buddhism-inspired modality invented by Japanese psychiatrist Shoma Morita in the 1920s, enjoyed a short-lived popularity in Chinese psychiatry. This was prompted by the assumption that Japan, a country with a similar cultural background, would offer a more suitable model of psychotherapy (see Tseng et al., 2005, p. 260). Many psychiatric hospitals set up Morita therapy wards, which later turned into psychosomatic wards when the trend diminished.

In terms of the contributions to the recent psycho-boom, nothing comes close to the Sino-German Course (*zhongde ban*); today many people equate its history to the field's origins (see Haaß-Wiesegar et al., 2007; Simon et al., 2011). The history began with a personal journey of a German therapist, Margarete Haaß-Wiesegart, who first came to study at Peking University in 1976. She completed her studies of family therapy in West Germany. Later, she returned briefly to Peking University, and learned that China's mental health system did not have psychotherapy. Determined to bring it to China, she found several allies, including Chen Zhonggeng, the founder of the clinical psychology programme at Peking University, Wan Wenpeng, President of the Yunnan Province Psychiatric Hospital in Kunming, and Yang Huayu, Professor at Anding Hospital in Beijing. She recruited a group of German therapists and held the first symposium in Kunming in 1988, followed by two similar events in Qingdao in 1990 and Hangzhou in 1994. In 1997, the group launched a new training programme based on the so-called "continuous training" (*lienxu peixun*) model: six week-long episodes dispersed over the span of three years. The first and the last episodes were held in Kunming where their Chinese collaborators Wan Wenpeng and his disciple Zhao Xudong, who had just received a PhD in family therapy from Heidelberg University, were located. Beijing, Shanghai, Wuhan, and Chengdu hosted the intervening episodes. The programme had three sections: psychoanalysis, systemic family therapy, and behavioural therapy (including hypnosis). All the 130 trainees were young, promising psychiatrists or psychologists handpicked by their home institutions. From this cohort emerged many of the most influential figures of the psycho-boom period. Referring to the institution where many of the commanders on both the Nationalist and the Communist sides were trained, the programme became known as the "Whampoa Military Academy" of Chinese psychotherapy.

Psychotherapy and psychology in general also inched into non-professional or popular domains during this period. The boundary between the professional and the popular was very thin, as those who wrote on psychotherapy usually conceived a broad readership that included patients, their families, and the general public. The early signs of popular interest lay in the rise of various art forms in which individual emotions and private experiences loomed large. Throughout the 1980s, a new wave of literature as well as popular music and television shows from Hong Kong and Taiwan found an enormous audience. In the latter half of the 1980s, publications on psychoanalysis, including several of Freud's books in translation, suddenly appeared and were read voraciously by college students (see Guo, 2009, pp. 1–3; Ju, 1987). This so-called "Freud fever" turned out to be as transient as the coeval infatuation with other western cultural icons such as Nietzsche and Sartre. But many of the members of the first Sino-German Course encountered psychoanalysis during this fever. While books filled with abstract musings were popular among the soul-searching youth, a crude form of popular psychology or self-help publications also emerged (Farquhar, 2012; Kleinman, 1988, pp. 143–144). In the 1990s, advice columns, radio call-in programmes, and hotlines (Erwin, 2000; Palmer, 1997) offered new channels for seeking psychological help. However, the communicative practices one could find through these channels or at the psychological counselling clinics in hospitals were marked by a practical, didactic orientation and had limited room for the exploration of inner depths.

THE PSYCHO-BOOM (EARLY 2000S–THE PRESENT)

China entered a new phase of economic growth after entering WTO in 2001. Within a decade, the nation had remade itself into a looming superpower whose achievements and potentials were showcased at the Beijing Olympics in 2008 and the Shanghai Expo in 2010. In 2010, China surpassed Japan as the second largest economy when the developed world was caught up in the global economic crisis. Despite the principal role that manufacturing has long played in its economy, the country is experiencing a rapid expansion of the middle class and a transition to becoming a major global consumer. The psycho-boom has emerged during this period and is often associated with these trends. In the popular imagination, the psycho-boom has gained a dual character—it is both an outgrowth of economic progress and the remedy for the ailments that progress gives rise to. People suppose that the boom reflects the increased purchasing power and the rising demand for quality healthcare services at a time when the perils of prosperity are rampant, as evidenced by the surging rates of depression, anxiety, and so on (see Huang et al., 2008; Kolstad & Gjesvik, 2013; Lee et al., 2009). The projected results of the ground-breaking study by Michael Phillips and colleagues (2009)—173 million adults in China have a mental disorder and 158 million of these have never received any type of professional help—are particularly appalling; these widely circulated numbers suggest a mental health crisis whose scale is beyond imagination.

Both academic psychology and psychiatry have experienced substantial growth during this period. Psychology is no longer a small discipline—the number of psychology departments could have reached 300 (J. Zhong, personal communication, 15 January, 2015). More than 100 universities offer Master's programmes in applied psychology, the official category that includes counselling psychology. Providing counselling services in schools has become common, not only in universities, but also in primary and secondary schools (Thomason & Qiong, 2008; Zhou, 2007). Psychiatry has made great strides after the state initiated a public mental health reform in the aftermath of the SARS epidemic in 2003. The centrepiece is the "686 project" that aimed to establish a nationwide management and intervention system for major psychoses (Liu et al., 2011; Ma, 2012). Meanwhile, the state also works with the professional associations to promote standardised residency training. However, the association between the psycho-boom and the development of these two disciplines should not be taken for granted. Psychotherapy remains very marginal in psychiatry, and is rarely part of the residency training even at the country's top institutions. It receives more attention in psychology, but much of the expansion of the related programmes followed rather than preceded the advent of the boom.

What truly distinguishes the psycho-boom is that psychotherapy and its training are no longer exclusively controlled by academic psychology and psychiatry, which are based in universities and hospitals and are largely confined to the public sector. A new sector that is privately owned, market-driven, and open to the broader society has taken centre stage. At the heart of this change are the commercialisation of psychotherapy "training" and the frenzy among the middle class to participate in these activities. This might contradict the popular impressions, but the boom seems to be more about the consumption of these training programmes than gaining access to psychotherapy services. In the local parlance, the notion "training" (*paixun*) entails a wide range of motivations that are not necessarily related to the pursuit of a professional career. This is because psychotherapy has been imagined and promoted so differently that it is able to travel in flexible forms, suiting the expectations of the urban middle class that finds psychology more pertinent to their life. The psycho-boom is driven by multiple forces: a state that is able to implement major policy changes, the disciplines of psychology and psychiatry that have striven to amplify their clout, and the market in which new commodities and business models are introduced to capitalise on the desires of consumers (see Huang, 2014). A succession of projects that occurred during the 2000s became the vehicles through which these forces could exert their influences. Despite not being coordinated, they produced synergic effects that led to the psycho-boom.

The first and the most crucial among these projects is a training and certification programme administered by the Ministry of Labour and Social Securities (MOLSS). In 2001, the ministry announced that "psychological counsellor" (*xinli zhixun shi*) would be a new addition to the National Vocational Qualification (NVQ), a UK-inspired system that was the outcome of the massive labour reform in the latter half of the 1990s. This was immediately followed by two other certification systems: one for "psychotherapists" (*xinli zhiliao shi*) that was administered by the Ministry of Health, and the other for "mental health promotion worker" (*xinli baojian shi*) that was managed by the quasi-official China Health Care Association. However, their impacts were nowhere close to the MOLSS system, which was launched provisionally in 2002 and officially in 2005. Like many successful projects in the post-reform business world, it derived from collaboration between the ministry and a private company specialising in distance learning technology named Huaxia Xinli, which invited Guo Nienfeng, an eminent psychologist at the IOP and then Vice President of the CAMH, to be the mastermind behind the project. As a disciple of Li Xintian, Guo was a proponent of psychological counselling in the 1980s and had since then presided over a correspondence learning programme at the IOP. The new system inherited many elements of this programme with a pivotal distinction: commercial agencies were the major suppliers. The entry requirements were deliberately lowered to accommodate more trainees. The programme could be completed in a few months on a part-time basis; it mainly concerned exam preparation and had little to do with practice. Huaxia Xinli and other training agencies produced a marketing campaign that built on the official discourse about a mental health crisis to suggest that there were rosy prospects for those who graduated. They further promoted the image that being a psychotherapist was a financially rewarding profession based on private practice—a sharp contrast with psychologists and psychiatrists in China who, as public sector employers, were paid modestly. These messages were well received by the public; people began to ignore the fact that the vocation of psychological counsellor, as certified through the NVQ, was meant to be low-skilled in the first place.

Popular media is another key factor in fuelling enthusiasm for psychotherapy training. At the end of 2004, the state-run China Central Television launched a new programme called *Psychological Interviews* (*xinli fang-*

tan), which featured real, edited twenty-minute in-studio therapy sessions. This daily show became an immediate success. It made its most frequent guests—Yang Fengchi and Li Zixun, both graduates of the Sino-German Course—household names and offered a convenient channel for common people to familiarise themselves with the imported therapy and the psychological ways of thinking (Krieger, 2009). Concurrently, a new breed of fashion/lifestyles/women's magazines turned to psychology, providing space for the celebrity therapists-cum-writers and helping to foster an aura of taste and distinction around psychotherapy. The most notable example was the Chinese edition of the French magazine *Psychologies* that was first published in 2006. The MOLSS training had become quite popular around 2006 or 2007. In Beijing, Shanghai, and other major cities, tens of thousands of people rushed to register in these programmes. Some of them wished to pursue a career in psychotherapy practice, but others were simply interested in learning something about psychology or making friends through these activities. Foreseeing the potential market for training beyond the MOLSS level, those in the training industry put forward programmes that were of shorter duration (typically 2–5 days) and pertaining to specific theories, techniques, or topics. These companies found eloquent and charismatic figures from academic psychology and psychiatry to teach these programmes. The most successful ones would emerge as "masters" who embarked on a journey no one had trodden before—to give lecture tours around the country.

While the boom was developing, psychotherapy moved toward the centre of the state's attention. In 2006, the Central Committee of the Communist Party published a major policy statement that proclaimed "psychological harmony" (*xinli hexie*) as a pillar of the official discourse of "harmonious society" (*hexie shehui*). What turned this pledge into action was the Wenchuan earthquake in May 2008. In the aftermath of the disaster, the state embraced "psychological aid" (*xinli jiuyuan*) or "psychological crisis intervention" (*xinli weiji ganyu*) as an essential component of the relief programme. Massive media attention was splashed on the state-orchestrated efforts and the psychological consequences of the disaster. Such media fanfare lasted for several months and became a new wave of the publicity campaign for psychotherapy. The psycho-boom further heated up after the Wenchuan earthquake; the most telling sign was the rapid escalation of treatment and training fees and the greater variety of courses offered by the training industry. Once the boom caught the attention of international media (e.g., Osnos, 2011; Tatlow, 2010; Wan, 2010), therapists from overseas, including Hong Kong and Taiwan, also swarmed to Beijing and Shanghai to give lectures or workshops. Two other fields grew hand in hand with the training industry: corporate psychological services, the so-called "employee assistance programme" (EAP), and the supply of artefacts with which one might wish to furnish a psychotherapy office. Concurrently, the boom made further headway in the public sector. Apart from school counselling, the military, the police, prisons, and the community services system also installed elementary forms of psychological assistance (see Yang, 2013a,b). In many instances, the Ministry of Labour and Social Securities training was employed, as it was a convenient, officially approved solution.

The psycho-boom used to be dominated by psychoanalysis. When I began my fieldwork in 2008, many celebrity therapists, practitioners, and trainees identified themselves with this particular orientation. In fact, psychoanalysis nearly became a generic term for the entire world of psychotherapy. The local understanding of the term differed sharply from that in the west, as formal training was not available and short-term courses were the only means of transmission. However, the popularity of this label suggested a penchant for things that are deep and emotionally resonant, which might account for the utter unpopularity of cognitive–behavioural therapy that had become the mainstream in the west since the 1980s.

The dominance of psychoanalysis was closely linked to the first Sino-German Course cohort. Out of this group emerged many of the most celebrated teachers, including Zeng Qifeng, who earned the moniker of "seeding machine" (*bozhongji*)—an allusion to Mao's (1965, p. 145) famous comment on the Long March of the Red Army in the 1930s—by ceaselessly touring around the country. It also included Shi Qijia, whose stylish demeanours and penetrating insights established him as another "master". Additionally, several of their peers occupied leadership positions in key institutions and were able to garner institutional resources to advance their cause. The most influential was Xiao Zeping, who, during her long tenure as President of the Shanghai Mental Health Centre, hosted the psychoanalytic section of the Sino-German Course with Alf Gerlach (see Gerlach, 2014; Xu et al., 2011). In Beijing, Yang Yunping, Chief of the Clinical Psychology Division at Anding Hospital, organised an equally important programme—the Sino-Norwegian Course (*zhongnuo ban*)—with the Norwegian analyst Sverre Varvin. In Wuhan, Tong Jun presided over the first and only hospital that featured inpatient psychotherapy in the country—Wuhan Hospital for Psychotherapy—and made it into another hub of training activities.

Outside the Sino-German group, two senior therapists stood out in the deep psychology scene. The long-awaited Jungian voice anticipated by Blowers (2000) was represented by Shen Heyong, a psychology professor at Fudan University in Shanghai and a disciple of the eminent translator of Freud, Gao Juefu. Affiliated with the international Jungian community, he published profusely on the integration of Jung's ideas and traditional

Chinese thoughts. Apart from these theory-building efforts, he made a more noticeable impact through the dissemination of sandplay therapy—every school counselling room I visited in China was equipped with sandplay instruments. On the other hand, Huo Datong, a philosophy professor at Sichuan University, was the leader of a small but dedicated Lacanian group in Chengdu. Trained in Paris and known in France as an icon of Chinese psychoanalysis (see Haski, 2002), he argued that the unconscious was structured not just like a language, as Lacan proclaimed, but like the Chinese language. In addition to the broadly defined deep psychology, family therapy (particularly the Satir model, the systemic approach associated with the Sino-German Course, and the structural approach associated with the Hong Kong-based therapist Lee Wai Yung), humanistic–existential therapy (partly due to the influence of Irvin Yalom, whose works were widely read in the circle), NLP (neuro-linguistic programming), Bert Hellinger's family constellation, and, more recently, Eugene Gendlin's focusing, mindfulness, and dance/movement therapy were well received.[3] The number of schools being introduced into China quickly increased after the Wenchuan earthquake, giving rise to a scene of "one hundred flowers blooming" envisioned earlier by Chang and her colleagues (2005).

However, referring to particular schools as well received could be misleading, as it implied proficiency, commitment, or a relatively mature stage of professional development. This seldom existed in China. The psychoboom involved two seemingly contradictory processes: a popular movement concerning the participation in psychotherapy "training" and the building of a new profession of experts. Existing scholarship tends to emphasise the latter dimension (Chang et al., 2013; Gao et al., 2010; Hou & Zhang, 2007; Qian et al., 2011), but it is the former that made up most of the flourishing scene. While official statistics were not available, it was estimated by many leading figures in the field that by mid-2011 over 300,000 people had attained the MOLSS certificates. In Beijing, Shanghai, and some other major cities, people engaged in learning psychotherapy formed large and thriving communities. The majority of these people were young or early middle-aged women who were relatively well to do in financial terms. They tended to spend a lot of time socialising with friends who shared this passionate hobby. These local scenes were further connected through the Internet. There were numerous web-forums, chat rooms, and online communities specifically for people who were involved in the psycho-boom. Lately, the country's native social networking programmes such as *weibo* (micro-blogging) and *weixin* (WeChat) have become the major arena for online interactions.

Only a small portion of the psycho-boom participants—though still a rather large number—went on to practise psychotherapy. They mostly worked in private counselling centres or individual private practice that had burgeoned in the regulatory vacuum. These facilities, unlike private medical practice that was strictly regulated by the health authorities, were not governed by any public agencies or professional organisations. As systematic training was seldom available, practitioners had to assemble their own curricula out of a rapidly expanding pool of courses whose students had widely varied motivations. Moreover, the career prospects were nothing close to the reassuring suggestions they heard from the media or the training industry. Up until 2011 or 2012, when the feverish scene had persisted for several years, most of the therapists I knew found it difficult to find even one or two regular clients, and therefore they tended to work on a part-time basis. Most of the time the client asked for a one-time consultation—a huge discrepancy existed between the psychodynamic psychotherapy that these therapists claimed to master and what their clients actually demanded.

Despite these challenges, the "professional core" of the movement—those who worked or trained at reputed universities or hospitals and lay practitioners who were committed to the career—benefited greatly from the intense international exchanges that were concentrated in Beijing, Shanghai, Wuhan, and a few other metropolises. These endeavours saved the elite members of the psycho-boom the travails of going abroad and expedited their professionalisation. Here, I provide a brief sketch of the most respected programmes in the psychoanalytic domain that are but a small part of the whole picture. The two long-established programmes—the Sino-German Course and the Sino-Norwegian Course—continued to offer training in the "continuous training" format at both the introductory and advanced levels. They also helped the local community to establish ties with the International Psychoanalytical Association (IPA). IPA set up a China Committee and initiated a direct candidate programme in Beijing in 2008, followed by a similar programme in Shanghai in 2011. Local candidates were in analysis with Irmgard Dettbarn, a German analyst who resided in Beijing during 2007–2010, and Hermann Schultz, another German analyst, who began to divide his time between Frankfurt and Shanghai in 2011. China American Psychoanalytic Alliance (CAPA) arrived at a later time; it began to offer a two-year programme in psychoanalytic psychotherapy to students in several major cities in 2008. Led by Elise Snyder, a New York-based psychoanalyst, it had evolved into a large organisation that mustered over 300 analysts from various corners of the USA. Its programme included lectures, group and individual supervision, and personal treatment, all of which were conducted through Skype (see Fishkin et al., 2011; Fishkin & Fishkin, 2014). Taught on a weekly basis, it resembled the one-or-two-year fellowship programmes offered at many psychoanalytic institutes in the USA. A two-year advanced programme was added in 2011, and a training programme in supervision was initiated recently.

CONCLUSION:
RECENT DEVELOPMENTS AND FUTURE PROSPECTS

In June 2011, the State Council for the first time released the draft of the Mental Health Law. The draft included several articles related to psychotherapy. They could be summarised as two points. First, it made a distinction between "psychotherapy" and "psychological counselling"—the two terms that had been used interchangeably since the early 1980s. The draft stipulated that psychotherapy was a medical treatment that had to be carried out by medical personnel in medical facilities. Because of the predominance of public hospitals and the immense difficulty of attaining permission for private medical practice from the health authorities, this would, in effect, restrict psychotherapy practice to psychiatric hospitals and psychiatric departments in general hospitals. Second, the draft specified that psychiatric facilities needed to hire psychotherapists. Although the requirements of these positions were not mentioned, this suggested that a new profession would be added to the psychiatric team that had, throughout the past several decades, consisted of physicians and nurses. Some leading psychiatrists speculated that the law might refer to the certification system for "psychotherapists" that had been administered by the Ministry of Health since 2003. The system had remained small and of little significance, as the job was offered at a mid-level rank (*zhongji zhicheng*) within the medical system.[4]

Between then and May 2013, when the minimally revised law (see Chen et al., 2012) was enacted, people who were involved with the psychoboom engaged in fierce debates on the nature of psychotherapy and the prospects for local development. Their views often reflected their personal experiences and standpoints. Many of the therapists in private practice thought that the law unjustly deprived them of the right to practise psychotherapy. Some of them were even worried that the state might launch a crackdown on the private practice scene. Members of academic psychology were upset that the law, which had been drafted by the country's leading psychiatrists, strongly favoured psychiatry by the adoption of a medical definition of psychotherapy. They felt that their expertise had been excluded from consideration in the legislation. Psychiatrists, who were the least affected, generally welcomed these changes, including the addition of psychotherapists to their teams.

Almost two years after the law was promulgated, its direct effects are limited. The health authorities have not taken any serious regulatory actions. The most visible change seems to be that the therapists in private practice now avoid using the term psychotherapy and stick to calling their practices "psychological counselling". The MOLSS programme continues to thrive, and the number of people certified might have reached 600,000 by the end of 2014. Only a small number of psychiatric institutions have begun to recruit psychotherapists. In early 2015, the National Health and Family Planning Commission (created through the merger of the Health Ministry and the Population and Family Planning Commission) announced that its certification for "psychotherapists" would soon be offered at a junior rank (*chuji zhicheng*) and open to people who hold psychology degrees. This new policy will be implemented later this year. While larger-scale structural shifts are yet to be seen, during the past two or three years the psycho-boom, particularly in its most developed centres such as Beijing and Shanghai, has experienced some significant changes.

1. The rise of the Registry System: as early as in 2006, the Clinical and Counselling Psychology Division of the Chinese Psychological Society set up its Registry System under the leadership of Qian Mingyi, Professor at Peking University who was also a member of the first Sino-German Course cohort. The system differed from other professional associations (mainly the several committees related to psychotherapy under the China Association for Mental Health) in setting down codes of ethics and registration criteria that were comparable to the western standards (see Qian et al., 2009). While the system included most of the leading figures in academic psychology and psychiatry, as of the announcement of the draft in mid-2011, its influence was weak. None the less, in the debates that ensued, the system was vocal in espousing its values, and has since then become much more visible. The system now has about six hundred members and has recently begun the accreditation of training courses, degree programmes, and internship sites.

2. The differentiation between professional and popular purposes: the individuals and agencies associated with the psycho-boom are devel-oping a clearer distinction between the professional and the popular. Many of them replace the elusive notion of "training" with terms that do not have a professional connotation, for example, "growth" (*chengzhang*) or "well-being" (*jiankang*). In the meantime, some insti-tutions try to offer more systematic curricula or more advanced courses to meet the needs of dedicated trainees. Among the practitioners and those who are interested in pursuing such a career, the importance of rigorous training has become more widely acknowledged.

3. The increase in younger participants: the psycho-boom used to be dominated by people who were born between the mid-1960s and the late 1970s. In the past few years, people who were born after 1980 or even 1985 have quickly moved to the centre of the flourishing scene. This new generation has much greater chances of receiving formal training in psychology. They are also more accustomed to psychologi-cal language and ways of thinking, as their early adulthood coincided with the unfolding of the psycho-boom.

4. The growth in the numbers of clients: the most intriguing difference, in my view, is the substantial growth in the numbers of clients. Now I know several dozens of therapists in Beijing and Shanghai who are seeing more than ten or fifteen regular clients. Although the number might look modest, it is very different from three years ago, when no more than ten of my informants had a caseload that large. For these people, psychotherapy has really become a job and a way of making a decent living.

Given the fluidity and rapid pace of change, any conclusion about the psycho-boom in China is tentative at best. In the near future, it could maintain its dual identity as a popular movement and a new profession and continue to evolve on both fronts. However, the recent trends mentioned above are hints that part of the psycho-boom is moving closer and closer to what many of its leading figures have long wished to achieve: a profession of private practitioners. A considerable number of its participants have committed to practising psychotherapy. Correspondingly, more clients have walked into therapists' offices, taking the first steps on their personal journeys of therapy. The growth in the numbers of clients might reflect the maturation of the therapeutic community as well as the effects of the psycho-boom on the popular culture—urbanites in China have been exposed to all things psychological through the media and other channels since the early 2000s. These popular effects also foster a distinction between psychotherapy, which is associated with the middle class and urban lifestyles, and psychiatry, which is deeply connected to serious mental illness and stigma (see Guo & Kleinman, 2011).

At this moment, it is important to remember that the development of psychotherapy in China has never been met with a straightforward reception. Instead, it has a meandering trajectory deeply entangled with, and affected by, the social, political, and economic transformations during the past century, as I delineate above. The eminent psychiatrist Lin Tsung-Yi, who visited China as a WHO consultant in the early 1980s, once challenged the then long-held view that psychotherapy was not suitable for the Chinese. He argued that this conviction was premature because psychotherapy had not been "properly and sufficiently applied to Chinese patients by well-trained Chinese psychotherapists" (Lin, 1983, p. 865). As Chinese therapists and clients engage more deeply with psychotherapy, we are finally moving toward the answer to this question. It is expectable that the therapeutic project will be able to tell us more about the inner and interpersonal lives of Chinese individuals, which have experienced tremendous transformations during the reform period (see Hansen & Svarverud, 2010; Kipnis, 2012; Kleinman et al., 2011). The Chinese therapists, working with the problems derived from these transformations, may begin to make more significant contributions to the field that they have been enamoured with.

ACKNOWLEDGEMENTS

My deepest gratitude goes to all the therapists I met during my fieldwork in China. I am particularly grateful to Qiu Jianyin, Sheng Li, Xiao Zeping, Xu Yong, Yang Yunping, Yu Xin, Zhao Xudong, and Zhong Jie for helping me to navigate the psycho-boom from their disciplinary standpoints. I am also thankful to Ba Tong, Cao Xiaoou, Li Binbin, Li Ying, Ma Hongmei, Ma Xiquan, Miao Shaojiang, Si Jiyuan, Wu Yanru, Xu Hang, Zhang Lili, and Zhao Chengzhi. I benefited from the discussions with clinicians who are involved with or interested in the psycho-boom in China: Elise Snyder, José Saporta, James Dalsimer, Yang Ming-Min, Wang Hao-Wei, Shan Yu, Chien Yi-Ling, Wang Sheng-Chang, Liu Shu-Tsen, Chen Jia-Shin, and Chou Jen-Yu. I am indebted to Arthur Kleinman and Byron Good for their mentoring during the research. I also thank Elisa Nessosi and Thomas Cliff for their comments on a previous draft. Research for this article was supported by a Desmond and Whitney Shum Fellowship, a Harvard-Yenching Doctoral Student Fellowship, and a Chiang Ching-kuo Doctoral Fellowship. Finally, I thank David Scharff and the two anonymous reviewers at *Psychoanalysis and Psychotherapy in China* for their helpful suggestions, which have been incorporated into this final version.

NOTES

1. In China, popular media often granted the designation *re* (fever or heat) to the frenzied trends that had seized large proportions of the population in the post-reform period. These included the so-called "qigong fever" (*qigong re*), "culture fever" (*wenhua re*), "stock fever" (*gupiao re*), "national learning fever" (*guoxue re*), "nurturing-life fever" (*yangsheng re*), and so on. What I describe as the "psycho-boom" is a new addition. I borrow this term from the therapists who used it to characterise the proliferation of groups and workshops in 1970s Germany (Bach & Molter, 1976; Schülein, 1978). These phenomena derived from the encounter group and human potential movements that emerged slightly earlier in the USA. While these movements had their origins in academic and professional psychology, more precisely its humanistic school, they emerged as popular movements that engaged hundreds of thousands of participants who were interested in self-exploration and growth (see Grogan, 2012). As I reveal later in the article, the psycho-boom in China also allows the pursuit of various non-professional interests. The crucial distinction is that in China psychiatry and the counselling/clinical branch of psychology were far from well established when the psycho-boom emerged. This contributes to a greater conflation of professional and non-professional pursuits.

2. For the internal history of Chinese psychology, see the two ambitious book projects led by the eminent psychologist Gao Juefu (2005) and Yang and Zhao (2000). Unlike psychology that has long regarded "history of psychology" as a legitimate sub-discipline, Chinese psychiatry has been less effective in composing its disciplinary history. The collection of biographies and summaries edited by Chen and Chen (1995) has remained a valuable sourcebook. Additionally, scholars from overseas (e.g. Lin, 1985; Livingston & Lowinger, 1983; Pearson, 2014; Yip, 2005) offer some historical overviews of the discipline.

3. It should be noted that the therapeutic landscape described above is seen from Beijing and Shanghai, the two cities that are generally seen as constituting the heart of the psycho-boom. While these two centres have a paramount influence over the periphery, other routes of transmission flourish in the psycho-boom, creating substantial regional variation. For example, anthropologist Li Zhang (2014) discovered in Kunming that the Satir model, cognitive–behavioural therapy, and sandplay are the most popular modalities. Also, it is not easy to gauge the popularity of a specific school based on its visibility in academic publications. For example, the publications on the Taoist cognitive psychotherapy (e.g., Zhang et al., 2002), which was invented by the eminent psychiatrist Young Derson and his disciple Zhang Yalin, have received considerable attention. However, one can hardly find any training courses on this topic.

4   This means that only medical personnel (including doctors, nurses, and technicians) who have finished their junior-rank services (typically five years) are eligible for the certification. These rules technically exclude people who are outside the medical system, including those who hold psychology degrees, as one needs to have a health-related degree to attain a junior-rank employment in the medical system. The system has certified merely two or three thousand people since its inception. For a critical evaluation of the system and the related articles in the Mental Health Law (see Zhao, 2014).

REFERENCES

Allodi, F., & Dukszta, J. (1978). Psychiatric services in China or, Mao versus Freud. *Canadian Psychiatric Association Journal, 23*(6): 361–369.

Bach, G. R., & Molter, H. (1976). *Psychoboom: Wege und Abwege Moderner Therapie* [Psycho-Boom: Ways and Byways of Modern Psychotherapy]. Reinbek bei Hamburg: Rowoholt.

Bermann, G. (1968). Mental health in China. In: A. Kiev (Ed.), *Psychiatry in the Communist World* (pp. 233–261). New York: Science House.

Blowers, G. (2000). The prospects for a Jungian psychology in China. *Journal of Analytical Psychology, 45*: 295–306.

Blowers, G. (2004). Bingham Dai, Adolf Storfer, and the tentative beginnings of psychoanalytic culture in China: 1935–1941. *Psychoanalysis and History, 6*(1): 93–105.

Blowers, G. (2014). Gone with the west wind: the emergence and disappearance of psychotherapeutic culture in China, 1936–68. In: H. Chiang (Ed.), *Psychiatry and Chinese History* (pp. 143–160). London: Pickering & Chatto.

Brown, L. B. (1981). *Psychology in Contemporary China*. Oxford: Pergamon Press.

Cautin, R. L. (2011). A century of psychotherapy, 1860–1960 In: J. C. Norcross, G. R. VandenBos, & D. K. Freedheim (Eds.), *History of Psychotherapy: Continuity and Change* (pp. 3–38). Washington, DC: American Psychological Association.

CCP Central Committee (2006). Guanyu gojian shehui zhuyi hexie shehui ruogan zhongda wenti de jueding [Resolution on certain major issues concerning building a socialist harmonious society] [Press release]. Accessed at: http://news.xinhuanet.com/politics/2006–10/18/content_5218639.htm.

Cerny, J. (1965). Chinese psychiatry. *International Journal of Psychiatry, 1*: 229–247.

Chang, D. F., & Kleinman, A. (2002). Growing pains: mental health care in a developing China. *The Yale–China Health Journal, 1*: 85–98.

Chang, D. F., Cao, Y., Shi, Q., Wang, C., & Qian, M. (2013). Building capacity to serve 1.3 billion. In: R. Moodley, U. P. Gielen, & R. Wu (Eds.), *Handbook of Counseling and Psychotherapy in an International Context* (pp. 182–192). New York: Routledge.

Chang, D. F., Tong, H., Shi, Q., & Zeng, Q. (2005). Letting a hundred flowers bloom: counseling and psychotherapy in the People's Republic of China. *Journal of Mental Health Counseling, 27*(2): 104–116.

Chen, H. H., Phillips, M. R., Cheng, H., Chen, Q. Q., Chen, X. D., Fralick, D., Zhang, Y. E., Liu, M., Huang, J., & Bueber, M. (2012). Mental Health Law of the People's Republic of China (English translation with annotations). *Shanghai Archives of Psychiatry, 24*(6): 305–321.

Chen, N. (2003). *Breathing Spaces: Qigong, Psychiatry, and Healing in China*. New York: Columbia University Press.

Chen, X., & Chen, X. (1995). *Zhongguo xiandai shenjing jingshen bing xue fazhan gaikuang* [The Development of Modern Neurology and Psychiatry in China]. Beijing: Zhongguo Kexue Jishu Chubanshe.

Chin, R., & Chin, A.-I. (1969). *Psychological Research in Communist China: 1949–1966*. Cambridge, MA: MIT Press.

Cushman, P. (1995). *Constructing the Self, Constructing America: A Cultural History of Psychotherapy*. Reading, MA: Da Capo Press.

Erwin, K. (2000). Heart-to-heart, phone-to-phone: family values, sexuality, and the politics of Shanghai's advice hotlines. In: D. S. Davis (Ed.), *The Consumer Revolution in Urban China* (pp. 145–170). Berkeley, CA: University of California Press.

Farquhar, J. (2012). For your reading pleasure: self-health (Ziwo Baojian) information in Beijing in the 1990s. In: P. Mankekar & L. Schein (Eds.), *Media, Erotics, and Transnational Asia* (pp. 53–74). Durham, NC: Duke University Press.

Fishkin, R., Fishkin, L., Leli, U., Katz, B., & Snyder, E. (2011). Psychodynamic treatment, training, and supervision using Internet-based technologies. *Journal of the American Academy of Psychoanalysis and Dynamic Psychiatry, 39*(1): 155–168.

Fishkin, R. E., & Fishkin, L. (2014). Introducing psychoanalytic therapy into China: the CAPA experience. In: D. Scharff & S. Varvin (Eds.), *Psychoanalysis in China* (pp. 205–215). London: Karnac.

Frank, J. D., & Frank, J. B. (1991). *Persuasion and Healing: A Comparative Study of Psychotherapy.* Baltimore, MD: Johns Hopkins University Press.

Gao, J. (Ed.). (2005). *Zhongguo xinlixue shi* [The History of Chinese Psychology]. Beijing: Renmin Jiaoyu Chubanshe.

Gao, X., Jackson, T., Chen, H., Liu, Y., Wang, R., Qian, M., & Huang, X. (2010). There is a long way to go: a nationwide survey of professional training for mental health practitioners in China. *Health Policy, 95*(1): 74–81.

Ge, M. (1965). Zheshi yanjiu xinlixue de kexue fangfa han zhengque fangxiang ma? [Is this the scientific method and correct path of doing psychological research?]. *Guangming Daily,* October 28.

Gerlach, A. (1995). China. In: P. Kutter (Ed.), *Psychoanalysis International: A Guide for Psychoanalysis throughout the World* (pp. 94–102). Stuttgart-Bad Cannstatt: Frommann-Holzboog.

Gerlach, A. (2014). German psychoanalysis in China and the start of group therapy work. In: D. Scharff & S. Varvin (Eds.), *Psychoanalysis in China* (pp. 216–224). London: Karnac.

Grogan, J. (2012). *Encountering America: Humanistic Psychology, Sixties Culture, and the Shaping of the Modern Self.* New York: Harper Perennial.

Guo, B. (2009). Gaige kaifang sanshi nien lai zhongguo jingshen fenxi de lilun yanjiu yu linchuang yingyong huigu [A review of the theoretical studies and clinical applications of psychoanalysis during the three decades of reform in China]. In: Q. Shi & W. Senf (Eds.), *Zhongguo xinli zhiliao duihua* [Chinese Psychotherapy in Dialogue], Vol. 2: Psychoanalysis in China (pp. 1–6). Hangzhou: Hangzhou Publishing.

Guo, J., & Kleinman, A. (2011). Stigma: HIV/AIDS, mental illness, and China's nonpersons. In: A. Kleinman, Y. Yan, J. Jing, S. Lee, E. Zhang, T. Pan, F. Wu, & J. Guo (Eds.), *Deep China: The Moral Life of the Person* (pp. 237–262). Berkeley, CA: University of California Press.

Haaß-Wiesegart, M., Zhao, X., Xiao, Z., & Qian, M. (Eds.) (2007). *Zhongde hezuo tuijin zhongguo xinli zhiliao shiye fazhan (1976–2007)* [The Chinese–German Cooperation for the Development of Psychotherapy in China (1976–2007)]. Shanghai: Deutsch-Chinesische Akademie für Psychotherapie.

Halberstadt-Freud, H. C. (1991). Mental health care in China. *International Review of Psycho-Analysis, 18*: 11–18.

Hansen, M. H., & Svarverud, R. (Eds.) (2010). *iChina: The Rise of the Individual in Modern Chinese Society.* Copenhagen: NIAS Press.

Haski, P. (2002). 1.3 milliard d'âmes et un seul divan [1.3 billion souls and one couch]. *Libération,* 16 July.

He, B. (1958). Jiji jinxing jingshenbing fangzhi de gongzuo [Fully committed to the prevention of mental illness]. *Zhonghua shenjing jingshen ke zazhi* [Chinese Journal of Neurology and Psychiatry], *4*(5): 343–347.

Hou, Z.-J., & Zhang, N. (2007). Counseling psychology in China. *Applied Psychology, 56*(1): 33–50.

Huang, H.-Y. (2014). The emergence of the psycho-boom in contemporary urban China. In: H. Chiang (Ed.), *Psychiatry and Chinese History* (pp. 183–204). London: Pickering & Chatto.

Huang, Y., Liu, Z., Zhang, M., Shen, Y., Tsang, A., He, Y., & Lee, S. (2008). Mental disorders and service use in China. In: R. C. Kessler & T. B. Üstün (Eds.), *The WHO World Mental Health Surveys: Global Perspectives on the Epidemiology of Mental Disorders* (pp. 447–473). Cambridge: Cambridge University Press.

Jia, X. (2004). *Xinling yu zhixu: cong shehui kongzhi dao geren guanhuai* [Mind and Order: from Social Control to Personal Care]. Guiyang: Guizhou Renmin Chubanshe.

Ju, W. (1987). Dui woguo chuxian folo yide re de fenxi [The analysis of the "Freud fever" in our society]. In: *Yishi yu wuyishi* [The Conscious and the Unconscious] (pp. 96–103). Shenyang: Liaoning Renmin Chubanshe.

Kipnis, A. (Ed.). (2012). *Chinese Modernity and the Individual Psyche.* New York: Palgrave Macmillan.

Kirsner, D., & Snyder, E. (2009). Psychoanalysis and China. In: S. Akhtar (Ed.), *Freud and the Far East: Psychoanalytic Perspectives on the People and Culture of China, Japan, and Korea* (pp. 41–58): Northvale, NJ: Jason Aronson.

Kleinman, A. (1986). *Social Origins of Distress and Disease: Depression, Neurasthenia, and Pain in Modern China.* New Haven, CT: Yale University Press.

Kleinman, A. (1988). *Rethinking Psychiatry: From Cultural Category to Personal Experience.* New York: The Free Press.

Kleinman, A., Yan, Y., Jing, J., Lee, S., Zhang, E., Pan, T., Wu, F., & Guo, J. (Eds.). (2011). *Deep China: The Moral Life of the Person.* Berkeley, CA: University of California Press.

Kolstad, A., & Gjesvik, N. (2013). Perceptions of minor mental health problems in China. *Mental Health, Religion & Culture, 16*(4): 335–351.

Krieger, J. (2009). Manufacturing psychological understanding: how China's first national psychotherapy TV show teaches viewers psychological narratives of Chinese family problems (PsyD thesis). Wright Institute, Berkeley, CA.

Larson, W. (2009). *From Ah Q to Lei Feng: Freud and Revolutionary Spirit in 20th Century.* Stanford, CA: Stanford University Press.

Lazure, D. (1964). Politics and mental health in New China. *American Journal of Orthopsychiatry, 34*(5): 925–933.

Lee, S. (1999). Diagnosis postponed: Shenjing Shuairuo and the transformation of psychiatry in post-Mao China. *Culture, Medicine, and Psychiatry, 23*(3): 349–380.

Lee, S., Tsang, A., Huang, Y.-Q., He, Y.-L., Liu, Z. R., Zhang, M.-Y., Shen, Y.-C., & Kessler, R. C. (2009). The epidemiology of depression in metropolitan China. *Psychological Medicine, 39*(5): 735–747.

Leung, P. W. L., & Lee, P. W. H. (1996). Psychotherapy with the Chinese. In: M. H. Bond (Ed.), *The Handbook of Chinese Psychology* (pp. 441–456). Hong Kong: Oxford University Press.

Leung, S. A., Guo, L., & Lam, M. P. (2000). The development of counseling psychology in higher educational institutions in China: present conditions and needs, future challenges. *The Counseling Psychologist, 28*(1): 81–99.

Li, C., Xu, Y., Geng, Z., & Wang, M. (1959). Shenjing shuairuo de moxie bingy-inxue wenti ji kuaisu zonghe liaofa de chubu tantao [Some etiological issues of neurasthenia and a preliminary examination of speedy synthetic treatment]. In: Ministry of Health (Ed.), *Qingzhu jianguo shinian yixue kexue chengjiu lunwen ji* [The Scientific Achievements of Medicine during the First Decade of the People's Republic] (pp. 539–545). Beijing: Renmin Weisheng Chubanshe.

Li, M., Chang, D. F., & Tong, H. (2006). Zhongguo xinli zhiliao de fazhan lishi [The history of the development of psychotherapy in China]. In: Q. Shi & W. Senf (Eds.), *Xinli Zhiliao: Lilun yu Shijian* [Psychotherapy: Theory and Practice] (pp. 10–20). Beijing: Zhongguo Yiyao Keji Chubanshe.

Li, X. (1960). Renshi huodong zai shenjing shuairuo zhiliao shang de zuoyong [The effect of recognition on the treatment of neurasthenia]. *Xinlixue bao [Acta Psychologica Sinica]*, *1*: 36–45.

Li, X. (Ed.). (1991). *Yixue xinlixue* (Medical Psychology). Beijing: Renmin Weisheng Chubanshe.

Li, X., Xu, S., & Kuang, P. (1980). Thirty years of clinical psychology in China. *Chinese Sociology and Anthropology, 12*(3): 97–123.

Lin, T.-Y. (1983). Psychiatry and Chinese culture. *Western Journal of Medicine, 139*(6): 862–867.

Lin, T.-Y. (1985). The shaping of Chinese psychiatry in the context of politics and public health. In: T.-Y. Lin & L. Eisenberg (Eds.), *Mental Health Planning for One Billion People: A Chinese Perspective* (pp. 3–41). Vancouver: University of British Columbia Press.

Liu, J., Ma, H., He, Y.-L., Xie, B., Xu, Y.-F., Tang, H.-Y., Li, M., Hao, W., Wang, X.-D., Zhang, M.-Y., Ng, C. H., Goding, M., Fraser, J., Herrman, H., Chiu, H. F. K., Chan, S. S., Chiu, E., & Yu, X. (2011). Mental health system in China: history, recent service reform and future challenges. *World Psychiatry, 10*(3): 210–216.

Liu, J. C.-H. (2004). Xin de fanyi [The translation of the heart]. In: *Xin de bianyi: xiandaixing de jingshen xingshi* [Perverted Heart: The Psychic Forms of Modernity] (pp. 121–157). Taipei: Maitian Chubanshe.

Liu, W.-S., & Leung, P. W.-L. (2010). Psychotherapy with the Chinese: an update of the work in the last decade. In: M. H. Bond (Ed.), *The Oxford Handbook of Chinese Psychology* (pp. 457–477). Hong Kong: Oxford University Press.

Livingston, M., & Lowinger, P. (1983). *The Minds of the Chinese People: Mental Health in New China*. Englewood Cliffs, NJ: Prentice-Hall.

Lu, L. (1989). *Shudao xinli liaofa* [Shudao Psychotherapy]. Shanghai: Shanghai Kexue Jishu Chubanshe.

Lumsden, D. P. (1992). Professional godfather: the role of Adolf Meyer and his students in Canadian and Chinese psychiatry. *Santé Culture/Culture Health, 9*(2): 217–252.

Ma, H. (2012). Integration of hospital and community services – the "686" Project – is a crucial composition in the reform of China's Mental Health Services. *Shanghai Archives of Psychiatry, 24*(3): 172–174.

Mao, Z. (1965). Lun fandui riben diguo zhuyi de qinlue [On resisting the aggression of Japanese imperialism]. In: *The Collected Works of Mao Zedong* (Vol. 1) (pp. 137–162). Beijing: Renmin chubanshe.

Murray, C. J. L., & Lopez, A. D. (1996). *The Global Burden of Disease: A Comprehensive Assessment of Mortality and Disability from Disability from Diseases, Injuries, and Risk Factors in 1990 and Projected to 2020.* Cambridge, MA: Harvard University Press.

Osnos, E. (2011). Meet Dr. Freud: does psychoanalysis have a future in China? *New Yorker, 86*(43): 54–63.

Palmer, S. (1997). Telephone counseling in China. *Counseling Psychology Quarterly, 10*(4): 473–479.

Pearson, V. (1995). *Mental Health Care in China: State Policies, Professional Services and Family Responsibilities.* London: Gaskell.

Pearson, V. (2014). The development of psychiatric services in China: Christianity, Communism, and community. In: B. Andrews & M. B. Bullock (Eds.), *Medical Transitions in Twentieth Century China* (pp. 146–170). Bloomington, IN: Indiana University Press.

Peng, H.-Y. (2009). Yige luxing de xiandaibing: xin de jibing kexue shuyu yu xin ganjue pai [A traveling malady – the "malady of the heart," scientific terminology, and the neo-sensation school]. *Zhongguo wenzhe yanjiu jikan* [Bulletin of the Institute of Chinese Literature and Philosophy], *34*: 205–248.

Peng, X. (2010). *Wujian* liaofa [Comprehensive Practice Therapy]. Beijing: Renmin Weisheng Chubanshe.

Petzold, M. (1987). The social history of Chinese psychology. In: *Psychology in Twentieth-century Thought and Society* (pp. 213–231). Cambridge: Cambridge University Press.

Phillips, M. R. (1998). The transformation of China's mental health services. *The China Journal, 39*: 1–36.

Phillips, M. R. (2000). Mental health services in China. *Epidemiologia e Psichiatria Sociale, 9*(2): 84–88.

Phillips, M. R., Zhang, J., Shi, Q., Song, Z., Ding, Z., Pang, S., Li, X., Zhang, Y., & Wang, Z. (2009). Prevalence, treatment, and associated disability of mental disorders in four provinces in China during 2001–05: an epidemiological survey. *The Lancet, 373*(9680): 13–19.

Qian, M., Chen, R., Chen, H., Hu, S., Zhong, J., Yao, P., & Yi, C. (2011). Counseling and psychotherapy services in more developed and developing regions in China: a comparative investigation of practitioners and current service delivery. *International Journal of Social Psychiatry, 58*(5): 1–8.

Qian, M., Gao, J., Yao, P., & Rodriguez, M. A. (2009). Professional ethical issues and the development of professional ethical standards in counseling and clinical psychology in China. *Ethics & Behavior, 19*(4): 290–309.

Qian, M., Smith, C. W., Chen, Z., & Xia, G. (2002). Psychotherapy in China: a review of its history and contemporary directions. *International Journal of Mental Health, 30*(4): 49–68.

Ratnavale, D. N. (1973). Psychiatry in Shanghai, China: observations in 1973. *American Journal of Psychiatry, 130*(10): 1082–1087.

Rose, A. C. (2012). Racial experiments in psychiatry's province: Richard S Lyman and his colleagues in China and the American South, 1932–1951. *History of Psychiatry, 23*(4): 419–436.

Sabbadini, A. (1990). Mental health in China: a personal account. *Free Associations* (1U): 181–197.

Schülein, J. (1978). Psychoanalyse und Psychoboom: Bemerkungen zum Sozialen Sinnkontext Therapeutischer Modelle [Psychoanalysis and the psycho-boom: remakers on the social meaning context of therapeutic models]. *Psyche, 32*(5–6): 420–440.

Seurre, J. (1997). Psychoanalysis with Chinese characteristics. *China Perspectives, 10*: 40–46.

Shih, S.-M. (2001). *Lure of the Modern: Writing Modernism in Semi-Colonial China, 1917–1937.* Berkeley, CA: University of California Press.

Simon, F. B., Haaß-Wiesegart, M., & Zhao, X. (2011). *"Zhong De Ban" oder Wie die Psychotherapie nach China Kam: Geschichte und Analyse eines Interkulturellen Abenteuers* [The Sino-German Course or How Psychotherapy Came to China: History and Analysis of a Cross-Cultural Adventure]. Heidelberg: Carl-Auer-Systeme Verlag.

Taipale, V., Taipale, I., & Helsinki, H. (1973). Chinese psychiatry: a visit to a Chinese mental hospital. *Archives of General Psychiatry, 29*, 313–316.

Tatlow, D. K. (2010). Freudians put China on the couch. *New York Times*, Oct 28.

Thomason, T. C., & Qiong, X. (2008). School counseling in China today. *Journal of School Counseling, 6*(11). Available at: http://jsc.montana.edu/articles/v6n11.pdf.

Tseng, W.-S., & Hsu, J. (1987). *Xinli zhiliao* [Psychotherapy]. Beijing: Renmin weisheng chubanshe.

Tseng, W.-S., Lee, S., & Lu, Q.-Y. (2005). The historical trends of psychotherapy in China: cultural review. In W.-S. Tseng, S. C. Chang, & M. Nishizono (Eds.), *Asian Culture and Psychotherapy: Implications for East and West* (pp. 249–264). Honolulu: University of Hawai'i Press.

Varvin, S., & Gerlach, A. (2011). The development of psychodynamic psycho-therapy and psychoanalysis in China. *International Journal of Applied Psychoanalytic Studies, 8*(3): 261–267.

Wan, W. (2010). Freud coming into fashion in China. *Washington Post*, October 11.

Wang, N. (1990). The reception of Freudism in modern Chinese literature Part 1 (1920–1949). *China Information, 5*(4): 58–71.

Wang, N. (1991). The reception of Freudism in modern Chinese literature Part 2 (1949–present). *China Information, 6*(1): 46–55.

Wang, W.-J. (2006). Dangxia weiren zhi daren: Dai Bingham de suren jingshen fenxi [The all-important job of being human at the present: Dai Bingham's lay psychoanalysis]. *Xinshixue* [New History], *17*(1): 91–142.

Wang, W.-J. (2011). Xinlixue de xiaceng gongzuo: xifeng yu 1930–1940 niandai dazhong xinliweisheng lunshu [West Wind Monthly and the popular mental hygiene discourse in Republican China]. *Keji, yiliao, yu shehui* [Science, medicine, and society], *13*: 15–88.

Wu, Z. (1959). Xin zhongguo jingshen yixue de chengjiu [New China's achieve-ments in psychiatry]. In: Ministry of Health (Ed.), *Qingzhu jianguo shinian yixue kexue chengjiu lunwen ji* [The Scientific Achievements of Medicine During the First Decade of the People's Republic] (pp. 521–529). Beijing: Renmin Weisheng Chubanshe.

Xu, Y., Qiu, J., Chen, J., & Xiao, Z. (2011). The development of psychoanalytic psychotherapy in Shanghai Mental Health Center. *International Journal of Applied Psychoanalytic Studies, 8*(3): 196–206.

Yang, J. (2013a). Peiliao: gender, psychologization, and psychological labor in China. *Social Analysis, 57*(2): 41–58.

Yang, J. (2013b). Song Wennuan,'sending warmth': unemployment, new urban poverty, and the affective state in China. *Ethnography, 14*(1): 104–125.

Yang, X., & Zhao, L. (Eds.) (2000). *Zhongguo jinxiandai xinlixue shi* [The History of Psychology in Modern and Contemporary China] (Vol. 2). Jinan: Shandong jiaoyu chubanshe.

Yip, K.-S. (2005). A historical review of the mental health services in the People's Republic of China. *International Journal of Social Psychiatry, 51*(2): 106–118.

Zhang, J. (1992). *Psychoanalysis in China: Literary Transformations 1919–1949*. Ithaca, NY: East Asian Program, Cornell University.

Zhang, L. (2014). Bentuhua: culturing psychotherapy in postsocialist China. *Culture, Medicine and Psychiatry, 38*(2): 283–305.

Zhang, Y., Young, D., Lee, S., Li, L., Zhang, H., Xiao, Z., Hao, W., Feng, Y., Zhou, H., & Chang, D. F. (2002). Chinese Taoist cognitive psychotherapy in the treatment of generalized anxiety disorder in contemporary China. *Transcultural Psychiatry, 39*(1): 115–129.

Zhao, G. (1995). Xinli zixun de jinzhan [The progress of psychological counselling]. In: X. Chem & X. Chen (Eds.), *Zhongguo xiandai shenjing jingshen bingxue fazhan zhuangkuang* [The Development of Modern Neurology and Psychiatry in China] (pp. 288–295). Beijing: Zhongguo kexue jishu chubanshe.

Zhao, X. (2009). Mental health in contemporary China: struggles and contradictions of psychiatrists and traditional healers. In: M. Incayawar, R. Wintrob, L. Bouchard, & G. Bartocci (Eds.), *Psychiatrists and Traditional Healers: Unwitting Partners in Global Mental Health* (pp. 135–148). Chichester: Wiley.

Zhao, X. (2014). Opportunities and challenges for promoting psychotherapy in contemporary China. *Shanghai Archives of Psychiatry, 26*(3): 157–159.

Zhong, Y. (1988). *Zhongguo xinli fenxi: renshi lingwu xinli liaofa* [Chinese Psychoanalysis: The Insight-Cognitive Therapy]. Shenyang, China: Liaoning renmin chubanshe.

Zhong, Y. (1995). Zhongguo xinli zhiliao de jinzhan [The progress of psychotherapy in China]. In: X. Chen & X. Chen (Eds.), *Zhongguo xiandai shenjing jingshen bing xue fazhan gaikuang* [The Development of Modern Neurology and Psychiatry in China] (pp. 296–301). Beijing: Zhongguo kexue jishu chubanshe.

Zhou, H. (2007). School psychology in China. In: S. R. Jimerson, T. D. Oakland, & P. T. Farrell (Eds.), *The Handbook of International School Psychology* (pp. 53–59). Thousand Oaks, CA: Sage.

Brief Intervention with a Chinese Family*

Jill Savege Scharff and David E. Scharff

Abstract

This paper is a case report of a brief intervention with a Chinese family, comprising a series of five hour-long interviews on successive days. The family presented in acute distress because of the suicidality of their fourteen-year-old only daughter. The intervention demonstrates basic techniques of analytic family evaluation and intervention, the intersection of an adolescent's development and issues of strain in the parents, the potential usefulness of crisis intervention in ongoing treatment, and the effect of the current mainland Chinese middle-class culture on development.

Key words: psychoanalytic family therapy, suicidality, adolescence in China, cultural diversity.

THE SETTING AND THE APPROACH

As part of our conducting an ongoing couple, family, and child analytic therapy training programme in Beijing, sponsored by the Beijing Mental Health Association and organised by Professor Fang Xin, Director of the Centre for Psychological Consultation and Treatment of Peking University, we are asked to provide brief consultations and interventions with volunteer families and couples in front of the group of trainees. The families hope to get help for their marriage or family issues from western "experts" and the trainees (all of them experienced mental health professionals) see analytic psychotherapy in action. We bring a level of clinical experience in psychoanalytic family therapy that is not yet readily available in China, and it is for the purpose of building a knowledgeable core of clinicians in China that we conduct this training and agree to our hosts' request for live demonstration interviews. At first, this was a pressured situation for us. We drew on our experience of live interviews in our residency training programmes, on our experiences on stage, and in making clinical videos in a television studio. By now we have done many of these demonstration interviews (D. E. Scharff & J. S. Scharff, 2011). We agree that the benefits outweigh the discomforts of being on display, warts and all, with no possibility of editing what has happened.

---

* This article was written for this journal and also for *Couple and Family Psychoanalysis* (*C&FP*), where it was recently published in Volume 5, Number 1, pp. 57–75. Joint publication by permission of the editor of *C&FP* and Phoenix Publishing House.

We present this background to set the context for the clinical material we will describe. We will not dwell on (although we may refer in passing to) our experience of doing demonstration interviews before a large group, our interaction with the group as it reacts to the clinical experience, or our training of leaders to facilitate small group discussion of the experience (Scharff & Scharff, 2000). Our focus in this paper is on our analytic family therapy approach to show our way of working (Scharff & Scharff, 1987) and to demonstrate what can be accomplished in a brief intervention. As the case report will demonstrate, there was a generosity about the family's determination not only to seek help for themselves, but to make their experience helpful to mental health professionals world-wide, as evidenced in their firm decision, taken as a family, to give us permission to publish an account of our work with them for the benefit of our colleagues and other families.

A brief introduction to our theory base and way of working will orientate the reader to this five-session intervention. We take our overall orientation from object relations theory (Bion, 1959, 1962, 1967; Bowlby, 1958; Fairbairn, 1952, 1963; Klein, 1946; Winnicott, 1963) expanded by the South American link theory of Pichon-Rivière (Losso et al., in press). Applying object relations theory, we view the individual unconscious as organised by taking in experience with important others and splitting and repressing those aspects that have felt too unpleasant for the immature ego to handle in consciousness. So, the personality forms with a conscious part of the ego connected to good objects and satisfied feelings, and an unconscious consisting of repressed parts of the ego connected to over-exciting and rejecting objects that bind the unpleasant affects of unmet longing, anger, and fear of annihilation (Fairbairn, 1952; Scharff & Scharff, 1987). Then, through continuous cycles of projective and introjective identification, the individual takes in and pushes out unpleasant experience in relation to significant others, continually communicating affectively and unconsciously with them (Klein, 1946). In a family, the processes of projective and introjective identification are continuous and mutual, each one shaping the other as they move through the life cycle. These interacting processes create "basic group assumptions" (Bion, 1959) renamed by Zinner and Shapiro (1972) in the context of the family group as "shared family assumptions" that govern the family and the development of its individuals. They create a network of conscious and unconscious object relationships into which the infant is born, one aspect of the link described by Pichon-Rivière. The link is organised by the interactions of all the involved individuals, and at the same time contributes to the continual reorganisation of each of those individual personalities (Losso et al., in press).

We draw our technique from Winnicott (1963) viewing ourselves as the environmental mother who provides a safe context for therapy, and as the object mother toward whom focused desires, fears, and hatreds are expressed. We also rely on Bion's (1962, 1970) concept of container–contained as we work towards transformation of unmanageable emotional experience to thought, by engaging with the family in process and review to find words that link emotion to words through which the experience can be communicated and managed. We approach the family we are interviewing or treating with an attitude of learning from them. We listen to communications, track the family's affective flow, work to enlarge the capacity for observation, and make interventions on several levels depending on where we are in the process, and on the family's capacity for insight. In a brief intervention, we begin by trying to understand what brings the family to seek help, and then note the members' way of interacting as they present their concerns. We explore the family history with them and work to strengthen their capacity for thoughtfulness about themselves in relation to previous generations, current social groups, and future goals. We try out interpretations to assess whether they can use our insight orientated approach. Finally, in an evaluation or brief intervention, we offer recommendations about next steps in therapy for their consideration.

The referral

A fourteen-year-old Chinese middle school girl whom we will call Clover had been failing in school, staying up on the phone and online, cutting herself, putting Chinese stones[1] into her mouth, was afraid of strangers, and had become preoccupied with love and suicide. She had been sexually provocative, falling in and out of love with male and female teachers. When she joined suicide chat rooms and erotic porn sites, and formed a suicide club at her elite school, her teachers became concerned and informed her mother, who taught at the same school. Clover's mother Cindy, an authoritative, accomplished, and well-respected teacher, felt humiliated that her daughter had been open with others and not with her. Her father, Hong, an engineer, was more laid back, but both parents perceived the need for help. Clover began weekly individual therapy, while the parents went into parent–couple counselling, but family therapy had not been tried. The parents' couple co-therapists suggested the possibility of a family consultation with us as visiting senior teachers and analytic family therapists, and Clover's therapist agreed, knowing that we would be accompanied by a translator and observed by the trainee group. The family met with us for a five-session family therapy intervention.

We were somewhat apprehensive about the parents' participation in such an open setting, given their concerns about others knowing too much about their child. It seemed that they circumvented any discomfort in order to accept the teaching setting and get the clinical help they wanted. Their shame would emerge later, delivered right into the transference where it could be worked on. But at the point of meeting them, we could not know this. We could imagine the parents' tremendous worry about their only child whose life was so precious and who was so determinedly interested in death. From previous experience with Chinese families we know that the only child is under immense pressure to perform academically so as to become a good earner who can support both parents and grandparents in their old age. At the same time, a girl carries the hope for a grandchild who will enlarge the family and continue the line. Many families in China have been openly more proud of having a son than a daughter, so we would look out for disappointment about the girl, though we might not find it, because, as a result of this attitude, there are now too many men and not enough women for them to marry, and so girls are in a position of greater power than formerly.

We carry this type of knowledge as background, but we set aside assumptions and meet the family with minds open to learning about their reality. We approach the family with our usual analytic attitude of benign interest, waiting to hear what they want to bring up for discussion. We proceed in a friendly but reserved manner, equally partial to each member in the group. We think of the family as a small group with the task of supporting its members through the life cycle, dealing with challenges at various developmental stages. So, we look at the family in terms of recurrent patterns of interaction that reflect shared family defences, sub-group formations, and unconscious family assumptions that connect to their current anxieties at this stage of development and their family history within their culture. We follow the affect, work with our countertransference until meaning emerges from inside our experience with the family, and at that point we make an interpretation and listen to see whether it is accepted or needs to be fine-tuned by the family (Scharff & Scharff, 1987).

Session 1

We were seated opposite the family, the translator sitting slightly behind and between us. Clover smiled at us, while her mother, Cindy, seemed close to tears and her father, Hong, anxiously checked that his family had enough water and tissues. Clover sat between them, looking at one and the other parent as if holding them together and keeping them apart at the same time.

Cindy began. She explained that Clover is more sensitive to criticism from teachers than other children in her highly competitive school. She worried that she and Hong had been too demanding about her falling grades. She told us that this concern would be like that of any other parents of children at that school. Clover had then felt pressure both at home and school and so they had tried to lessen the pressure by lowering their expectations. Cindy said, "I used to set standards for her, give her a work plan, but I have stopped because life comes before success. It is OK to be average. I have given up expecting more." Hong agreed that they had backed off confronting their hypersensitive, secretive daughter and missed the child who used to talk to them freely. He said, "We can't accept her actions, her extreme thoughts, her wish to hurt herself. We can't understand her inner world." With no apparent empathy for her parents' distress, Clover said amusedly, as if to end the worry, "I don't want to live. It's just my style. It's no big deal." They were at an impasse. We tried to encourage conversation, but they did not know what else to say.

We felt that Clover's suicidality was about much more than falling grades, something to do with the usual worries of adolescents about family, friends, social life, and sexual questions, wishes, and fears. As the family did not volunteer information, David, feeling some anxiety about making the meeting a good clinical experience for the family and good material for the audience to learn from, began asking questions to reach these areas, but he kept not getting answers until we felt that we too had hit a wall. In the first part of the first session, already the family problem had been delivered into the therapeutic space. Facing a family in distress before an audience of our peers and trainees, we felt that our performance was slipping (like Clover) and, at the same time, that we were being demanding (like her parents who wanted more) and getting nowhere in our attempts to communicate and understand (like the whole family with one another). Our usual way of working is to reflect on our countertransference and then speak to our experience as a way of understanding and clearing the way for open communication. We do discuss our countertransference experiences outside the session (and, in this setting, with the audience) in preparation for the next day as needed, but our ideal is to have the discussion right there at the moment in the session when we become aware of it.

Jill said, "I feel we are becoming part of the pressure. I think it is hard sitting here wanting help and not knowing how to offer it, in front of these observers."

Hong admitted, "With so many people out front of us, I feel nervous. It is hard for us Chinese to reveal what is buried deep in our hearts. I feel that there must be something lacking in our way of being as a family."

David asked, "There is such a block to telling us about how you feel, it makes me wonder if Clover is being unhappy for all of you?"

Cindy said, "No, my marriage is stable." (Clover started to cough, and Hong offered her water.) "But every family has conflicts, and I'm not sure if our occasional quarrels stress her out or not. Mostly I am complaining about trivialities, like he didn't sweep the floor well enough, or he should have closed the kitchen door. He is in charge of science homework but she doesn't want to learn from him."

Hong intervened, "My wife just likes to complain. I support her, I do things again, I smile, and I laugh it off. I know I don't do a good job, but I don't think it matters. I'm easy going. It is difficult to change."

Clover said simply, "I can't meet their standard. I am lazy, and I let it go. I'm like my Dad. Everyone has a lazy part. But I don't feel bad for being lazy. I don't cry at night about that."

Jill said, "Clover, you don't cry about it: you jump right into cutting and thinking about killing yourself."

Clover nodded.

Jill continued, "And Mum cries all the time. In your family when you were growing up, Cindy, who was perfect, and who was lazy?"

Cindy replied, "My father was very relaxed, and my mother was industrious. My older sister is high achieving, good at maths and science, a very successful accountant. My mum preferred my sister because she was more obedient and better than me. My dad preferred me. When I was in middle school, I liked to play. I was relaxed and busy with social life. I didn't like to work too hard, but I was not lazy. It was in high school that I started to work because of a particularly good teacher."

Jill said, "You liked to play, and Clover likes to play with her friends on the Internet, but it takes the form of playing with her body in scary ways, cutting and playing about suicide."

David said, "Clover, I sense that you think it is better to die than be unhappy yourself, and then somehow the unhappiness falls upon your mum and dad who want you to live. Then there is a family argument about living and dying."

Discussion of Session 1

By the end of the first session we felt we knew little. We had few clues as to why this attractive, lively young girl would want to die. What might she be escaping from and to? The audience was most concerned with Clover's suicidality as a response to academic pressure. We felt that in telling her friends and teachers all about it, she seemed desperate to be known and understood. Yet, in keeping her thoughts from her devastated parents, and to a large extent from us, she wanted to remain private and undisturbed. Her secrecy seemed partly a typically adolescent stance, and partly a dissociative response to deep and disturbing conflict. We noticed that the focus was on death, not sexuality, suggesting that sexuality was even more upsetting to Clover than death thoughts or academic expectations of teachers and parents. The parents seemed traumatised both by the knowledge of their daughter's preoccupations, and by the humiliation of not having learnt of them directly from her.

There seemed to be an unconscious shared family assumption that death is preferable to unhappiness, and that excellence is the best defence against criticism and shame. But perfection blocks chaos and conflict, and that leads to the death of hope and belief in evolution and progress.

Session 2

The session began with Cindy speaking about how she had learnt of Clover's suicidal nature from her co-teachers and had been dismayed that they knew about it when she had not. It moved on to a discussion of Clover's tendency to feel numb or to forget what was said. Then, in response to our asking about her adolescent physical development, the family joined in talking about her first menstruation as a joyful event that speaks of life in the future as a woman and possibly a mother. We noted that, nevertheless, now they live in fear of death. We asked about anger at the parents, thinking that angry moments might connect to the underlying "bad thoughts". Cindy told a story: in fourth grade Clover had been furious with her for saying she could not play with her grandmother's lamb because she had not done her homework. Clover said she had strong feelings from that event, but she could not remember them. The more Clover backtracked, or simply said "No!" in response to our attempts to explore the parents' experiences, the more stupid we felt at not getting through to her or her family. As before, we spoke to our countertransference as a way to communicate our understanding of their experience.

> Jill said, "We are having an experience of feeling controlled, and then helpless, and desperate, as you parents must feel, stupefied by your situation. Clover, that makes me wonder if you want us to know that feeling puzzled is how you feel, too."

> Cindy said, "That's exactly how I feel—helpless and stupid. I don't know what to say or do, and there's no feedback."

> David said to Clover, "I think you feel helpless inside about thoughts you can't share."

Nodding, Clover said, "Yes".

David continued, "And these thoughts are driving you, like you drive your parents."

Clover again said, "Yes."

David continued, "Clover, you are in the grip of forces that you are too frightened to talk about. Your parents and teachers value your life, and we do too. I think there is a part of you that values your life too, because I see that part of you sitting here, full of life and laughter and teasing. We are searching in the dark, but the dark is really in you, Clover. You're more frightened of talking with your parents and us than you are of being in the dark by yourself."

Clover said, "Inside me there are many thoughts and there are many selves flying around."

Jill asked, "Can you tell us about them? How are the selves different? What do they do?"

Clover gradually explained, "One is talking normally; one is judging me; one is having wild thoughts; one is killing herself; and there is also an observer."

We closed by saying we would look forward to a chance to hear more about the four selves the next day, and Clover nodded.

Discussion of Session 2

We tried to open the space for the couple and Clover to think, feel, and talk together more openly than before, so that they could become curious about one another's experience. We noticed that Hong, in his desperation to care for his family, left no space for Clover (or indeed Cindy) to experience need, and so Clover appears to have found a perverse way of achieving separation. Commenting on the countertransference of feeling stupefied and frightened ourselves allowed Clover to acknowledge the helpless feeling inside her. We talked to each other aloud during the interview about how each of us was feeling stupefied, and how to proceed, and that open conversation was different from the parents' way of working and withdrawing. In discussion after the afternoon's interview, audience members referred to David's telling Clover that he could see that she was also full of life, and one of them called it "a golden moment".

Session 3

The family did not arrive on time. After ten minutes, Hong hurried into the room out of breath. He said that his wife and daughter had had a terrible fight in the car on the way here and he could not deal with it. His wife had erupted at Clover, saying that she was so upset that all her colleagues knew about Clover's bad thoughts, and that they were looking at her now with sympathy. She had said to Clover, "If you are going to kill yourself, why don't you go ahead and do it, and I'll follow you." Hong was horrified. He did not know what to do. He tried to get them to come in and talk, but they refused. So he had left them in the car and had run straight to the interview room.

David went out to the car with the translator while Jill remained in the therapy space. He found the women huddled in the back seat as if in a state of fusion, Cindy in tears and Clover glued to her. Sobbing, Cindy described her humiliation in front of her colleagues. When David used the word "humiliation", it did not seem to mean anything to Cindy, but when he then said that he could understand her "loss of face", Cindy agreed readily. After a bit more talk about her situation, she agreed to return to the interview room with Hong, but Clover stayed outside the room with her parents' therapist to keep her company.

Back in the room in front of the audience, Cindy repeated that she now feels so ridiculous, and has so much loss of face, that she is not able to face going to school at all. She hoped that David would give her a doctor's note so she could miss school. Jill responded by empathising with her "humiliation and shame", but Cindy disagreed. David, knowing that Cindy had previously accepted his comment about "loss of face" and that loss of face is a more culturally accurate phrase for what in western culture we would call shame, modified Jill's comment by saying again to Cindy that it was her "loss of face" that had been intolerable. Cindy readily agreed to this way of putting the emotional situation. (It later occurred to Jill that it might also have been the female sympathy that Cindy could not accept, rather than a semantic difference creating a block in understanding.)

The session continued to focus on Cindy's upset about not knowing.

After a few moments, Jill spoke of feeling lost, deeply split off from David, who had not briefed her on where Clover was or about his experience at the car. She felt in the dark and disempowered. (In this way, the session repeated the situation that Cindy herself had been in for those terrible months.)

When Cindy was close to tears again, Hong instantly offered her water, then tissues, both of which she refused. We asked what that refusal was like for him. He responded in terms of what it must be like for her. We guessed that it must feel as if there were too many sympathetic people too close in, including teachers, counsellors, Cindy, and Hong, all trying to help Clover.

Cindy apologised that her outburst in the car had spoiled the opportunity to talk about Clover's four selves, because her upset and Clover's reaction to it kept that from happening. So she had ruined their chances of understanding, and she would have trouble accepting her mother's solicitousness when she would return to their apartment in the evening.

Jill said, "Therapists' kids are like teachers' kids. They feel their parents know too much, and therefore there is no private space, which Cindy and Clover both want." Hong smiled at Jill's saying that therapists' kids feel this. He told us that Clover had sent a message to her classmates that said, "It is hard to be the child of a teacher!" He and Cindy took this to mean that there is no room to think because the teachers know everything about their topics, rather than that Cindy knew too much about Clover and her life at school. Learning that the families of both Cindy and Hong were teachers, David asked about their treatment during the Cultural Revolution, wondering if they had been sent to the countryside, seeking to know if there might be intergenerational trauma to account for the anxiety around Clover. Cindy and Hong agreed that neither of the two families had been affected because their parents trained after those years of persecution for academics, Cindy being forty-one now, Hong forty-four. They get along well with both families, and gave no sign of any cultural trauma or unease with current or past societal changes. (Histories of other families have alerted us to the widespread social trauma in the period of the Cultural Revolution between 1966 and 1976, and so we now routinely ask about the impact of those times on parents and grandparents. We have seen the effects of that type of unspoken, unmetabolised trauma transmitted to the younger generation.)

Hong said that talking about old things was too hard, and maybe it is better to "let painful things alone". But Cindy shook her head in firm disagreement, insisting, "No. I know now that we have to talk!" Hong said then, "I think you should tell Clover your experience here of talking, and then feeling better. And I think you should apologise for your outburst. It is better if Clover comes here, because it is best for the family." Cindy agreed.

They left looking somewhat cheerful and determined.

Discussion of Session 3

As Clover was about to reveal things about her inner world that had been withheld from her parents, her mother "cracked" and said things that *she* had been too frightened to say. Her anger, clearly a factor in Clover's suppressed anger with her parents, had felt too dangerous to express. Instead both parents had become depressed and helpless, while quietly also seething at Clover's covert attack on their love and support. This paralleled Clover's anger at the way their lifelong solicitousness and demands had invaded her and her sense of well-being. Pressure to get into the best schools and universities is felt widely throughout the Chinese middle class, because the best education ensures the best earning potential in a country where there is no safety net, and only one child to take care of two parents in old age.

When David heard Cindy's "loss of face" and her anger displayed openly for the first time in the car, he felt a sense of relief that the encapsulated rage had burst to the surface, and felt cautiously hopeful that the family might begin to build on this event, since it had brought into the open the venomous feelings that had been buried because they were felt to be too dangerous to be aired. For much of the session, Jill felt left in the dark in a way that echoed Cindy's being locked out of Clover's inner world, until she and David could straighten out this omission after the family left the interview. This is the kind of dramatic, and sometimes cornerstone, session that makes or breaks a crisis intervention.

Session 4

Cindy began. "I feel so good about all this. I am thinking that if I get better, Clover will feel better. And if Clover is better, the whole family will feel better."

Clover said, "I don't need your help," and continued to refuse to have a conversation.

David began to speak about academic pressure, the need for space, social anxieties, and so on, as if giving a lecture to fill the space. There was a kind of desperation to help in his delivery. (David later thought that in giving a kind of speech like this, he had enacted the parents' giving Clover help when she wanted to be free to think things through for herself.)

There was no response, and David said, "What do you think, Jill?"

Jill replied (in an almost teasing way), "I think you should stop talking! We need to allow space so Clover doesn't feel smothered here, too. By her reticence and her one-word answers, she does evoke the wish to give her help. If we keep asking questions, all we will get are answers, but no conversation." (We would learn during the discussion that the audience was surprised and later reported that they felt Jill had been rude to David. But David did not lose face over this, because he appreciated the wisdom of the remark.)

Hong said, puzzled, "You mean we should chat freely? I can't think about what to chat about. Can you give us a hint?"

The parents spoke about meeting, falling in love, studying together, and having fun. They also told us that Clover had frequently been up late at night on her mobile phone, texting her classmates and on Internet chats. They had tried to take the phone away at night, but Clover had begged, saying she needed it because she could not sleep, so they had given in. We noted that Clover had managed to be in charge of what happened, and that the parents had been unable to set limits because they were so worried.

Later in the interview, Jill said to Clover, "I feel you don't want anyone to know of your longings and your various selves. Is there a place where you do talk about them?"

Clover said, "There are girls at school who say they love me. It can appear to be a homosexual thing, but it's not. It's part of a whole family. For instance, I am in a family at school. But I am a father because this girl asked me to have a family with her. So I got her as a wife. We have one child. In that family I have a father who is a girl. All the boys are called sisters."

Cindy concurred. "I have seen this in my class. I know her 'wife'. She's the class monitor."

Jill said, "Now that you are an adolescent, there is a next step that is missing. Where is the dating before thinking of a family?"

Clover said, "We don't do that because we would mature too early. So we make a family out of our schoolmates and that is safer."

David said, "What do the four parts of yourself think about your family?"

Clover said, "They don't feel anything about it. And they don't think anything about it. They just tell me what to do."

Hong said, "I am very confused. What is happening here? You have a good time with your family at school. Parts of you are a wife, a father, a girl and yet not a girl?"

Cindy explained, "If there is someone Clover likes, that person takes a role in her family. She will say, 'I treat him well because he is my sister.' I think it is to cover her true feelings."

Discussion of Session 4

They had all returned, but it was difficult at first to get the discussion going again. The family members were unfamiliar with the culture of family therapy, saying whatever comes to mind, and associating freely to what one another is saying. We had a sense of pressure and awareness of the limitation of time remaining. When Jill and David spoke together about the wish for more space and about the pressure they were feeling in the interview, Clover became more connected to the process. We learnt about her complex social world, about her and her peers' invention of a play reality to bridge the gap between latency and adulthood in creating virtual experiences of life, death, and family relationships, but we noted that she did not explore the various selves that had piqued our interest before Cindy's collapse had diverted attention from it. We regretted that loss, but recognised that there are limits to what is possible in such brief interventions. We speculated that Cindy's blow-up on the previous day must have been partly triggered precisely because she must have been frightened at the possibility of hearing about Clover's secret inner world, perhaps out of some personal resonance with it.

Session 5

Jill began: "Clover, I've been thinking about your families at school. There is a life family in the classroom and a death family on the Internet." (We could see that Clover could not connect with this idea of a split between life and death.)

Cindy said, "Yesterday she told me she has stopped having those thoughts about suicide! I am 50% glad and 50% still concerned. My husband really supported me and my child witnessed my despair. I met with my principal, and he supported me too. I feel much stronger today and I feel I can manage now. If a colleague expresses compassion, I can tell her the story without feeling loss of face."

Hong said, "After these days of counselling, we can sit together with a new way of communicating. I am happy about that."

Cindy said, "I am much better, but not totally happy. The problem is not gone. Yes, I got a message from her class teacher that Clover no longer has the thoughts about suicide, but I don't know if they could return. Clover says she doesn't know either. Can you suggest how to keep her stable? Do you have any advice for us?"

David said, "It's true that Clover might feel down again, and then the thoughts might return, but the difference is that now you can talk about it, and talking is what helps. Jill, do you have anything to add?"

Jill said, "Our advice is that both parents should agree. Talking is one part of it, and another is that you need to have the confidence to set limits. As we said yesterday, one limit we suggest is that there should be no mobile phone after bed-time."

Cindy said, "I get the idea. After Clover had those bad thoughts, she became the one in charge."

David said, "Yes, because you were so frightened. Then she can't stop, feels more guilt, and feels out of control with no one who can help her. When she can't stop, it keeps getting worse."

Cindy said, "Hong thought I was too strict. But mostly he followed what I thought."

Hong said, "Sometimes she will overdo it, but mostly she is right. About the mobile phone, I thought, after the quarrel the child was very upset and couldn't get our support, and so the mobile phone became her friend. Her therapist told us that she might feel worse without it."

During this exchange Hong kept trying to pass water to Cindy even though she did not want it, and it reminded us of the earlier session when Hong opened a bottle of water for Clover even though she had not wanted it.

Jill said, "I think Hong is afraid that Clover won't be his friend. Indeed if you take away her mobile phone she will be mad at you."

Hong said, "Her mother will have to take it away. I'm not that assertive."

Cindy said, "I am the bad one. He is the good one. I didn't allow her to play videogames, and he sneaked them into the house for her, and he would watch them with her. I was very angry about it, but they did it again, and I was angry again."

David said, "The worst thing for you, Clover, is to come between your parents. Clover, you'll feel best if they support each other."

Shaking her head, Clover said, "I don't know about that."

Jill said, "I would rather Clover be angry with both parents than so angry with herself and guilty that she has to hurt herself and think of suicide."

Clover said, "It is none of my business."

David repeated, "You're right. It's the parents' job to say 'No' when 'No' needs to be said, and to take the anger together. It's hard to do, and it's why you have to be a grown-up to be in charge."

Cindy said, "Hong and I do agree mainly. I can take the anger, but I can't bear the silence and the upset."

David said, "But that is how Clover expresses her anger. She gives you the silent treatment. You have to be able to understand that's what it is, and you have to be able to take it."

Hong said, "There are different kinds of anger in different people. When she is silent, it's so suffocating. It's harder than a fight."

Clover said again, "This is none of my business."

David said to the parents, "So our advice is, you have to talk together, make a decision, and stake out your position. We know it is hard to do, and that is why we advise you to continue therapy in this family format if you think it is a useful way to work, and if your current therapists agree. Jill, do you have any closing remarks?"

Jill summarised what had been achieved and what had not been addressed. Jill said, "You came together as a family to work on things. The stress of doing this brought about a crisis of despair in Cindy, which you survived and which brought important things to the surface so that we could discuss them. Hong stepped up as the father to keep the appointment when you could not, and then brought you in to face your despair here. That helped you to recover and enjoy some good family time. You have improved your communication. We have understood the pressures of parenting, the intense academic pressure on Clover, and the appeal of the Internet over the ordinary work of middle school. We have heard about a time when Cindy herself used to play, and yet recovered her ambition by the time she was at high school. We have learned about Clover's creation of a life and death family as a way of exploring life and death anxieties, but we have not dealt with the social and sexual anxieties of adolescence. We began to hear from Clover about her inner selves, but we didn't learn more from each of them. It is important that Clover tells her therapist about these inner selves, and that her therapist talks with them."

Hong stepped forward to take his leave of us and of the audience. He explained that they were grateful for the help, and gave us a gift of a stone on which our names had been etched. On its end a character had been carved for stamping letters or drawings. Handing us a red inkpad, Hong explained proudly that Clover herself had made this gift yesterday for the family to bring to us. We were moved by the gratitude, and the choice of the gift, and encouraged by its being a creative product of play, work, and carving on stone, a much better activity than cutting her skin. Clover explained that the character she had chosen to design for us said, "calm and harmony".

Discussion of Session 5

Advice to parents of the sort we gave in this last session also functions as a psychodynamic interpretation to the whole family. We knew that Clover could not use direct interpretations about guilt and anxiety to help her regulate her behaviour, but the family therapy setting allows for us to speak to her through the device of speaking to the parents. We had not forgotten that Clover sees herself as having multiple selves, one or more of which is an observing, more mature part that can identify with her parents. So, in giving advice, we were simultaneously saying to the family group that it needed to be governed by an integrated parental ego, which operates best through the thoughtful, mature collaboration of the parental couple. That couple had been invaded by the fear of losing love and losing face, and this had disabled them so that they could not set ordinary limits to help Clover with her mounting adolescent anxiety—limits they themselves would have preferred. Clover was pairing with her father in a sneaky plea-sure that was forbidden by her mother. In this way, Clover's developmen-tally appropriate sexual interest and curiosity were constrained by the gratification of oedipal triumph or were switched into guilty excess with peers. Unable to tolerate her guilt and shame, Clover short-circuited her anxiety by turning it into a self-punishing suicidal idea that went viral by contagion in the adolescent peer group. Clover's anxiety about confronting her parents directly with her anger, guilt, and sexual longing had turned into malignant self-punishment and self-harm.

Clover's individual therapist and one of the parents' couple co-therapists were in the audience watching and learning from our way of working and from the contributions of their peers to the large group discussion. It was not our task to consult to them, or to change their way of working. Their approach has been parallel therapy for the adolescent and her parents, a common approach in the child guidance model, and one that has a history of being effective. We have found family therapy more conducive to developing shared understanding of the family difficulties, a shared approach to solving problems, and more effective group strategy for moving on through the life cycle. Our task was to augment the didactic teaching on theory and technique of analytic family therapy by demonstrating our way of working, from which Chinese therapists could take whatever aspects they might find applicable in their work in their culture.

CONCLUDING REMARKS

Any treatment of a family occurs within the context of the culture in which the family lives. Of course, there are many similarities of family and adolescent development, but there are cultural differences. The highly competitive Chinese educational system that is so important to the family tends to exert pressure on children and parents far greater than we generally see in the western countries. We are familiar with the pressures of school on adolescents and their parents, but we have to explore and adjust our approach to the circumstances of the Chinese family. This includes giving family members permission to speak freely, encouraging their free association, and adopting language that fits with their way of understanding, for instance using the term "loss of face" when shame is not adequate for conveying our understanding that "loss of face" feels worse than death. In the US, the parents are free to choose the size of their family. In China, urban parents have been forbidden to have more than one child. This "One Child Policy", in effect in China for thirty-five years, has meant that the degree of investment in that child's future feels unbearable for all concerned. Added to that is the effect of the culture in the specific middle school in which mother and child teach and learn. It is the most prestigious of the local schools and likely to open the door to a first-rate university.

Clover's play "family" was her particular expression of adolescent culture in response to concerns about sexual maturation and gender roles. The play family puzzled Clover's father, but it made sense to her teacher-mother, who knew the school culture, but we had never heard of that in the North American, Central American, or British adolescents and families we have interviewed and treated. We understood it as an adaptation specific to Clover's family and school environment in China. Clover sought a space of her own with her young adolescent peers in the world of burgeoning sexuality and romantic preoccupation with death, a space apart from her loving parents whose investment and interest in her felt intrusive. That is similar to what we work with in the west; allowing freedom and setting limits, offering discretion but not secrecy, are conflicts that western families wrestle with. This has been our experience in China; things are different and yet the same. With attention to culture in general and the particularities of conflict and loss unique to each case, we can adapt our work to the needs of Chinese families and couples.

When family therapy offers an opportunity to dissolve the shared tensions of growing trauma in a family, turning pain and self-inflicted harm into a positive experience for the family, therapists feel hopeful. This family showed us the potential for shared self-exploration, mutual support and concern, and trust in a therapeutic experience, despite the unusual barriers of being translated and observed. We left the situation feeling that the family would do well in ongoing family therapy with a Chinese therapist, but the responsibility for the ongoing therapy plan rests with the current therapists for Clover and her parents.

NOTE

1. Chinese stones are square columnar stones with a carved stamp on one end for signing paintings or calligraphy.

REFERENCES

Bion, W. R. (1959). *Experiences in Groups.* New York: Basic Books, 1961.

Bion, W. R. (1962). *Learning from Experience.* London: Heinemann (reprinted London: Karnac, 1984).

Bion, W. R. (1967). *Second Thoughts.* London: Heinemann (reprinted London: Karnac, 1984).

Bion, W. R. (1970). *Attention and Interpretation.* London: Tavistock (reprinted London: Karnac, 1984).

Bowlby, J. (1958). The nature of the child's tie to his mother. *International Journal of Psychoanalysis, 39*: 1–24.

Fairbairn, W. R. D. (1952). *Psychoanalytic Studies of the Personality.* London: Routledge.

Fairbairn, W. R. D. (1963). Synopsis of an object relations theory of the personality. *International Journal of Psychoanalysis, 44*: 224–225.

Klein, M. (1946). Notes on some schizoid mechanisms. *International Journal of Psychoanalysis, 27*: 99–100. Reprinted in *Envy and Gratitude & Other Works 1946–1963*. London: Hogarth Press, 1975.

Losso, R., Setton, L., & Scharff, D. E. (2015, in press). *Enrique Pichon-Rivière: A Pioneer in Psychoanalysis.* Lanham, MD: Rowman and Littlefield.

Scharff, D. E., & Scharff, J. S.(1987). *Object Relations Family Therapy*. Northvale, NJ: Jason Aronson.

Scharff, D. E., & Scharff, J. S. (2011). The impact of the social link on group dreaming. In: *The Interpersonal Unconscious* (pp. 85–97). Lanham, MD: Jason Aronson.

Scharff, J. S., & Scharff, D. E. (2000). *Tuning the Therapeutic Instrument: Affective Learning of Psychotherapy*. Northvale, NJ: Jason Aronson.

Scharff, J. S., & Scharff, D. E. (2011). The impact of Chinese cultures on a marital relationship. *International Journal of Applied Psychoanalytic Studies, 8*(3): 249–260.

Winnicott, D. W. (1963). Communicating and not communicating leading to a study of certain opposites. In: *The Maturational Processes and the Facilitating Environment* (pp. 179–192). London: Hogarth Press, 1975.

Zinner, J., & Shapiro, R. (1972). Projective identification as a mode of perception and behaviour in families of adolescents. *International Journal of Psychoanalysis, 53*: 523–530. Reprinted in J. S. Scharff (Ed.), *Foundations of Object Relations Family Therapy* (pp. 109–126). Northvale, NJ: Jason Aronson, 1989.

A Commentary on
"Brief Intervention with a Chinese Family", by Jill and David Scharff

Gao Jun

Abstract

This commentary by the interpreter in Jill and David Scharff's case description of their brief intervention with a Chinese family focuses on the cultural issues most relevant to the family's difficulties, especially the subtlety in Chinese culture of nuanced differences between humiliation and loss of face. It makes suggestions for the clinical usefulness of these differentiations.

Key words: translation of psychotherapy; humiliation, loss of face.

COMMENTARY

After I accepted the invitation from Drs David and Jill Scharff to write a commentary for this intriguing family consultation, my idea was not to write anything about the theoretical understanding of the case or about the therapeutic technique, but, rather, to add some perspective as the interpreter for the consultation and as a Chinese clinician.

I tried first to search in my own memory to write down any impressions I had of this family and the five hours of therapeutic work before actually reading the description of them written by the authors. I hoped, thereby, to offer a chance to compare and contrast my memories and perspectives with that of the authors' record and understanding of the case. Three memories or impressions stood out. The first memory was about Clover. She had rather big black eyes, compared with her thin face. Before meeting with the family, Drs David and Jill Scharff and I already had some information about Clover's major difficulties, as revealed by her school counsellor. This included her being sexually provocative and visiting erotic pornography sites. When I saw Clover for the first time, I was surprised at how young and "asexual" she looked. She reminded me of a fawn, alert and vulnerable. She always looked at her parents first whenever she was asked to answer a question about herself. It was difficult to get to know her, since her answers were usually brief. Although, as the translator sitting between the Drs Scharff, I was only speaking their words and the words of the family, I often had the feeling that Clover was reluctant to say anything in front of her parents. It seemed that her most important task here was constantly to track her parents' reactions, especially those of her mother.

The second memory was of when the father started to describe how he first met his wife. He had found her so attractive that he fell in love with her almost at first sight. He also mentioned her large, charming eyes. I was deeply touched at that moment, for the way he told the story was full of love and passion. As far as I could remember, this was the only moment when I felt there was a deep connection, emotionally and sexually, between the couple. However, I could not recall how the mother reacted to her husband's words, I think because she was so preoccupied by the fact that her daughter was suicidal, and because she was so ashamed that many of her colleagues knew her daughter's difficulty when she did not, that her mind seemed to have little room for her husband and for a couple state of mind.

The third memory was about the "crisis" during the third session, when the father rushed into the room to tell us the mother had had a fight with Clover and that Clover refused to come to the session. I was shocked when the father told us that his wife had been so agitated and depressed that she had said to Clover that if Clover really wanted to kill herself, she should do so and that she, the mother, would follow her in death. However, I also had a strange sense of relief when I heard her words. It felt as if the lid of a steaming pot had finally blown off. Now the aggression, the despair, and the shame within the family were revealed to everyone. The mother's words were oddly familiar, too. One probably could find similar versions in Chinese television dramas, words that a desperate parent, usually a mother, shouted at a child whose "out of control" and "outrageous" behaviours threatened to bring humiliation to the family.

I also want to highlight one other scenario from the five-hour consultation. This scenario did not come to mind until I read the case study written by the Drs Scharff. Then I immediately recognised the special value of this case report for illustrating important aspects of the Chinese cultural context within which this family was created and in which its drama continued to unfold. I was also struck by the fact that I did not remember it through my first attempts to recall things about the family. I believe a principal reason for this was that since I share the same cultural background with the family, these scenarios and their underlying dynamics were just too familiar to me, so that, in a way, from inside our shared cultural assumptions, it was difficult for me to identify them and recognise their importance.

I think of this scenario as the contrast between "losing face" and "humiliation". When David Scharff came to the car park to talk to the mother and Clover in order to try to resolve their crisis, I went with him as translator, and so I translated when he first used the word "humiliation" to describe how the mother might be feeling when she found out that all her colleagues knew of Clover's problems. The mother did not react positively to this word, so Dr Scharff used another expression, which was "her loss of face". The mother found this expression more accurate and meaningful, and she immediately agreed with him. David Scharff probably knew Chinese culture well enough to know the phrase "loss of face", which is indeed a phrase commonly used in China. So, reading this case report has prompted me to ask, "What is the difference between humiliation and losing face?" Why did the mother find it hard to accept the word "humiliation"? These are interesting questions. In general, the two concepts are both from the same family of emotions, namely shame. Since China has been regarded by many scholars as a "shame culture", it is not surprising that the emotion of shame is quite important here in China. Unlike English, which only has a few words to describe the concept of shame and its gradations – for instance embarrassment or humiliation—there are many Chinese words to differentiate aspects of shameful intense negative feeling about one's self. The Chinese translation of the word humiliation is "耻辱 (Chi-ru)". Chi-ru describes a situation in which a person feels that because of his/her wrongdoing—usually severe moral transgressions or major personal failures—he/she is looked down upon by others. The contempt and disgust implied in this word is strong, and the consequence can be fatal: he/she may lose reputation and respect from others completely, and might even run the risk of being expelled by his/her group. The word "humiliation" can also indicate a strong sense of aggression from others. The image of a bad, disgusting self is forced upon the person by others, either in the reality or in the person's imagination.

On the other hand, the phrase "losing face" is far less negative and painful compared to the word "humiliation". There are two differing translations for the phrase "loss of face". One is "丢面子 (*diu mian zi*)" and the other is "丢脸 (*diu lian*)". There is a subtle but important difference between the two. The meaning of the first (*diu mian zu*) is similar to the English word embarrassment, usually indicating a social inadequacy or mistake that one makes in front of others, and indicates that these faults or inadequacies do not fit the status or the role that a person occupies in his/her social network. The second (*diu lian*) is more negative in the sense that it indicates a more severe social inadequacy or even a moral transgression.

Another difference between "humiliation" and "losing face" concerns the personal reaction towards these shameful experiences. In Chinese, we have phrases such as "earn face", or "win back your face", indicating that if a person tries to redress his wrongdoings afterwards, or correct his social inadequacy, he can restore his reputation and be accepted once more as a worthy member of the group. In this sense, when a Chinese person feels or is told that she has lost face, she is usually quite motivated to get it back. However, it is far more difficult to "wash away your humiliation with others' blood", as the Chinese phrase indicates. Besides, to get rid of your humiliation also implies quite a lot of aggression towards those people who made you feel humiliated.

From this perspective, I would say that the mother's refusal of the word "humiliation" and her willingness to accept the phrase "losing face" may have several implications about the dynamics that operated within her as well as within the family. On the first level, the mother might not have regarded Clover's difficulties and the revelation of these difficulties as something severe enough to be admitted as a moral stain or major personal failure of the kind that would bring humiliation to her and her family. Based on her own account about how her colleagues treated her with sympathy, she seemed to feel that there had been little aggression from them. However, she did indicate that her daughter's falling grades were a great concern for her and her husband, at least before they knew she was suicidal. Children's poor academic performance is indeed a common reason for Chinese parents to feel that they lose face. Clover's mother also readily said that her daughter's difficulties made her feel inadequate and helpless as a mother. Therefore, from her point of view, losing face was probably a more accurate term to describe her feelings. By admitting that she had lost face because her colleagues knew of her daughter's problems might also indicate her strong motivation for her to "win back face", probably by helping her daughter to overcome her problems. This strong motivation for helping her daughter, if utilised properly, would be likely to facilitate the therapeutic process. Moreover, the mother's denial of feeling humiliation might also be a positive sign, indicating that she did not have strong negative opinions about herself or her daughter, or, in other words, that she did not severely disparage herself and her daughter, and suggesting that she was closer to believing that things could get better. Thus, Dr Scharff's first attempt to empathise with the mother by using the word humiliation can be understood as a clinical mismatch, stemming from the fact that he came from such a different culture.

However, there might be another possibility. The mother might indeed have felt humiliated because of her daughter's problems, but have found it too painful or threatening to admit that she felt so badly about her daughter and herself, or that she was so helpless and angry towards her daughter. The mother might also have felt that her daughter was attacking her by having so many problems. For instance, she had said several times that Clover had been such a happy girl and had always been a source of happiness in her mother's life. It must have been ironic indeed for such a "happy girl" to have so many dark secrets hidden from her parents. By revealing her secrets to her school counsellor and several other teachers who were her mother's colleagues, Clover was able to set the stage for her mother to feel indeed humiliated. Clover's actions were, in my view, full of despair and aggression. Moreover, it seemed that the parents only knew part of Clover's problems, the part that her grades were falling and that she was suicidal. They seemed to know little about her being sexually provocative and visiting erotic porn sites, since the school counsellor reported that she did not reveal that to them, even though this information was imparted to the consultation group. It was likely that the Drs Scharff, by knowing more of Clover's "dark secrets" than the mother did, pointed out the desperate situation the mother faced and might have contributed to the mother's humiliation. In this way, in the transference, it was too much for the mother to take because she was still somewhat blind to her daughter's struggles and the level of aggression within the family. Therefore, by acknowledging "her loss of face", the mother might indeed turn away from looking behind the "faces" of Clover, her husband and herself, where more difficult feelings around more powerful humiliation remained still hidden in the dark.

Projective Identification in Group Therapy in China

Xu Yong

Abstract

Western concepts such as projective identification, containment, mentalization and aspects of identification are useful in China for the conduct of psychodynamic group psychotherapy. This paper describes those concepts, and, through clinical illustration, focuses on the elucidation of issues through clinical use of projective identification in a Chinese therapy group.

Key words: projective identification, group psychotherapy in China, containment, mentalization, identification.

INTRODUCTION

Western concepts have proved useful in the conduct of psychodynamic group therapy in China. They are employed to help patients to think about their behaviour and its effects on others. These are primarily projective identification (Klein, Ogden), augmented by containment (Bion), mentalization (Fonagy), and concordant and complementary identification (Racker).

The term projective identification, conceptualised by Melanie Klein (1946), describes an unconscious mental mechanism in infancy whereby the infant finds relief from painful and undesirable feelings by splitting them off from consciousness and in unconscious fantasy putting them into the mother. The infant then feels them to be coming from the mother and cannot differentiate between self and mother. The child, and later the adult, might continue to use this defence habitually or might return to it at times of great anxiety, attempting to find relief by projecting unpleasant feelings into other figures such as spouse or therapist.

Since Melanie Klein, many psychoanalysts have broadened this concept from one concerning individual unconscious phantasy to one that includes the components of interpersonal interaction and communication. Bion (1962) wrote that the analyst should

> observe and interpret the operation of the phantasy as a mental phenomenon deducible from the evidence and also observe signs that the patient is sufficiently adjusted to reality to be able to manipulate his environment so that the phantasy of projective identification appears to have substance in reality. (1962, p. 32)

Psychoanalysis and Psychotherapy in China, Volume 1, 2015: pp. 55–62.

It was Bion's (1967) later concept of containment that broadened projective identification from an intrapsychic mechanism to include its effect on the other. Bion held that the infant projects unthinkable anxiety into the mother who transforms it by her own reverie into something that is thinkable and, therefore, manageable. When therapists experience anxiety engendered in them by the action of the patient's projections, they subject it to process and review so that the experience can be thought about and so managed.

Ogden (1979) clarified three phases in the process of projective identification. In the first phase, the projector projects a part of the self or an internal object on to another person, and in order to get rid of and control anxiety about the projected part exerts pressure "on the recipient of the projection to experience himself and behave in a way congruent with the projective fantasy" (p. 359). The recipient registers the projection and is either taken over by it or modifies it for reinternalisation by the projector. Later, Ogden (1982) made his views even clearer, describing projective identification as "a statement about the dynamic interplay of the two, the intrapsychic and the interpersonal" (p. 3). Thus, one person can cause another to behave in a specific way, even if this person is not inclined to this behaviour. When someone projects some undesired parts of the self on to the other person in an interaction, the projector starts to perceive the recipient as possessing those characteristics and behaves towards that person accordingly. In an active but fundamentally unconscious way, this evokes in the recipient, who identifies with the projection, behaviour that matches the projection.

Ogden (1983) made another important observation concerning projective identification as the basis of transference. He wrote,

> It is my experience that projective identification is a universal feature of the externalization of an internal object relationship, i.e. of transference. *What is variable is the degree to which the external object is enlisted as a participant in the externalization of the internal object relationship.* In other words, there is always a component of the therapist's response to the patient's transferences that represents an induced identification with an aspect of the patient's ego that is locked in a particular unconscious internal object relationship. (p. 237, my italics)

That means that the external object, for example, the therapist in the therapeutic relationship, also makes a contribution to the projective identification process. Therapists receive projections and might or might not identify with them, and might actually evoke them because we have our own internal structures and reactions to projections. In other words, we more or less identify with our patients' projections in our own way. As Gabbard (1995) wrote,

The analyst's countertransference reactions will involve a joint creation of contributions from both patient and analyst, suggesting that part of what the analyst experiences reflects the patient's inner world. One of the analyst's tasks in collaboration with the patient, then, becomes to work his or her way out of the transference–countertransference enactment and understand interpretively with the patient what is going on. (p. 482).

Fulfilling this collaborative, interpretative task depends on the analyst's awareness of feeling, thought, or fantasy provoked or evoked by each projection. This job is not easy. When the patients, especially those with early disturbance that has led to massive splitting, project bad and aggressive parts of self or objects on to their therapists, the pressure on the therapists is so high that they have have almost no space to reflect on what is happening in their own experience and in interaction with the patient. They find that they cannot think, let alone formulate an interpretation about projective identification. However, knowing about projective identification helps them to develop insight about what has happened in the interaction, so that later they are able to analyse the content of the patient's fantasy, the perceptions and behaviour that it evokes, and the part played by their own internal structures.

Because projective identification is unconscious, patients cannot be aware how it happens, or how their internal structures, projections, and perceptions of others interact with the traits of others on to whom they are projecting. They do not see the connection between their emotional experience and their perception, between internal experience and behaviour, and between their behaviours and others' reactions. Having an interpretation about the *content* of their unconscious fantasy is not enough. Patients need to experience and learn from the interactive *process* of the therapeutic relationship.

To gain insight into this process, patients have to repeatedly experience affect in a therapeutic environment, and become more tolerant of it. Then they can identify their emotions, and become increasingly aware of the relationship between emotion and behaviour, and the impact of their behaviour on others. This brings me to Fonagy's useful concept of mentalization, which comes from the literature of attachment theory (Fonagy, 2001). Mentalization is defined as "the mental process by which an individual implicitly and explicitly interprets the actions of himself and others as meaningful on the basis of intentional mental states such as personal desires, needs, feelings, beliefs, and reasons" (Bateman & Fonagy, 2004, p. xxi). Mentalization is different from insight, which traditionally refers to gaining awareness of unconscious mental content. However, insight about content does not secure lasting therapeutic change. Patients also have to understand their involvement in process. Therapists need to use their feelings and reactions to help their patients to recognise the process, mentalize their experience of self and other, and modify their behaviours. From these interactions, patients not only gain insight about content and process, but also internalise a new experience of interpersonal communication.

In the following section, I will show how mentalization and projective identification are useful in psychodynamic group therapy and how group therapy is useful for illustrating the action of mentalization and projective identification.

PROJECTIVE IDENTIFICATION IN THE GROUP

Helping patients mentalize the influence of their actual behaviour on others by linking their behaviours with their perception of others and helping them to recognise the connection to unconscious projective identifications and contain anxiety by process and review, instead of discharging it by projection, are the essential activities of therapeutic action in psychodynamic group therapy.

In individual psychoanalysis, projective identification operates as though the patient unconsciously directs a drama, with roles that are determined by internal object relationships unconsciously assigned to the analyst by the patient. Because of the complexities of the patient's internal object relationships, the analyst has to play many roles as the various objects of the patient's projection while being the interpreter of the projection. Then the therapist must react to the patient in a way other than he or she would expect. This is the way to modify the projective identification.

The same is true in group therapy. The group therapist is the object of the group's projection of unconscious group fantasy, but the group therapist abstains from establishing focused interactions with individuals, instead directing remarks to the group as a whole. Deprived of intense individual attention, group members pair with one another, and this targets projective identifications to one another in the group. The group provides many objects for a group member's individual projections and many opportunities for all the group members to experience and reflect upon their own and others' experience. In the framework of psychodynamic group therapy, the stage becomes larger than in individual therapy or analysis. The therapist is neither the sole object nor the sole interpreter. Every group member can behave like a co-therapist and can provide different views. As Kauff (2009) has pointed out, member-to-member communication can be more easily received and processed in therapy groups than patient-to-therapist communication in individual therapy. Therapist, members, and even the whole group can be targets for projection. For some patients in individual psychoanalysis, it is difficult to project bad or aggressive parts on to the therapist, because they fear retaliation from the therapist. It is much easier for patients in groups to select a member with the valency to receive their projections that fit with their own internal structures, because the group member, unlike the therapist, is not an authority figure from whom retaliation might be feared.

The group therapist and various group members can be projectively identified with the self or object pole of an individual member's internal object relationship recreated in interaction in the group. Having studied the countertransference of therapists to individual patients, Racker (1968) identified their concordant and complementary identifications with the patient's projections. Racker meant that the individual therapist might identify with a projected part of the patient's object pole of an internal object relationship (complementary identification) or with the self pole of the internal object relationship (concordant identification). In group therapy, some members identify with a projected aspect of the projector's self (concordant identification), while others identify with a projectively disavowed internal object (complementary identification), depending on their valencies. If the therapist uses group members' differing reactions effectively, the internal structure of the projector is arrayed in the group for all to observe and learn from. As a result of his steady presence in the face of many projections, and the containing function of the group itself, the group therapist helps the members to improve their capacity for the containment of anxiety.

CASE EXAMPLE

The group I will describe is a slow-open, outpatient psychodynamic group with nine members, meeting once a week in China. Most of the members have been in the group more than two years. I am not intending to describe the group-wide dynamics or the system of projective identifications. I will instead focus on one patient's experience within the group to illustrate mentalization, containment, and projective identification. I am following the example of Horwitz in describing one patient in a group (2014, p. 206, 224; Scharff, 2015).

> Mrs J, thirty-five years old, is a doctor in a municipal hospital. She joined the group because she had difficult relationships with family members, colleagues, and friends. She has been married once and is now divorced. From her individual evaluation, I knew she had a strict, critical, devaluing father. From a young age, she felt that her father did not love her and preferred her younger sister. In the group, Mrs J frequently complained that she was honest and authentic towards others, but that they did not reciprocate her honesty. She often felt cheated and was easily hurt. Therefore, she either avoided powerful people or developed angry conflicts with them.

At the beginning, Mrs J seemed warm-hearted, helping group members, giving advice, and showing sympathy. But her difficulty in establishing stable relationships gradually emerged. She became hurt and angry when someone did not agree with her, or when someone reported feelings towards her that she could not understand. Gradually, she developed conflicts with many group members, which repeatedly made her want to quit the group. With my encouragement, she stayed, gradually becoming more tolerant and familiar with the meaning of her conflicts with others. She found that the conflicts in the group were not as destructive as those in her real life. She gradually became more accepting when other group members, who also experienced conflict, offered her understanding and support. When she could begin to tolerate conflict in the group, and see how her hurt and anger operated there, she was gradually able to identify the traits of those members who developed conflicts with her, and the situations in which she was prone to feel hurt. Later, she could link those features with people in her daily life with whom she also had conflicts. She was able to mentalize her experience in relation to others.

Mrs J told the group, "When someone in my life looks powerful and assertive, I feel insecure and am easily hurt when they don't agree with me. It's similar to what happens here in the group." With her increasing tolerance, she could accept feedback and stand more confrontation both from group members and group leaders. When she complained about a powerful man in the group, another member said to her, "I feel he chose to talk with you, not others in the group, because he trusted you. Why do you feel he bulldozed you?" Another member challenged her on her tendency to make snap judgements: "I feel you often change your impression of someone just because of one sentence." Another member spoke of being scared of her because of the way she spoke sometimes: "Every time you say something, I just feel you are putting a knife on the table. I was scared and didn't know if I should tell you my feelings." Such heartfelt confrontation helped Mrs J become curious about her own and others' internal worlds and about the relationship between her emotions and her external relationships. These interactions helped improve her mentalizing.

In one session, Mrs J wanted to help another member, Ms K, who felt inferior to her colleagues and became anxious in their company. When Mrs J gave advice about what to do, Ms K refused the advice politely. Mrs J became irritated and angry, and exerted pressure on Ms K to accept her point of view. The next week, Mrs J told the group that, on reflection, she could understand Ms K's feeling in the previous session when she tried to give her advice. She told the group that at dinner with her parents and her sister, when she told them about some difficulties in her hospital, her father and her sister tried to help her by giving her advice. She said, "Although I know they were trying to help me, I just felt they didn't understand. They became more and more angry with me, until I felt wronged and upset. After that, I thought of the interaction with Ms K in the last session. Ms K must have had a similar feeling to mine with my father and sister." Then Mrs J took the next step, owning her projective identification. She said, "I behaved just like my father and sister towards Ms K." Mrs J realised that her overbearing behaviour had evoked in Ms K the suffering Mrs J had experienced in relation to her critical primary objects.

With improved mentalizing and ability to own her projections, Ms J gradually brought what she learned in group into her daily life. Her avoidance of others decreased, and when she felt hurt, she was more able to tolerate emotional pain and maintain contact with others. Those "powerful people" were now felt to be less dangerous, just as Ms K had become less threatening herself. She could see them more fully, look at things from their point of view, and in her eyes they became more fully developed in their own right.

We can see how, in her daily life, Mrs J either avoided her weak and vulnerable feelings by projecting bad and aggressive parts on to others, which fulfilled her prophecy of being punished or abandoned. The group acted as a container for her fear about this part of herself. Since the group gave her no room to run, she repeatedly experienced her typical conflicts there and could see them anew. What was different from her outside life was that instead of being punished or abandoned, her internal experience was confronted and understood. Through this constructive interaction, she had an opportunity to identify her own and others' inner worlds and understand the links between her own behaviour and the behaviour of others and their connection to their inner worlds via the action of projective identification. Because these interactions improved her tolerance of emotional discomfort, she became able to reduce her splitting of objects into good and bad and so could see members of the group as whole persons, not part objects misidentified as causing her distress. As her need for using projective identification to deal with her weakness and vulnerability lessened inside the group, she became slowly able to transfer her new capacity for mentalizing and containing to her daily life.

CONCLUSION

Projective identification is not just a defence mechanism; it is the vehicle for powerful unconscious interpersonal communication, as seen so clearly in psychodynamic group therapy. It is important for patients to understand the processes of projective identification and for the therapists to use their understanding as a pathway to help patients re-own their projections and contain them. Psychodynamic group psychotherapy offers an effective environment for improved mentalizing, the emergence and exploration of projective identification, and better containment, thus facilitating personal growth.

REFERENCES

Bateman, A. W., & Fonagy, P. (2004). *Psychotherapy for Borderline Personality Disorder.* New York: Oxford University Press.

Bion, W. R. (1962). *Learning from Experience.* London: Heinemann.

Bion, W. R. (1967). *Second Thoughts.* Northvale, NJ: Jason Aronson.

Fonagy, P. (2001). *Attachment Theory and Psychoanalysis.* New York: Other Press.

Gabbard. G. O. (1995). Countertransference: the emerging common ground. *International Journal of Psychoanalysis, 76*: 475–485.

Horwitz, L. (2014). *Listening with the Fourth Ear.* London: Karnac.

Kauff, P. (2009). Transference in combined individual and group psychotherapy. *International Journal of Group Psychother.apy, 59*(1): 29–46.

Klein, M. (1946). Notes on some schizoid mechanisms. *International Journal of Psychoanalysis, 27*: 99–110.

Ogden, T. H. (1979). On projective identification. *International Journal of Psychoanalysis, 60*: 357–373.

Ogden, T. H. (1982). *Projective Identification and Psychotherapeutic Technique.* New York: Jason Aronson.

Ogden, T. H. (1983). The concept of internal object relations. *International Journal of Psychoanalysis, 64*: 227–241.

Racker, H. (1968). *Transference and Countertransference.* The International Psycho-Analytical Library. London: The Hogarth Press and the Institute of Psycho-Analysis.

Scharff, J. S. (2015). Book Review. Listening with the Fourth Ear: Unconscious Dynamics in Analytic Group Psychotherapy. *Journal of the American Psychoanalytic Association, 63*: 182–191.

Somatic Countertransference:
A Chinese Perspective

Adrienne Margarian

Abstract

When somatic experiences such as headaches, nausea, and sleepiness are felt in the psychotherapist's body, they are acknowledged as somatic countertransference in western psychotherapeutic practice. This paper researches somatic countertransference from a Chinese perspective by exploring the cultural notions of Qi, Yin and Yang, and psychic blockages addressed by the process of "talking acupuncture" known as psychotherapy in the west. Data provided by Chinese psychotherapists and clinical experts who acknowledge somatic countertransference or who work with Chinese medical, spiritual, and healing practices are referenced to describe and discuss these new cultural contributions to the field of somatic countertransference research.

Key words: China, somatic countertransference, Qi, Yin and Yang, psychic blockage.

INTRODUCTION

The notion of somatic countertransference, whereby the therapist's body becomes activated, enlivened, or deadened in relation to the transference, has encouraged clinical musings and empirical research for some time (Margarian, 2014a). Headaches, nausea, pain, sleepiness felt by the therapist in relation to their client bring with them an opportunity to enrich clinical insight and explore the unfolding relationship between client and therapist. Western ideas about intersubjectivity inspired by relational psychoanalysis and the mutual zone of unconsciousness described by Jung suggest ways of understanding how a therapist can experience a physical sensation that manifests in his or her body that may be meaningful and related to what is occurring in the psychotherapeutic relationship (Jung, 1954; Stolorow et al., 2002). Current research has endeavoured to extend our ideas about this aspect of psychotherapy by referencing Chinese ideas about intersubjectivity, a holistic approach to mind and body, and the general notion of Qi equating with the unconscious.

This paper explores findings presented from doctoral research undertaken in the area of somatic countertransference from a Chinese perspective. Referencing the responses from twenty-nine Chinese psychotherapists and several experts in the area of somatic countertransference, Chinese medical, healing, and spiritual practices, some tentative conclusions are drawn about understanding somatic countertransference from a Chinese perspective. The paper commences with a short overview of the concept of somatic countertransference, a brief outline of the research project and methodology, followed by some Chinese ideas on somatic countertransference provided by the cross-cultural research. The four cultural notions of Qi, Yin and Yang, psychic blockages, and "talking acupuncture" will be explored in particular. While it is apparent that differences between western and Chinese ways of exploring and defining somatic countertransference could occur, this paper focuses primarily on areas of overlap through the cultural notions of somatic countertransference, Qi, and Yin and Yang.

SOMATIC COUNTERTRANSFERENCE: A BRIEF OVERVIEW

When Freud first conceived of the idea of countertransference in the psychotherapeutic relationship, he considered it to be a hindrance (Freud, 1912e, Gelso & Hayes, 2007). Yet, today, in the broader field of psychoanalysis and psychotherapy, countertransference is worked with in numerous ways and given varying degrees of importance for therapeutic exploration and process (Gelso & Hayes, 2007).

For clarity's sake, a definition of the psychoanalytic terms employed in this paper is required. The term transference denotes the unconscious relationship transferred to the analyst or psychotherapist that bears close resemblance to an earlier experience with important parental figures. Countertransference in this instance is defined as feelings, thoughts, and images experienced by the therapist in relation to the transference enacted in the psychotherapeutic relationship. Somatic countertransference builds on the traditional description of countertransference by including the somatic dimension, whereby any physical sensations felt in the body of the psychotherapist are considered to be countertransference. This term notably has evolved from the traditions of body psychotherapy, and dance and movement therapy. Additionally, somatic countertransference has been explored in various clinical depictions from psychoanalysis to analytical psychology (Margarian, 2014a). Yet, while rich clinical examples are explored in the literature, little attempt has been made to understand how somatic countertransference manifests in the psychotherapy session.

None the less, it is noted that the notion of intersubjectivity, according to the school of relational psychoanalysis and Jung's seminal ideas on the mutual zone of unconsciousness discussed in his *Collected Works*, provide some sense that therapist and client can mutually infect and affect each other (Jung, 1954; Stolorow et al. 2002). Specifically, Jung suggested that there is a line of communication that occurs between analyst and patient at an unconscious-to-unconscious level (Jung, 1954). Accordingly, these ideas are significant western attempts to understand how a psychotherapist can pick up in his or her body something physical that, when explored in the psychotherapeutic process, holds clinical importance and relevancy. Specifically Jung wrote,

> For two personalities to meet is like mixing two different chemical substances; if there is any combination at all, both are transformed. In any effective psychological treatment the doctor is bound to influence the patient; but this influence can only take place if the patient has a reciprocal influence on the doctor. You can exert no influence if you are not susceptible to influence. (Jung, 1954, p. 71)

This statement made by Jung emphasises the mutuality of the psychotherapy experience and suggests that underpinning this relationship is a zone of shared influence. As such, there is the sense that both therapist and client will infect/affect each other via a shared zone of unconsciousness. More specifically, Jung notes that the role of the psychotherapist is to become infected with the patient's material as if he develops a psychic infection (Jung, 1954). It is this idea that I think sits comfortably with the possibility that somatic countertransference is transmitted, or perhaps facilitated, in the psychotherapeutic relationship. Somatic countertransference, therefore, becomes a psychotherapeutic tool, an indicator of important psychic material that is surfacing in the process.

From a post-Jungian perspective, it was Andrew Samuels, a Jungian analyst who researched and developed the idea of embodied countertransference. After interviewing thirty-two psychotherapists, Samuels discerned notable nuances in countertransferential material provided by his participants (Samuels, 1985). Samuels surmised that there is an observable subset of countertransference that he termed embodied countertransference. Samuels describes it in this way:

> There is a considerable difference between, on the one hand, my reflecting of the here-and- now state of my patient, feeling just what he is unconscious of at the moment, and, on the other, my embodiment of an entity, theme or person of a longstanding, intrapsychic, inner world nature. One problem for the analyst is that, experientially, the two states may seem similar. (Samuels, 1985, p 52)

The embodied countertransference is, therefore, more elusive and uncanny in how it manifests in the psychotherapist. It can represent a past inner object, such as the punitive mother, or an unsymbolised and unprocessed experience that Joyce McDougall spoke about in her important work, *Theatres of the Body*. MacDougall surmised that remnants from a mistuned attachment could surface as inexplicable body states in the patient (McDougall, 1989). Following on, similar states surface in the body of the psychotherapist as somatic countertransference (Dosamantes-Beaudry, 1992; Iannaco, 2000; Stone, 2006). Returning to Samuels, he provides an excellent example of feeling extremely thirsty in the presence of his analysand. When he describes this to her in terms of feeling parched like a desert, this leads the analysand to surface unexplored and unacknowledged material relating to her parents. Samuels reports that the effect of this is profound for the unfolding psychotherapy process (cited in Merchant, 2012). As such, I sense that somatic countertransference is a subset of the embodied form whereby the therapist experiences, in physical terms, material that has been split off and unacknowledged from the client's psyche. As Samuels states, it can be difficult to grasp and convoluted in the way that it is tracked back to important inner psychic states (Samuels, 1985).

In thinking about somatic countertransference and that it surfaces from a zone of mutual unconsciousness, or, in contemporary terms, the intersubjective space, I noted that these theories were largely western and, therefore, underpinned by Cartesian dualism. Both Bloom and Shaw have critiqued our knowledge to date on this basis, that our understanding has developed from theories influenced by western philosophy informed by a mind–body division (Bloom, 2007; Shaw, 2004). Accordingly, they encourage an exploration of eastern spiritual and healing practices, specifically, Chinese approaches to working with energy in order to reach an understanding from a holistic viewpoint. This is commensurate with Orbach's warning that when we work with bodily experiences in the psychotherapeutic space, we are naturally inclined to analyse the body, therefore endorsing a mind–body split rather than sitting with the body to experience it for increased clinical insight (Orbach, 2004). When I interviewed Susie Orbach for this research project, she clearly emphasised the need to make the body "primary" rather than "secondary" by subjecting it to mentalist processes (Orbach, 2013). Encouraged by Bloom, Shaw, and Orbach, this research project therefore endeavours to seek out information and ideas about somatic countertransference from a culture that approaches the mind and body holistically (Bloom, 2007; Orbach, 2004, 2013; Shaw, 2004).

THE RESEARCH PROJECT

In acknowledging that to date our understanding and ways of working with somatic countertransference are largely inspired by western philosophy, this quantitative research project aimed to look beyond that. Accordingly, I interviewed twenty-nine Chinese psychotherapists from China, Hong Kong, and Singapore and several experts and academics either working with somatic countertransference or with an interest in Chinese medical, healing, and spiritual practices. All participants were recruited voluntarily by "snowballing" methods and agreed to participate in an interview. The

China America Psychoanalytic Alliance (CAPA), South China Normal University, and the Hong Kong Institute of Analytical Psychology all agreed to facilitate a snowball email for recruitment of participants. Each participant's identity was protected by a pseudonym commencing with the letter T and assigned a number, to ensure confidentiality in accordance with ethical procedures and guidelines set by Deakin University.

All twenty-nine Chinese psychotherapists had studied and were practising psychotherapy with a range of professional experience from one to twenty years. Their nominated professions ranged from counsellor, psychologist, psychotherapist, psychotherapy intern to psychiatrist. In terms of the experts, I approached each person individually and they agreed to reveal their participation as they are considered to be established within their field of expertise. As such, they were sought out for their opinions to enrich the clinical data and findings from the research project.

The research process entailed each of the Chinese participants being interviewed for up to two hours on the research topic of somatic countertransference. A set of questions to guide the conversation was emailed to all participants prior to the interview. After completion of the interview, each participant was assigned a pseudonym to protect their identity and provided with a transcript to enable them to edit their responses to ensure that a mutually agreed version of the interview data was established. Post collection of the data, the interviews were analysed for recurring themes and areas of interest according to a discourse analysis approach. After this initial stage of investigation, several experts in psychoanalysis, analytical psychology, Qi Gong, and traditional Chinese medicine (TCM) were interviewed about their understanding and experiences of somatic countertransference from their cultural perspective. Their contributions augmented the data obtained from the original interviews of Chinese psychotherapists. The process of interviewing the Chinese psychotherapists and experts occurred over an eighteen-month period either via Skype or in face-to-face format when possible. As such, some interviews were conducted in China, Hong Kong, Malaysia, and Australia.

In terms of the focus of the research project, two essential questions were posed; do Chinese psychotherapists experience somatic countertransference and if so, how would they account for it from their cultural, spiritual, and medical practices? For the purposes of this paper, only the findings relating to question two are taken up for discussion.

A CHINESE PERSPECTIVE ON SOMATIC COUNTERTRANSFERENCE

Exploring somatic countertransference from a Chinese perspective brought about some interesting findings and ideas for understanding how it evolves and how best to work with it clinically. Importantly, it was noted that some similarities between the western notions of transference, countertransference, and somatic countertransference occurred with Chinese cultural ideas of Qi, Yin and Yang, and the concept of psychic blockages and the corresponding remedy of "talking acupuncture". For the purposes of this brief overview of a culturally complex and vast terrain, it is only the similarities between the Chinese and western psychotherapy that are focused upon.

Prior to considering these cultural notions, however, it is important to consider that two themes emerged from the data analysis. On the one hand, there was the sense that cultural knowledge had been lost since the Cultural Revolution. Yet, conversely, for some psychotherapists cultural ideas were freely integrated and adapted into psychotherapy styles. Commensurate with the integration of cultural ideas and knowledge were some theories to explain somatic countertransference with reference to TCM, Taoism, and the practice of Qi Gong. TCM is an indigenous system of holistic medicine that has been developed and refined over 5,000 years, while Taoism, according to Sun, is "The order of nature, the way in which the Universe works" (Sun, 2013, p. 253).

Similarly, Qi Gong is noted to be the practice of Qi enabled by tailor-made exercises that harness and enhance the personal flow of Qi. From these spiritual and medical practices, the notions of Qi, Yin and Yang, psychic blockages, and the idea of "talking acupuncture" are relevant aspects of the material uncovered from this exercise. These cultural notions are explored in turn.

QI

The Chinese concept of Qi is integral to Chinese health and well-being. As described by Master Chunyi Lin, Qi Gong Master, and John Dolic, TCM practitioner, two recruited experts I interviewed, it is the energy force that is within all life matter (Dolic, 2014; Lin, 2013). According to Sun, it is succinctly noted as "The vital force in the body, which is the synergy of Yin and Yang" (Sun, 2013, p. 252).

While it is not immediately visible, it reportedly flows within and between people. That being said, Qi is likely to be similar to the western notion of the unconscious. This explanation was taken up by numerous Chinese psychotherapists. Additionally, there was a sense that one's Qi could affect another person's Qi, as noted by interviewee T3 in the following.

It is potentially, maybe it is useful in a sense in a more comprehensive way for your body to pick up and catch all those underlying issues and material rather than verbal. So when you become more fully aware of that, it might be a valuable truth. Just like the thermometer or detector that is picking up the sense. What if the therapist can produce a response such as the kind I am thinking of through this way? Because when you mentioned about the culture, in Chinese, there is Qi.

The Qi, now it may sound a little bit far-fetched, but I think it could be explained too, that is the somatic, that is exactly the somatic. [You receive it] [t]hrough your Qi and then you transmit it back to your client.

In a sense, it is possible I think. But probably not me, not my experience. I am talking about some theoretical things. In another way, the somatic counter-transference could be interpreted for the Qi principal. (T3)

In the above statements made by T3, a psychiatrist with knowledge of the I Ching and Taoism, he is sounding out the possibility that Qi can flow between people and this experience would account for somatic counter-transference experienced by the psychotherapist. Similarly, another Chinese psychotherapist, T14, says the following:

I never thought of it before in a cultural way, I mean, [that] from the Chinese culture [we] can explain this. I never thought of this before. In Chinese culture, we have a word: it is Qi.

It is another definition of unconsciousness. It is a term we [describe] in that way but maybe it is the same thing. (T14)

Another participant articulates the following:

You have a Qi area, you have some Qi around you and other people will be influenced by your Qi and they can feel your Qi and it can control other people, this Qi. It can influence other people. So some people who are powerful, we can feel the[ir] energies are powerful, the Qi is stronger and intense and peaceful or passionate, Qi is different from other people. It is Qi. Maybe some substance or some description but in China we call it the Qi. (T4)

It is like the air, the Qi is like the air. I think people from other cultures could-n't understand the Chinese knowledge about the Qi. When it is a substance or a subjective description or like the Chinese medicine, we think that the patient has a different cure (acupuncture point); even the traditional Chinese people didn't have a machine to detect where it is, we can describe it and find it, where it is and how it flows from one place to another. [Acupuncturists] can use needles to push it, to push the flow. Later, when [there is] some research about it, they can find the place exactly: it is the right place for something that has happened. So I actually think that Qi is like a substance and it could influence other people as an energy, even when they didn't have [a] machine to detect it. We can feel it, like our traditional Chinese medicine. The Chinese doctors, we can find such a place. (T4)

In bringing these three separate statements from different Chinese psycho-therapists together there is a sense that unconscious processes in Chinese culture are equal to Qi energy. Additionally, it suggests that Qi occurs within a zone of mutuality whereby people can affect each other. This is consistent with Jung's notion of the zone of mutual unconsciousness, whereby Jung espoused the idea that an unconscious-to-unconscious line of communication could occur between analyst and patient (Jung, 1954).

In terms of how it could explain the manifestation of physical sensations in the body of the therapist and how it could relate to psychotherapeutic process, T3 expressed it in terms of a Chinese character and he described it in the following way:

> This picture gives you the impression that humans are something in between the sky and the earth and it is a being that can respond to the other in between the sky and the earth. So human actions will give this sort of resonance and that is my understanding of the I Ching. It is a system of inaction. So why do we have this sort of response? The whole I Ching is talking about the synchronicity, this kind of response, so if you ask me is this something with the culture, then I think of that um, the main feeling in the I Ching is the kind of synchronic response between humans. It is also compatible with the sort of sympathy response that has provided my understanding on that.

During our interview, T3 drew a Chinese character that was described in the above extract and illustrates synchronic resonance between humans that he felt was experienced as bodily sensations in everyday life and psychotherapy. As such, this Chinese character captures, in Chinese cultural terms, the western notion of somatic countertransference. The image following is the first character that T3 drew, which denotes the human, with the second character illustrating the human between the heaven and earth. This implies the human-to-human flow of communication that can often be experienced as synchronicity, or the unconscious-to-unconscious resonance implied by Jung (1954).

人 denotes human 天 denotes human between heaven and earth.

YIN AND YANG

Yin and Yang, a core concept from TCM, is integral for understanding the sense of balance within and between all living matter. As Sun describes it,

> A Taoist concept that in nature, events and matters always exist in pairs of contrasting states. Within the context of health, disequilibrium between yin and yang is deemed to be responsible for feelings and sensations of distress and discomfort. (Sun, 2013, p. 254)

As such, there is an immediate applicability of the Yin and Yang concept when two people meet whereby a balancing of Qi energy between two people occurs. This has implications for the idea of the zone of mutual unconsciousness and, by extension, the manifestation of somatic material in the body of the psychotherapist. Chinese psychotherapist T6 was keen to articulate the concept of Yin and Yang in terms of the therapeutic dyad. He says,

> Even when the person enters the room, you and the person you will be one; this is tai chi. It is the Yin and the Yang. You are the wholeness, you and the patient find a balance point, and the tai chi will stable; even if you are not in a balanced point, your patient will realise that it is not stable. (T6)

T6 explains that everybody possesses Qi and when therapist and client enter a room, two sources of Qi encounter each other and thereby morph into a Yin and Yang configuration. This parallels Jung's important statement on the mixing of two chemicals when therapist and patient meet (Jung, 1954). In my interview with John Dolic, TCM practitioner, he validated this explanation and stated,

> So if [I] have more Yin, you have less Yang, that is how they work. If you have more darkness, you have less brightness, more heat, less cold, so that is how they work. Ah, you have positive energy and you have negative energy. Positive energy is the one that protects us: you have your positive energy, I have mine. Everybody has positive energy, as along as we are alive. If your positive energy has gone, you die. Negative energy would be a disease of any kind; that is seen as Yin, Yang is protective. If you are suffering from a lot of negative energy, like patients of any kind, then they deal with it in their own way but you also deal with their energy.

> They come with their problems; that is seen as negative energy that I am exposed to and then as my positive energy builds, I am able to keep the balance—but maybe this is my explanation.

> So when my positive energy was stronger, then I was protected, so it could not harm me . . . it was like you have this darkness and then you have light. So if my light was not very strong, then it is really dark. But when the light becomes strong, the darkness diminishes and it is gone. As I say, that is just how I explain it, but in truth that is what was happening. I could take their problems and I would be protected, but it only worked, I guess, because I have had a lot of experience dealing with patients and also I practise Qi Gong. (Dolic, 2014)

Dolic is expressing many things about the interplay of Yin and Yang between two people. He described how each person has their own internal state of Yin and Yang and that when in the company of another, this balance of Yin and Yang is again changed. Furthermore, while he is validating the notion of mutual influence, he adds the potential of harm occurring when two energetic forces meet. He points out that his practice of Qi Gong enables him to process and work through any negative effects resulting from being infected by the other. While not discussed in this paper, this highlights the importance of greater self-care when working closely with patients and, by association, their Qi.

As an indication of the negative effects of Qi and, by extension, somatic countertransference, T6 says the following:

> Yes, I talked earlier about [the fact] that I felt so exhausted after seeing some patients. It is as if they gave their Qi, their negative Qi, to me and they took a lot of my positive Qi away, so I felt exhausted, as if I am constantly stretched. Sometimes it feels like a battle, they can see their Qi win over mine. I, consciously or unconsciously, will not let them make their Qi overwhelm mine. So in a session we might have this kind of invisible battle. (T6)

This is a telling statement of the potentially debilitating effects of Qi and working with unconscious processes. Importantly, T6 demonstrates an openness to, and awareness of, this material that he is able to work with in a conscious way in order to minimise harm to himself as a clinician.

MIND BODY FUSION: PSYCHIC BLOCKAGES AND "TALKING ACUPUNCTURE"

While not a direct explanation for somatic countertransference from a Chinese perspective, an interesting finding emerged from the data, that being the idea of "talking acupuncture". A surprising correlation between psychotherapy and TCM was elucidated in the responses made by T17 and T16. Both Chinese psychotherapists independently perceived psychotherapy to be a form of "talking acupuncture". T17 expresses it as such:

> Yes, I think it would be a good beginning: the talking acupuncture, because acupuncture can't be used with the metal needle, [but] it can be applied with another [kind of] needle, you can use your words. Like Winnicott's ideas, the holding environment is not only provided by arms [and] with [a] blanket, it can also be provided by [the] words of the therapist, of the analyst . . .

> With the patient's free association, you can also find the blockage. There are a lot of blockages. Your interpretations are like acupuncture. (T17)

Likewise T16, unknown to T17, expresses something very similar by stating,

> This is something from my own experience. Therapy is very much like a massage. You find a point or several points of the patient where they feel sour, but the therapist is doing the work to massage this painful point which does not really exist, but you can find several points where the patient cannot really . . .

how can I say this? Which is not exactly painful but has that kind of a feeling of sourness, this is like the relationship between the one who is doing the massage and the one who is being massaged, [it] is very close, because you can really feel . . . (T16)

While these statements do not shed light on somatic countertransference immediately, the use of the metaphor "talking acupuncture" is an important one. It implies that in the same way as acupuncture aims to reduce Qi blockages, the process of psychotherapy enables a similar process to occur. The implication is that both words and needles can reduce blockages. This very idea is discussed at length by Zhang and Chi in their article that explores the intersection between psychoanalysis and TCM practice (Zhang & Chi, 2013). In this article, they astutely parallel psychoanalytic aims of supportive and expressive process with the TCM notions of reinforcing and reducing (Zhang & Chi, 2013).

Another unrelated but essential finding from this research was the propensity for conflating feeling and physical states when discussing countertransference examples. On numerous occasions, when I asked for clinical examples of somatic countertransference, I was presented with examples of feeling-type countertransferential states. It was not until I interviewed T17 that it became clear that I had been limiting the notion of countertransference by imposing a split through the very act of asking for "somatic" countertransference examples. As T17 states,

Countertransference has the somatic dimension whether you are aware of it or not, or [are] sensitive enough to it or not. You regard it as trash or regard it as treasure . . . they are the same ontologically but they are two dimensions . . . Yes, images, associations, the body feelings, they are the same. Like this cup has many faces. (T17)

Bringing these two ideas together, as the data largely demonstrated, feeling and bodily sensations are intricately linked according to my research cohort, and, therefore, the process of "talking acupuncture" is highly intuitive. In terms of understanding how somatic countertransference evolves, that is not immediately relevant here; rather, the learning from these connections are that mind and body states are fully integrated, within the psychotherapeutic relationship, threaded together by Qi and balanced according to Yin and Yang principles. It brings to mind the numerous endeavours to understand whether psychoanalysis can be applied to the Chinese (Chen & Swartzman, 2001; Hwang et al., 2003; Markert, 2011; Ng, 1985; Shi & Scharff, 2011; Sun, 2004; Zhong, 2011). As such, this analogy of "talking acupuncture" for psychotherapy process provides a unique metaphor illustrating that psychoanalytic thinking can be utilised and applied in psychotherapy in China. In bringing together the ideas of psychic blockages and body and feeling fused states noted as somatic countertransference, the therapist's body is likely to behave as "a tuning fork" in that it picks up material from the mutual zone of unconsciousness in this unusual way (Stone, 2006, p. 109).

While not addressed in this paper, by exploring cultural explanations of somatic countertransference many ideas for working effectively with the therapist's body as a tool of clinical intuition were provided in the research findings (Margarian, 2014b). In addition, spiritual and healing practices further provided the means for heightening and refining sensitivity to picking up material from the mutual zone of unconsciousness. Moreover, the exploration of cultural practices encouraged and provided the means for increased self-protection against the negative effects for somatic countertransference, psychic infections, and Qi blockages. Qi Gong and meditation practices were seen as both refining and protective in their application to therapeutic process and practice (Margarian, 2014b).

THE ROLE OF RELATIONSHIPS

Following on from the notion of Qi and Yin and Yang, the importance of the psychotherapy relationship was noted with reference to the role of the body. As such, the emerging relationship in the room was both integral and facilitating of unconscious processes and somatic expressions. This idea fits neatly with Jung's concept of the mutual zone of unconsciousness and how the psychotherapist naturally becomes infected during the process of psychotherapy (Jung, 1954).

T17, a psychotherapist who suggested that somatic countertransference occurs 100% of the time as mind and body work in unison, stated the following, which articulates the role of relationships.

> When people are together, their bodies also build a relationship. The body is a temple. Even though they have not shaken hands, do not kiss each other, did not have sex. But the first thing is two bodies are together. This is the most primordial one. Your bodies are together. So there must be a lot of communication between the two bodies, whether you are aware of it or not. The bodies are the root for all experiences because the so-called advanced communications were based on soma. Mostly, I am Bionian; Bion speaks about beta and alpha elements. So once the communications starts [it is] with beta element. The beta element starts between the boundary between somatic and psychic surfaces; it is where our communications start . . . (T17)

In essence, this brings focus to an important ingredient in the psychotherapeutic process, that being the relationship between the two bodies in the room. It further validates T3's ideas of synchrony between bodies between heaven and earth, which he illustrated with the drawing of the Chinese character. As such, underpinning mutual unconsciousness, psychic infections, and the ebb and flow and balancing of Qi is the idea that relationships between two bodies between heaven and earth are the crux of the matter. It implies that the body plays a role in facilitating this relationship. In essence, the foundational role of the relationship is noted in both current western and eastern thinking.

CONCLUSION

While a lot has been written about whether psychoanalysis and the practice of psychotherapy can be accepted and worked with by the Chinese, this research project was endeavouring to seek counsel from Chinese psychotherapists to gain a cultural understanding of the role of the therapist's body in the psychotherapy process. Detailed elsewhere are examples of how Chinese psychotherapists work with somatic countertransference (Margarian, 2014b). The research project provided insight into the way Chinese psychotherapists understand the role of the body in psychotherapy practice, specifically known as somatic countertransference in western terms. It was noted that there was a propensity to conflate body and mind states when describing somatic countertransference, which is consistent with a more holistic approach to healing. By exploring Chinese medical, healing, and spiritual practices, several ideas were highlighted for enriching our understanding of somatic countertransference. Specifically, the ideas of Qi and Yin Yang were shown to describe the mutual unconscious effects that therapist and client will have on each other in psychotherapy. These ideas appear consistent with Jung's seminal concepts of the mutual zone of unconsciousness and the process of psychic infection. In addition, it was discovered that some Chinese psychotherapists are referencing the TCM practice of acupuncture to describe the psychotherapy process in which psychic blockages are reduced by verbal psychotherapy intervention. It was acknowledged that uniting western and Chinese approaches to grasping the complex topic of somatic countertransference was the understanding that the relationship between patient and therapist is integral for elucidating the psychotherapy process and enabling the role of the therapist's body.

Finally, while this research project is a tentative beginning towards understanding the role of the body in psychotherapy cross-culturally, it encourages future research to explore the inherent differences between western and Chinese psychotherapy practices for greater depth and a more complete clinical picture.

ACKNOWLEDGEMENT

I want to thank the Chinese American Psychoanalytic Alliance, South China Normal University, Hong Kong Institute of Analytical Psychology, and Deakin University for their support and participation in this research project.

REFERENCES

Bloom, K. (2006). *The Embodied Self: Movement and Psychoanalysis*. London: Karnac.

Chen, X., & Swartzman, L. C. (2001). Health beliefs and experiences in Asian cultures. In: S. S. Kazarian and D. R. Evans (Eds.), *Handbook of Cultural Health Psychology* (pp. 389–410). San Diego, CA: Academic Press.

Dolic, J. (2014). Personal communication, 17 January.

Dosamantes-Beaudry, I. (1992). The intersubjective relationship between therapist and patient: a key to understanding denied and denigrated aspects of the patient's self. *The Arts in Psychotherapy, 19*: 359–365.

Freud, S. (1912e). Recommendations to physicians practising psychoanalysis. *S. E., 12*: 111–120. London: Hogarth.

Gelso, C. J., & Hayes, J. A. (2007). *Countertransference and the Therapist's Inner Experience: Perils and Possibilities*. Mahwah, NJ: Lawrence Erlbaum.

Hwang, K. K., Liu, T. W., Han, D. Y., & Chen, S. H. (2003). Somatisation, emotional expression, and Confucian ethics in Chinese culture. In: Wai On-Phoon & I. Macindoe (Eds.), *Untangling the Threads: Perspectives on Mental Health in Chinese Communities* (pp. 47–80). New South Wales: Transcultural Mental Health Centre.

Iannaco, G. (2000). The therapist's body. *Psychodynamic Counselling, 6*(4): 533–537.

Jung, C. (1954). Problems of modern psychotherapy. General problems of psychotherapy. *C. W., 16*. London: Routledge & Kegan Paul.

Lin, C. (2013). Personal communication, 21 November.

Margarian, A. (2014a). A cross cultural study of somatic countertransference: a brief overview. *Asia Pacific Journal of Counselling and Psychotherapy*, DOI: 10.1080/21507686.2014.894922.

Margarian, A. (2014b) A cross-cultural study of somatic countertransference (unpublished doctoral thesis). Deakin University, Melbourne, Australia.

Markert, F. (2011). The Cultural Revolution—a traumatic Chinese experience and subsequent transgenerational transmission: some thoughts about intercultural interpretation. *International Journal of Applied Psychoanalytic Studies, 8*(3): 239–248.

McDougall, J. (1989). *Theatres of the Body: A Psychoanalytic Approach to Psychosomatic Illness*. London: Free Association.

Merchant, J. (2012). *Shamans and Analysts. New Insights on the Wounded Healer*. New York: Routledge.

Ng, M. L. (1985). Psychoanalysis for the Chinese—applicable or not applicable? *International Review of Psycho-analysis, 12*: 449–460.

Orbach, S. (2004). What can we learn from the therapist's body? *Attachment and Human Development, 6*(2): 141–150.

Orbach, S. (2013). Personal communication, 18 December.

Samuels, A. (1985). Countertransference, the 'mundus imaginalis' and a research project. *Journal of Analytical Psychology, 30*: 47–71.

Shaw, R. (2003). *The Embodied Psychotherapist: The Therapist's Body Story*. New York: Psychology Press.

Shi, Q., & Scharff, D. E. (2011). Cultural factors and projective identification in understanding a Chinese couple. *International Journal of Applied Psychoanalytic Studies, 8*(3): 207–217.

Stolorow, R. D., Atwood, G. E., & Orange, D. M. (2002). *Worlds of Experience: Interweaving Philosophical and Clinical Dimensions in Psychoanalysis.* New York: Basic Books.

Stone, M. (2006). The analyst's body as tuning fork: embodied resonance in the countertransference. *Journal of Analytical Psychology, 51*: 109–124.

Sun, C. (2013). *Themes in Chinese Psychology.* Singapore: Cengage Learning.

Sun, L. J. (2004). The deep structure of Chinese culture. Guangxi: Guangxi Normal University Press.

Zhang, P., & Chi, X. (2013). Reinforcing and reducing: dialogue between traditional Chinese medicine and psychoanalytic psychotherapy. *International Journal of Applied Psychoanalytic Studies,* DOI: 10.1002/aps.1358.

Zhong, J. (2011). Working with Chinese patients: are there conflicts between Chinese culture and psychoanalysis? *International Journal of Applied Psychoanalytic Studies, 8*(3): 218–226.

Practising Analytical Psychology in East Asia: A Post-Jungian Italian Perspective

Marta Tibaldi

Abstract

Two years after "Jung, Asia and Inter-culture: Jung across Cultural Borders", the first-ever International Conference on Carl Gustav Jung and his *Red Book*, held in Taipei, Taiwan, in October 2013, the author presents an updated reflection on her experience with East Asian trainees and clients and on some of the characteristics and difficulties that it entails from a post-Jungian Italian perspective. First of all, the encounter with a different culture such as the East Asian one requires the Jungian analyst to be aware of any cultural projection or countertransference he/she might have had beforehand, processing at the same time any possible cultural transference or projections on the part of the trainees and clients. A second reflection focuses on the use of English, usually the working language in East Asia, as a paradoxical bridge that might facilitate the analytic encounter, highlighting the quality of the analytical relationship and indicating the client's inner dynamics. The last reflection is about the need to interweave psychic experiences common to all human beings with the cultural images through which they are declined, aiming at achieving a cross-cultural imaginal narrative thanks to the method of active imagination. "Active deep writing", a new form of active imagination through writing, developed by the author and tailored to the East Asian trainees' and clients' cultural characteristics, is then briefly described as a cross-cultural way to process the personal, cultural, and archetypal aspects of their analytical experience.

Key words: Carl Gustav Jung, analytical psychology, East Asia, east–west dialogue, cross-cultural analytical practice, post-Jungian identity, active deep writing.

> We cannot clap with only one hand
> (Chinese proverb)

PREMISE

I am just back from Taipei, Taiwan, two years after the International Conference "Jung, Asia and Inter-culture: Jung across Cultural Borders", the first-ever International Conference on Carl Gustav Jung and his *Red Book*, held in that city in October 2013. At that time, I was invited to present a paper on my experience as Jungian analyst in East Asia (Tibaldi,

Psychoanalysis and Psychotherapy in China, Volume 1, 2015: pp. 78–96.

2013a), an opportunity for me to take a first stock of my work in Hong Kong and in Taipei, since I am currently in charge as Training Analyst and Supervisor of the International Association for Analytical Psychology (IAAP) in the Hong Kong Institute of Analytical Psychology (HKIAP).

After two years, I further focused my way of practising analysis in East Asia and this paper is an updated reflection on my experience from a post-Jungian Italian perspective. A perspective that, differently from how Andrew Samuels defines the four post-Jungian main identities (Samuels, 1986, 1998), I would call a "radical post-Jungian" one, meaning a way of practising analytical psychology mainly based on the extensive use of the Jungian method of active imagination, following the publication of Jung's *Red Book* (Jung, 2009).

Opening the 2013 Conference, Hao-Wei Wang, the president of the Taiwan Institute of Psychotherapy (TIP), noted that the development of psychotherapy in Taipei dated only back to the 1980s. In effect, twenty years before, in the 1960s, Taiwan was still dominated by the martial law imposed by Chiang Kai-shek and people were even forbidden from talking about any social issues or politics:

> The only possible way to resist is through the movement of Cultural Enlightenment, introducing Western thoughts into Taiwan. Among all these Western discourses, psychology was one of the most essential and important. Books by Jung, Freud and Fromm have brought the most impact to our minds. In that era, Jung's works *Modern Man in Search of a Soul, Man and his Symbols* and *Psychology and Literature* were translated into Chinese and became popular" (Jung, Asia and Inter-culture, 2013).

Despite this, no clinical work was involved with that cultural movement and only many years after was clinical psychology introduced in Taiwan:

> In the beginning the development of psychotherapy in Taiwan was focusing on Freudian Psychoanalysis and Cognitive Behavior Therapy. In the mid-90s, while André Lefebre introduced the Transpersonal Psychology to Taiwan, it merely touched the edge of the Jungian Psychology. The first systemic introduction of Jungian Psychology was organized by the Shiuhli Memorial Foundation in late 90s. (Jung, Asia and Inter-culture, 2013)

Since then, many things happened within the Taiwanese psychological scenario, including the foundation of the Taiwan Institute of Psychotherapy (TIP) in 2001 and the establishment of the Taiwan Sand-play Association in 2002; the acceptance from the International Association for Analytical Psychology (IAAP) of the Taiwan Jung Developing Group in 2010 and the many Jungian analysts coming to Taiwan for seminars and workshops; the first International Conference on Jung in 2013 and the always increasing exchange and dialogue between east and west; the regular arrival in the city of Jungian analysts providing personal analysis and supervision. Jungian analytical psychology is now an operating theoretical and clinical reality in Taiwan and the climate of lively confrontation with western analysts opens "a new model of communication between East and West in the field of human psychology, and inspires each other with different thoughts to meet in a common spiritual path" (Jung, Asia and Inter-culture, 2013).

In following this process, my paper aims to consider the importance of an active interface between western analytical psychology and the East Asian way to understand and to approach it, in the direction of the development of a cross-cultural Jungian practice.

THE "CHINESE" AND "WESTERN" IN OUR MIND

Working with the Italian trainees of the Associazione Italiana di Psicologia Analitica (AIPA) and reflecting on some current negative attitudes towards the Chinese in our country, I noticed that by a certain time—I could say since their presence grew massively in Italy—there has been an increase in collective movements against them, often not supported by any knowledge of the Chinese and of their culture or by any serious enquiry. A sudden surge of interest in the reality of life for the Chinese occurred in Italy in 2013 only as an emotional reaction to the tragedy in Prato (Florence), when some Chinese workers died due to the shed in which they were working catching fire. Nevertheless, the way in which this event was approached was western orientated and lacked an attempt to understand the different customs, habits, and ways of living of the Chinese (Corriere della Sera, 2013).

Generally speaking, in Italian fantasy the image of "the Chinese" tends to form an unconscious negative reaction, probably based more on the fear of the unknown and of what is culturally completely foreign to we westerners than on any real knowledge of cultural differences. Although, on the one hand, the Chinese are assimilated with the many immigrants who arrive in Italy from all over the world, on the other, they are experienced as more different than others—for example, a *leitmotiv* of complaint labels them as a closed community (is that because they are a community?). The Chinese are perceived then as more incomprehensible and frightening than others, and that seems to be one of the reasons why the image of the Chinese tends to comprise deep unconscious layers of psychic personal, cultural, and collective shadow.

As you know, in Jungian psychology, the notion of *shadow* refers to all those unconscious and unrecognised aspects of personality and of culture that tend to be thrown out. The more your cultural shadow's parts are unconscious, the more they are projected outside, on to the other. In Jungian analysis, "coming to terms with the shadow" means to develop an awareness of the personal and cultural triggers that are likely to form your shadow projections, moving towards integration (Galimberti, 1999, p. 711). But, as Jung writes in *Memories, Dreams, Reflections,* "Where danger is, there is salvation also . . . [and] the salvation lies in our ability to bring the unconscious urges to consciousness with the aid of warning dreams" (Jung, 1995, p. 274). When the projection is seen through, its energy therefore lessens, the basis for the projection is analysed, and the opportunity for dialogue and increased awareness is possible in both the inner and the outer world (von Franz, 1985). Approaching analytically the western personal and cultural image of the Chinese in our minds might lead to the discovery of a real unconscious treasure trove of information, which is an undeniable prerequisite of self-awareness for any analyst who wants to practise analytical psychology in East Asia.

From this perspective, the western analyst has actively to come to terms, both in the sessions and beforehand, with his/her cultural countertransference towards the East Asian trainees and clients or his/her cultural projections, in order to overcome possible cultural shadows. This need for enlightenment also concerns, on the other side, the cultural projections or transferences of East Asian trainees and clients towards western culture and the western analysts they meet. A common transference towards me, for example, was that of being seen as "an elegant, independent, powerful woman", with all the emotions related to this transference image: a very interesting starting point to process, among others, women's cultural position in the Chinese culture and their collective story of suffering (Ma, 2010; Tibaldi, 2015a).

From the Italian side, to give you a practical example of the need for active confrontation with the image of the "foreigner" in general and the image of the "Chinese foreigner" in particular, I shall report a segment of active imagination by an Italian Jungian trainee. During a seminar on the Jungian method of active imagination, it was her response to my request for an active confrontation with the unconscious image of the Chinese in her mind.

This is a brief part of the trainee's experience.

The first image that came to her mind was one scene from the film *Farewell My Concubine* (Kaige, 1993): "A very poor woman takes her little son to an acting school, but the owner refuses the child because he has a birth defect, a superfluous finger. The mother takes the child around the corner, gets a sharp knife, and cuts off the extra finger. Then she comes back to the owner and signs the contract with the child's thumb print in blood." Seeing this image, the trainee judges it as too superficial and she decides to wait for another image.

Then the image of Mao Zedong, the leader of the Chinese Cultural Revolution, appears, but the trainee lets it fade out immediately, because again she considers it too superficial: "Maybe I'm wrong to make these judgments," reflects the trainee, "but that's it!"

A third image appears. The trainee sees a white sheet, stained in deep-blue ink. She associates it to an image she saw in the film *The Last Emperor*, by the Italian director Bernardo Bertolucci (Bertolucci, 1987). The little Emperor forces his scribe to drink some dark ink. The scribe does it because he wants to show the Emperor his blind obedience, though he knows that he will die as a result. The trainee comments, "It seems that a part of my unconscious is linked to cruelty, violence, blind obedience, meaninglessness, sadism and masochism, the pleasure of the deadly game." During the night, the trainee has this dream: "I am at the top of a staircase in a very large and ancient building. I see the stairs from above. Then the image of the great Greek ancient philosopher Athenagoras appears. It seems to be a compensation dream in which my unconscious is sharing with me the image of my positive Old Wise Man."

Considering the information coming from this unconscious material, I would point out how, on the one hand, the images of the Chinese are charged by intense unconscious negative emotions, while the image of the Greek Athenagoras seems more reassuring and it is associated with wisdom. Also noticeable is the attempt, on the part of the trainee's ego-complex, to deny the disturbing images related to the image of the Chinese, considering them "too superficial".

Contrasting with this experience, East Asian trainees and clients tend to look at the western analysts and at western identity with an idealising atti-tude. Recently, a friend of mine told me that her daughter, who lives in China, dates a Chinese plastic surgeon who is growing rich because Chinese women want to have their eyes changed to look like those of westerners. A spontaneous question arises: what image of femininity and of female identity do these women project on western women to have surgery? Another western habit imported into Chinese culture is to get married wearing a white dress instead of the traditional red one (*quipao*). This choice brings a cultural clash because in China white is the colour of funerals and is definitely linked to death, while red is a positive colour, associated with prosperity and happiness: "In Chinese the expressions *bai shi* and *hong shi*, respectively 'white occasions' and 'red occasions', indi-cate mourning and celebration" (Casarin & Wang, 2012, p. 41). This also gives rise to a question: how much must western habits be idealised in China in order for brides to marry wearing the colour of mourning? During my most recent stay in Taipei, I noticed an interesting and creative cross-cultural outcome relevant to marriage and the colour traditionally associ-ated with funerals: the Chinese bride will wear three wedding dresses; in the morning, the traditional flowery red *quipao*, at lunch, the western white dress, and, in the evening, a third dress (the most interesting one), long and western in style, but finally red (Tibaldi, 2015b).

I shall take the image of the red wedding dress as a metaphor of my way of practising analytical psychology in East Asia: the search for a cross-cultural creative modality that might integrate the western Jungian approach to the psyche, while respecting the East Asian culture and style. From this perspective, I considered it to be a personal success when two Taiwanese trainees told me of their intention to compare the Jungian approach to the unconscious aspects of the mind to some traditional Chinese practices, such as the fortune-tellers' way of interpreting the indications coming from the sticks (*kau chim*), or the natural healing practices and knowledge used by the old aboriginal tribes in Taiwan.

Going back to the images of the Chinese and the western in our mind, they seem then to be overlain by unconscious contents that need enlightenment. When you start recognising that these are emotional unconscious images acting inside ourselves, you begin to come to terms with them, retreating from possible prejudices and projections. In this sense, the notion of *cultural unconscious* and the analysis of the cultural transference and countertransference in the analytic scenario becomes central in treating clients belonging to East Asian cultures:

> Cultural complexes are made conscious in the consulting room in the same way that most other unconscious conflicts become known, i.e., through paying close attention to personal, family and cultural history; through analyzing dream and fantasy material that emerges from the unconscious; through transference/countertransference reactions; through unconscious slips and through potent moods and/or the break-through powerful affect. (Singer & Kaplinsky, 2010, p. 15; cf. Singer & Kimbles, 2004)

As ethnologists in their work are asked to observe the culture and population they are studying without any preconceived position and to put aside, as far as possible, any form of ethnocentrism, western Jungian analysts wanting to practise in East Asia need to approach eastern patients and culture with, so to speak, "limpid thinking" and "pure heart", as some of Fellini's characters would say (cf. Fellini, 1965; Tibaldi, 2013b), clearing from any prejudicial projection the images they may have of that culture and those clients.

LANGUAGE AS A CROSS-CULTURAL EXPERIENCE OF ATTUNEMENT

When we practise analysis in East Asia, we use a working language, usually English. I am an Italian native speaker; I am not bilingual and I learnt English as an adult. This means that I process my English mainly at a conscious level. Lacking an unconscious mastery of the language rooted in childhood, when I practise analysis in English I pay attention to the words

I use in order to choose the "right" ones from an emotional and cognitive viewpoint. This linguistic awareness made me reflect on the different verbal relationships you can face in the analytical setting when you use a foreign language and how much they can also be a metaphorical image of the analytical relationships and of the inner dynamics inside the client.

Looking at the analytical experience and the perspective of the foreign language, you can focus on various matches: (a) a non-native English-speaking analyst practises with a non-native English-speaking client or trainee; (b) a native English-speaking analyst practises with a non-native English-speaking client or trainee. Of course, we could face other situations as well, such as, for example, (c) a native or non-native English analyst practising with a non-native English speaker who is bilingual (as normally happens in Hong Kong).

The first encounter is the one that interests me most, either because it reflects my personal situation or because both analyst and client are reciprocally engaged in creating a linguistic meeting point. In their analytical relationship, they are asked to be as precise as possible, linguistically speaking, reflecting continuously on what they wish to communicate. The linguistic barrier can also turn into an analytical resource, when it is considered as a sensor for the analytical relationship and as an indicator of the client's inner dynamics. Thanks to these linguistic transactions, the words became an aspect of "the intersubjective analytic third" in the field, as Thomas Ogden observes:

> I view the intersubjective analytic third as an ever-changing unconscious third subject (more verb than noun) which powerfully contributes to the structure of the analytic relationship. The analyst's and patient's experience in and of the analytic third spans the full range of human emotion and its attendant thoughts, fantasies, bodily sensations, and so on. The task of the analysis is to create conditions in which the unconscious intersubjective analytic third (which is always multi-layered and multi-faceted and continually on the move) might be experienced, attached to words, and eventually spoken about with the analysand. (Ogden, 1999)

The linguistic stance is more complicated—but also very challenging—when the analyst is not a native English speaker and the client or trainee does not speak English and needs a translator. I remember a very intriguing session in which an Italian was speaking English, the client was Taiwanese and was speaking Mandarin, and the translator was Taiwanese and translated Mandarin into English. The situation was rather paradoxical: each of us was saying something but none of us knew exactly if we really got what the other meant to say. Here, careful attention to the emotions in the field, the transference–countertransference movements between analyst and client, the analysis of the dreams, the expressive use of writing, and the active confrontation with the spontaneous images—in short, a flexible use of all the analytical tools the Jungian analyst has at his/her disposal—will be orientating and of great help.

As I said before, the apparent poison of the linguistic situation can also turn into the remedy: practising analysis with East Asian clients can increase your creativity, aiding the achievement of the ultimate goal of "coming to terms" with the unconscious thanks to the transcendent function:

> In actual practice, therefore, the suitably trained analyst mediates the transcendent function for the patient, i.e., helps him to bring conscious and unconscious together and so arrive at a new attitude. In this function of the analyst lies one of the many important meanings of the *transference*. The patient clings by means of the transference to the person who seems to promise him a renewal of attitude; through it he seeks this change, which is vital to him, even though he may not be conscious of doing so. (Jung, 1958, p. 74)

In this transference perspective, it is worth considering the emotional difference between dreams in which the client speaks in his/her mother tongue or those in which he/she dreams in English. As far as I can tell, dreaming in another language is already a sign of development of a new attitude, an indicator of the unconscious movement of the psyche towards a deep transformation. A client tells me, "After having started my analytic experience, I noticed that my dreams are in English. I cry out all my rage towards my parents and the Chinese culture and their not having accepted me being a girl and not a boy." In the analytical experience of East Asian trainees and clients, sometimes the English words allow the speaking out loud of what is otherwise unspeakable.

Paul Watzlawick, in *The Language of Change: Elements of Therapeutic Communication*, refers to the necessity of a conscious language in comparison with a "pathogenic prose". He assumes that although your words are able to make you sick psychically and physically, they can be, on the contrary, in the service of health and well-being as well (Watzlawick, 1993). Practising analysis in a different culture and in a different language compels you to be constantly aware of the characteristics of the words you are using, in the direction of a true "healthy prose". In this sense, the conscious use of the language can become another tool at the disposal of the analyst for investigating, describing, and integrating unconscious patterns acted out in the analytical field and in the inner world of the client. As you know, the first definition of psychoanalysis was "talking cure" (Freud, 1895d) but, as Paul Kugler writes, "talking cure" does not mean only a therapy that cures through words, but also that you as an analyst need to cure the words you use in your practice in order to make them fully effective (Kugler, 1982). This is why James Hillman said on his deathbed to "find the right words", because "Finding the right words is fantastic. It is so important . . . Words are like pillows: if put correctly they ease the pain" (Ronchey, 2011).

Taking a lead from Hillman's words, and following the interest I always had in the matter, in a paper of mine (Tibaldi, 2014a) I presented a clinical proposal for Eastern patients who cannot have regular sessions over time: an approach aimed at making each single session a complete session in itself also linguistically speaking as the result of the full attention to the words used by both the patient and the analyst. By sticking to the dreams or to deep images that the client brings into the session—as Hillman invites us to do—the analyst finds with the patient "the right words" that hold together the experience of the session and expresses it metaphorically. These words help the client to reflect clearly on the problem he/she and the analyst worked out in that single session, express the essence of the session itself, and provide the therapist and client an easy, clear link to reconnect to their previous session in the sessions that follow, irrespective of the distance in space and time between the sessions.

An example of the right words connecting one session with another:

A client tells me that for some months he has been having a recurring dream: he dreams that he has a denture in his mouth. In reality, this denture is redundant, because he has all his natural teeth. In order to overcome the problem, the dreamer swallows his dentures, but this action makes him feel suffocated and he wakes up full of anxiety.

Waking, he tries to interpret his dream rationally—"I need to swallow this and this, etc."—without sticking with unconscious images and what they are telling us *per se*, that is, the fact that he has a redundant denture (we have to assess why) that should not be in his mouth and that swallowing turns out to be the wrong solution. Working on the information coming from the images, we find these "right words" expressing the dream's message: "Spit out your dentures!"

When the dreamer speaks these words aloud, he "looks through" the images of his dream and he experiences emotionally that he has got "too many teeth in his mouth" (literal meaning) and he has "to spit them out" (symbolic meaning).

Recalling the words "Spit out your dentures!" in the following encounter, the client and the analyst will immediately get in touch again with the conscious and unconscious content they worked out in the previous sessions, linking it to the present situation and crossing the distance in time and space between their sessions.

Finding the right words to close a session is one of my ways of responding practically to Jung's legacy, when he suggests taking the images literally (in this case "there is a redundant denture in the mouth", that is, something that has to be spat out) but treating them symbolically ("what does it mean for the patient having redundant dentures in his mouth?") (Shamdasani, 2009), remembering also to shoulder the active responsibility of transforming the analytical knowledge in life: "It is . . . a grave mistake to think that it is enough to gain some understanding of the images and that knowledge can be the final point. Insight into them must be converted into an ethical obligation" (Jung, 1995, p. 218).

DIRECT AND INDIRECT APPROACHES TO THE UNCONSCIOUS IMAGES THROUGH ACTIVE WRITING

Practising Jungian analysis within a different culture represents a challenge for the western analyst on different levels. One of them is to recognise, differentiate, and integrate in an imaginal narrative what belongs to the client's personal and cultural history and what to his/her journey as a human being who is confronted with the essential facts of existence, such as birth, growth, love, separation, illness, and death. The awareness of these different levels of experience summons the Jungian notions of the personal, cultural, and archetypal unconscious that are to be worked with in the analytical practice.

In the Jungian model of the mind, spontaneous images—called "the transcendent function"—bridge the conscious and the unconscious psyche naturally, carrying information from one domain to the other. As Jung writes,

> The tendencies of the conscious and the unconscious are the two factors that together make up the transcendent function. It is called "transcendent" because it makes the transition from one attitude to another organically possible, without loss of the unconscious. (Jung, 1958, p. 73)

In analogy with what the transcendent function does spontaneously, the Jungian method of active imagination activates the same imaginal process intentionally. For Jung, this is the reason why the method of active imagination represents the "hermeneutic treatment of creative fantasies", or "the synthesis of the individual with the collective psyche, which revealed the individual lifeline" (Shamdasani, 2009, p. 51).

In *Symbols of Transformation*, Jung speaks also of

> two kinds of thinking: . . . a directed thinking, of which the highest form is science and which is based on speech; and a nonverbal, undirected, associative thinking, commonly called dreaming. These two modes of thought deal with two activities of man: adapting to outer reality, and reflecting on subjective concerns. (Rothgeb, 1992, p. 18)

Paul Watzlawick, in turn quoting Jung, describes two kinds of languages:

> One is the language of reason, science, interpretation and explanation. The other is the language of image, of metaphor, of the totality. (Watzlawick, 1993).

When I refer to Jung's "two kinds of thinking", I have in mind his experience of being "two personalities" at the same time. As Jung writes in *Memories, Dreams, Reflections,*

> One was the son of my parents, who went to school and was less intelligent, attentive, hard-working, decent, and clean than many other boys. The other was grown-up-old, in fact sceptical, mistrustful, remote from the world of men, but close to nature, the earth, the sun, the moon, the weather, all living creatures, and above all close to the night, to dreams, and to whatever "God" worked directly in him. (Jung, 1995, p. 61)

In the Jungian analytical practice, one of the goals is to develop an imaginal approach to these different dynamics, integrating your "two kinds of thinking", your "two languages", or what the neuroscientists call your "two brains" (Damasio, 2000, 2003, 2005, 2012; Gazzaniga, 2015; Schore, 1999, 2003a,b, 2012; Schore & Rothman Schore, 2012) in a co-constructed imaginal narrative. The Jungian method of active imagination is a way to achieve this goal, thanks to a verbal, direct, and intentional confrontation with unconscious spontaneous images.

As you know, Jung discovered the possibilities of this active and verbal confrontation during the years of crisis he experienced just after his break with Freud, and this was his way of integrating creatively his no. 1 and no. 2 personalities:

> The play and counter-play between personalities no. 1 and no. 2, which has run through my whole life, has nothing to do with a "split" or dissociation in the ordinary medical sense. On the contrary, it is played out in every individual. (Jung, 1995, p. 62).

Thanks to his verbal confrontation with the unconscious, he reached this new attitude towards the unconscious images that completely changed his way of treating clients (Tibaldi, 1995b). As Shamdasani writes,

> In 1912, in *Transformation and Symbols of the Libido*, he [Jung] considered the presence of mythological fantasies—such as are present in *Liber Novus*—to be the signs of a loosening of the phylogenetic layers of the unconscious, and indicative of schizophrenia. Through his self-experimentation, he [Jung] radically revised this position: what he now considered critical was not the presence of any particular content, but the attitude of the individual toward

it and, in particular, whether an individual could accommodate such material in their worldview. This explains why he commented in his afterword to *Liber Novus* that to the superficial observer, the work would seem like madness, and could have become so, if he had failed to contain and comprehend the experiences. (Shamdasani, 2009, p. 74)

Going back to my practice in East Asia, and because of my specific interest in the Jungian method of active imagination and in the use of writing in analysis (Tibaldi, 1995a, 2011), over time I developed a form of active imagination that was sensitive to some East Asian cultural characteristics that I called "personal–impersonal deep writing" (PIDW), but that I will rename here "active deep writing".

Active deep writing is a way to process the personal, cultural, and archetypal aspects of the psyche in a verbally active and intentional way, while respecting some cultural East Asian issues such as, for example, Asians being more indirect in approaching the unconscious images, at least at the beginning of their analytical experience. In some of their dreams, I noticed that when the dreamer has to face too strong or conflicting cultural emotions, such as those related to the issue of "face-saving" (Wenzhong et al., 2010), he/she will dream waking up inside the dream itself or he/she will ask someone in the dream to wake him/her up, then dream him or herself to sleep again: "I was dreaming I was in an embarrassing situation because of wrong behaviour on my part. In the dream I was with my friend Y. I asked him to wake me up in the dream so as not to face my embarrassment any more. He did that, my emotion calmed down, and I dreamt of falling asleep again."

The philosopher and Sinologist, Francois Jullien, who studied the differences between Greek and Chinese cultures, argues that westerners approach the world "from the front", while the Chinese approach it "across" (Jullien, 2000). According to Jullien, in politics and in poetry the Chinese, in direct comparison to westerners, prefer an oblique and indirect approach. That is the reason why, in China, strategies of knowledge and meaning take place in and follow a very different style from the west. That is also the reason why, according to Bollas (2013), the eastern use of poetry evolved as a collective way to house the individual self. Considering also that the East Asian people try to be in good connection with others (*guanxi*) and devote great energy to this because they want always be in "harmony" with others, I worked on the possibility of approaching these issues in session in a culturally sensitive way: the result was active deep writing, a way to deal in practice both with the Chinese "excess of connection" in social situations or with their "need to disconnect" emotionally in individual confrontation with the unconscious. Active deep writing is a form of active imagination through writing that gives the clients the possibility to distance themselves from personal and cultural experiences or to get closer to the archetypal ones.

Let me explain briefly how it works.

Active deep writing foresees two practical possibilities: one is to objectify the ego complex, effecting distance from it and making its style visible (double objectivication). The second is to experience an archetypal character, for example, from a fairy tale, in a direct but safe way (archetypal writing). The first modality "is aimed at offering the patient the possibility of differentiating their reflective attitude from the conscious and unconscious contents of their ego complex, enabling them to develop their ability to observe themselves from a detached position" (Tibaldi, 2004, 2014a, p. 153). The second is about the possibility of experiencing an archetypal character directly but in a safe way, using the past tense and opening the narrative with "once upon a time" in order to face the archetypal power of the character from inside and outside the story at the same time, thereby finding their personal reaction, position, and attitude towards archetypal or cultural experiences that do not immediately refer to their personal story but still affect their emotions deeply.

Here are short examples of each modality.

1. Double objectivation
The client tells the analyst a frightening dream. The analyst invites the client to write the dream down in the first person and then to turn it into the third person, using the present tense.

This is the dream written in the direct form:

> I dreamt a man was trying to suffocate me. He had his hands around my neck. I tried to cry for help but the voice didn't come out. I woke up in terror.

The same dream is written then in the indirect form:

> She dreamt a man was trying to suffocate her. The man had his hands around her neck. She tried to cry for help but her voice didn't come out. The girl woke up in terror.

When the client writes her dream in the third person, she can obtain distance from her disturbing emotions, looking at herself from outside and finding a possibly new imaginal answer to her inner frightening dynamics.

2. Archetypal writing
Working in a reading group on the Brothers Grimms' Fairy Tale number 31, *The Handless Maiden*, a trainee was invited to choose the character she liked most and to identify with it, re-writing part of the story according to her need. The only guidance from the analyst was to write the new text

in the past tense and start with the words "Once upon a time". The temporal displacement to the past is a measure of protection for the trainee, to avoid the risk of an inflating identification in the present with the archetypal power of the image.

This is the excerpt from the original text of the fairy tale *The Handless Maiden*, when the girl tells her father he can chop off her hands to avoid the devil's threats to kill him, followed then by the trainee's new version.

[The father] went to the girl and said, "My child, if I do not chop off both of your hands, then the devil will take me away, and in my fear I have promised him to do this. Help me in my need, and forgive me for the evil that I am going to do to you." She answered, "Dear father, do with me what you will. I am your child," and with that she stretched forth both hands and let her father chop them off.

The trainee rewrites the passage from her viewpoint (archetypal writing).

"Once upon a time my father told me that he wanted to chop off my hands to avoid the devil taking him away. As a good Chinese daughter I should have obeyed him, but I knew that what my father was asking me was unjust and destructive to me. I found the courage and said "no" to my father, although with guilt, and I left my home in search of my destiny. I was afraid but I knew I was on the right path to my freedom."

As you can see from this example, archetypal writing opened up to the trainee the possibility of taking an active position towards an archetypal character, freeing herself from the passive role of a victim.

* * *

The favourable reception of active deep writing by the East Asian trainees convinced me to use it extensively as a new form of active imagination, tailored to help them to deal with personal, cultural, and archetypal unconscious aspects through writing. The psychological material collected through active deep writing can be further processed in the analytical sessions as a starting point for analytical reflection, working, for example, on the transference implications of the imaginal material and processing them also as images of the inner dynamics of the client (Fordham, 1974; Sedgwick, 1994).

Going back to Jung's experience of being two personalities at the same time, actual evidence offers models to explain this scientifically, confirming Jung's and the Chinese's insights about the perception of being a duality—or "a thousand things"—which strives for unity in the individuation process and in the path of wisdom. I have in mind in particular Mark Solms' and Oliver Turnbull's neuro-scientific theory of *Dual-Aspect*

Monism (Solms & Turnbull, 2002). Briefly summarising, their elegant theory suggests that

> . . . we are made of only one type of stuff (that is why is a *monist* position), but it also suggests that this stuff is *perceived* in two different ways (hence, *dual-aspect* monism). The important point to grasp is the implication that *in our essence* we are *neither* mental nor physical beings—at least not in the sense we normally employ these terms. . . . These two things are one and the same thing—there really is only one "me"—but since I am the very thing that I am observing, I perceive myself from two different viewpoints simultaneously. (Solms & Turnbull, 2002)

According to Solms and Turnbull, if we accept that the mind–body problem is reduced to a mere question of viewpoint—a problem of observational perspective—and that the distinction between one's self and one's body (between mind and matter) is merely an artefact of perception, the complexity of the "complex problem" dissolves.

Jung knew intuitively, as he often said, that the aim of the individuation process and the analytical practice was about integrating the (apparent) duality you will experience in the inner and in the outer world thanks to symbolic images directly experienced through the method of active imagination. Jung was, then, aware, long before Solms' and Turnbull's theory, that the problem of duality—whatever pair of opposites it refers to, including the apparent opposite cultural approaches of east and west—is a "mere question of viewpoint, a problem of observational perspective" and then the same complexity of the "complex problem" dissolves. In Jungian practice, the imaginal perspective is the way that lets "the complex problem" dissolve, and, as Jung writes, "It is a way of attaining liberation by one's own efforts and of finding the courage to be oneself" (Jung, 1958, p. 91). Active imagination through writing is aimed at training the client to be a creative actor in his/her life at the personal, cultural, and archetypal level, incorporating Jung's individuation process and the Chinese path of wisdom.

CONCLUSION

In my life, one of my biggest wishes was always to work abroad, in another culture, speaking another language. There was a time when I thought my ideal place would be Germany—I loved their language and their way of living—and back then it did not occur to me that I could work outside Europe. My thoughts and wishes were kept within my western reality. Many years later, when I realised that I probably would never work outside Italy, a Jungian colleague asked me, "Would you like to go to China?" My immediate answer was "Yes" and that "yes" represented the first step of my

journey to East Asia, the one that brought me to Guangzhou, Hong Kong, Taipei, and Macau, and to the analytical experience I presented in this paper. Following Lao-Tzu when he writes that "A journey of a thousand miles begins with a single step" (Lao-Tzu, 1993), the considerations I presented represent for me the first steps of my journey to East Asian culture, in the direction of cross-cultural forms of practising analysis, in the symbolic and real space where west and east meet.

As I have tried to show up to now, practising Jungian analysis with East Asian patients is a challenge for western analysts in many respects, especially when you do not want it to turn into an experience of cultural exportation and "colonisation". In fact, practising analysis in East Asia compels you to focus your attention either on the "dominants" of analysis, in whatever context and culture you do it, or on the cultural specificities you face in the places where you are, knitting together these different levels of meaning and understanding and expressing them through imaginal words (Tibaldi, 2002).

In 1959, Jung painted the mandala of the Yellow Castle, noticing that it had something Chinese in it. Shortly afterwards, Richard Wilhelm sent him the text of *The Golden Flower* (Wilhelm, 1962), asking Jung for a commentary. Jung interrupted his work on *Liber Novus* and he wrote to Wilhelm that "Fate appears to have given us the role of two bridge pillars which carry the bridge between East and West" (Shamsadani, 2009, p. 85). The Taoist alchemical treatise, *The Secret of the Golden Flower*, gave Jung the confirmation of his ideas about the mandala and the circumambulation of the centre, and was the first event which broke through his isolation. As Jung noticed, thanks to it, "I became aware of an affinity; I could establish ties with something and someone" (Jung, 1995, p. 223). Jung then began his re-engagement with the world, giving many lectures and using the parallels with the Chinese text as an indirect way of speaking of the individuation process. His encounter with eastern wisdom was a turning point in his life.

In this spirit of encounter between western and eastern cultures, of the inner and the outer world, I conclude my reflection, recalling the image of the Golden Flower, but in my personal way and out of my direct experience in East Asia. If, on the one hand, the Golden Flower is the symbolic highest stage of enlightenment in the Chinese Taoist tradition and the representation of the individuation process in analytical psychology, on the other hand, the Golden Flower is also a real image you can admire in Hong Kong, just in front of the sea: a six-metre statue, representing a variety of local orchids (*Golden Bahunia*), given as a present by the Chinese government in 1998 on the occasion of the handover of the city and now a tourist attraction in Hong Kong (Tibaldi, 2014b). Observing that real Golden Flower, I could directly face the paradoxical nature of the analytical experience when west and east meet, understanding the meaning of the Chinese master's words: "when he affirms that the deepest secret of the secret is this: the land that is nowhere, that is your true homeland" (Jung & Wilhelm, 1931).

REFERENCES

Bertolucci, B. (Dir.) (1987). *The Last Emperor* (film).

Bollas, C. (2013). *China on the Mind*. New York: Routledge.

Casarin, E., & Wang, Y. (2012). *In Cina per lavoro. Usi, costumi e parole*. Bologna: Zanichelli.

Corriere della Sera (2013). Prato, rogo nella fabbrica dei cinesi. Sette morti e due ustionati gravi. 2 December.

Damasio, A. (2000). *The Feeling of What Happens: Body and Emotions in the Making of Consciousness*. New York: Mariner Books.

Damasio, A. (2003). *Looking for Spinoza: Joy, Sorrow and the Feeling Brain*. New York: Harvest Books.

Damasio, A. (2005). *Descartes' Error: Emotion, Reason and the Human Brain*. New York: Putnam Publishing.

Damasio, A. (2012). *Self Comes to Mind: Constructing the Conscious Brain*. New York: Pantheon.

Fellini, F. (Dir.) (1965). *Giulietta degli Spiriti* (film).

Fordham, M. (1974). Notes on the transference. In: M. Fordham, R. Gordon, J. Hubback, & K. Lambert (Eds.), *Technique in Jungian Analysis*. London: Heinemann.

Freud, S. (1895d). *Studies on Hysteria. S. E., 2*. London: Hogarth.

Galimberti, U. (1999). *Enciclopedia di psicologia*. Turin: UTET.

Gazzaniga, M. S. (2015). *Tales from both Sides of the Brain: A Life in Neuroscience*. New York: HarperCollins.

Jullien, F. (2000). *Detour and Access Strategies of Meaning in China and Greece*. New York: Zone Books.

Jung, Asia and Inter-culture. Jung Across Cultural Borders (2013). International Conference, Taipei (Taiwan), 17–20 October. Available at: www.tip.org.tw/tw-jung.

Jung, C. G. (1958). The transcendent function, *C. W., 8*. Princeton, NJ: Princeton University Press.

Jung, C. G. (1995). *Memories, Dreams, Reflections*, A. Jaffé (Ed.). London: Fontana Press.

Jung, C. G. (2009). *The Red Book. Liber Novus* (edited and with an introduction by S. Shamdasani). New York: W. W. Norton.

Jung, C. G., & Wilhelm, R. (1931). *The Secret of the Golden Flower*. London: Kegan – Trench – Trubner.

Kaige, C. (Dir.) (1993). *Farewell My Concubine* (film).

Kugler, P. (1982). *The Alchemy of Discourse. An Archetypal Approach to Language*. New York: Associated University Press.

Lao Tzu (1993). *Tao Te Ching*, S. Addis, S. Lombardo, & B. Watson (Eds.). Boston, MA: Shambala.

Ma, S. S. Y. (2010). *Footbinding*. London: Routledge.

Ogden, T. (1999). *The Analytic Third: An Overview.* Northern California Society for Psychoanalytic Psychology, psychspace.com.

Ronchey, S. (2011). Addio a Hillman, cosi si muore da filosofo antico. *La Stampa,* 10 October.

Rothgeb, C. L. (Ed.) (1992). *Abstracts of the Collected Works of C. G. Jung.* London: Karnac.

Samuels, A. (1986). *Jung and the Post-Jungians.* London: Routledge.

Samuels, A. (1998). *Will the post-Jungians survive?* In: A. Casement (Ed.), *Post-Jungians Today. Key papers in Contemporary Analytical Psychology.* Hove: Routledge.

Schore, A. N. (1999). *Affect Regulation and the Origin of the Self: the Neurobiology of Emotional Development.* Hillsdale, NJ: Lawrence Erlbaum.

Schore, A. N. (2003a). *Affect Regulation and the Repair of the Self.* New York: W. W. Norton.

Schore, A. N. (2003b). *Affect Dysregulation and Disorders of the Self.* New York: W. W. Norton.

Schore, A. N. (2012). *The Science of the Art of Psychotherapy.* New York: W. W. Norton.

Schore, A. N., & Rothman-Schore, J. (2012). *Reader's Guide to Affect Regulation and Neurobiology.* New York: W. W. Norton.

Sedgwick, D. (1994). *The Wounded Healer: Countertransference from a Jungian Perspective.* London: Routledge

Shamdasani, S. (Ed.) (2009). *Liber Novus. The Red Book of C. G. Jung.* New York: Norton.

Singer, T., & Kaplinsky, C. (2010). *The Cultural Complex* in *Cultural Complexes in Jungian Psychoanalysis: Working in the Spirit of C. G. Jung,* M. Stein (Ed.) (pp. 22–37). Chicago: Open Court.

Singer, T., & Kimbles, S. L. (2004). *The Cultural Complex: Contemporary Jungian Perspective on Psyche and Society.* London: Brunner-Routledge.

Solms, M., & Turnbull, O. (2002). *The Brain and the Inner World* (Foreword by O. Sacks). New York: Other Press.

Tibaldi, M. (1995a). Psicologia analitica, esperienza della scrittura e conoscenza di sé. *Rivista di Psicologia analitica, 52*: 19–31.

Tibaldi, M. (1995b). Jung a confronto con l'inconscio: una descrizione autobiografica del metodo dell'immaginazione attiva. *Studi Junghiani, 2*: 141–159.

Tibaldi, M. (2002). With heart and in facts. In: *Proceedings of Fifteenth International Congress of Analytical Psychology* (pp. 585–587). Cambridge: Karnac.

Tibaldi, M. (2004). Doppia oggettivazione e formazione dell'Io immaginale. In: G. M. Cerbo, D. Palliccia, & A. M. Sassone (Eds.), *Alchimie della formazione analitica* (pp. 329–338). Milan: Vivarium.

Tibaldi, M. (2011). *Pratica dell'immaginazione attiva. Dialogare con l'inconscio e vivere meglio.* Rome: La Lepre.

Tibaldi, M. (2013a). Practising Jungian analysis in East Asia. A western perspective. Paper presented to the First Jungian International Conference, "Jung, Asia and Interculture. Jung Across Borders", Taipei, Taiwan, 17–20 October (unpublished).

Tibaldi, M. (2013b). C. G. Jung e Federico Fellini. Un'introduzione. Conference held in Taipei (Taiwan) on 22 October.

Tibaldi, M. (2014a). Practising images. Clinical implication of James Hillman's theory in a multicultural reality and in a changing world. In: L. Huskinson and M. Stein (Eds.), *Analytical Psychology in a Changing World. The Search for Self, Identity and Community*. London: Routledge.

Tibaldi, M. (2014b). Il fiore d'oro esiste e si trova a Hong Kong. Available at: http://martatibaldi.blogspot.com, 27 March.

Tibaldi, M. (2015a). Mostrami il mio volto prima che io nascessi. In: S. S. Y. Ma (Ed.), *Con i piedi fasciati* (pp. 9–15). Bergamo: Moretti & Vitali.

Tibaldi, M. (2015b). Creative cross-culturality. Available at: http://martatibaldi. blogspot.com, 5 February.

Von Franz, M.-L. (1985). *Projection and Recollection in Jungian Psychology*. La Salle, IL: Open Court.

Watzlawick, P. (1993). *The Language of Change: Elements of Therapeutic Communication*. London: W. W. Norton.

Wenzhong, H., Grove, C. N., & Enping, Z. (2010). *Encountering the Chinese. A Modern Country, an Ancient Culture*. London: Intercultural Press.

Wilhelm, R. (1962). *The Secret of the Golden Flower. A Chinese Book of Life*. San Diego, CA: Harvest.

The Core Element of Sandplay Therapy: Analytic Atmosphere

Cai Chenghou

Abstract

Sandplay is a therapeutic method developed by Dora M. Kalff. It is based on the psychological principles of C. G. Jung. The sand, water, and miniatures are visible and tangible, and you can also understand the images through symbolic meaning. But there is one more important element in sandplay therapy, which is inexpressible and intangible, but is the core factor: the "analytic atmosphere". "This inner atmosphere is the metaphoric space in which analysis runs its course is the decisive criterion that nothing external can supplant" (Dieckmann, 1991, p. 148). This transparent analytic atmosphere is just like the magnetic field, which originates from the interaction between the conscious and the unconscious aspects of both the analyst and the analysand. As an analyst, to establish the "analytic atmosphere" three factors need to be considered: the first is the analytical attitude of the analyst, that is to revere the unknown world (unconscious) and show respect to it (敬); to understand and show sincerity to himself/herself and the analysand (诚); to love and show the compassion to himself/herself and the analysand (爱). The other is to practise what the analyst professes in his/her teaching and what he/she has learnt from the moral man. The last, but not least, is to develop himself/herself unceasingly.

Key words: sandplay, psychotherapy in China, Carl Jung, core element, unconscious, analytic atmosphere.

INTRODUCTION

Sandplay therapy is a therapeutic method developed by Dora M. Kalff (1980). It is based on the psychological principles of C. G. Jung. Sandplay is a creative form of therapy using the imagination. It is characterised by the use of sand, water, and miniatures in the creation of images within a "free and protected space" of the therapeutic relationship and the sand tray. A series of sandplay images portrayed in the sand tray create an ongoing dialogue between the conscious and the unconscious aspects of the client's psyche, which activates a healing process and the development of the personality. This therapeutic method may be successfully applied to individual work with both adults and children.

Psychoanalysis and Psychotherapy in China, Volume 1, 2015: pp. 97–106.

KEY FACTORS OF SANDPLAY THERAPY

Generally speaking, the following factors are crucial for understanding a client's sandplay images.

Oral description of sandplay

Getting the person's description of the production, such as, "I wish I could be powerful like the general who can command a large number of armies" (Figure 1).

But oral description is more likely to be connected with rational logic, which is on the cognitive level. However, many times the client's problem is just "thinking too much" to get out of the labyrinth of language and logic, even being helplessly trapped in it. Ruth Ammann (1991, p. 2) said, "The deeper the emotions and feelings are covered up, the more distanced from consciousness memories and a part of our personality have become, the less likely it is that we can find the words to express them." It could however it could be expressed by the playful creations in the sand" (Kalff, 2007). Sandplay therapy has its own "language" of the image.

Non-verbal expression

Sandplay therapy is also called non-verbal therapy. The sandplay images are presented in a non-verbal form. As Jung (1975) said, "An emotional disturbance can also be dealt with in another way, not by clarifying it intellectually but by giving it visible shape" (pp. 82–83). Hence, we can understand such expression through the analysis of archetypal images and symbols (Figure 2).

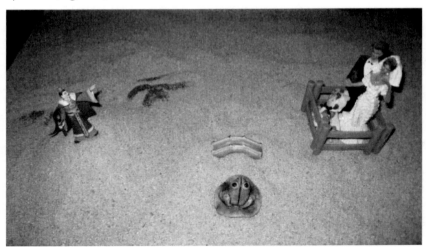

Figure 1.   The description of the general (photograph courtesy of the author).

Figure 2.   The image of a butterfly (photograph courtesy of the author).

Sandplay miniatures

Sandplay miniatures connect and balance the internal and external world. They are also the linkage between client and therapist. With these miniatures, the client could effectively express his/her unconscious contents, especially those that are difficult to describe with language. Sandplay miniatures are also an important healing factor. Dora Kalff (1980) gave advice as to its basic collection and composition, and described the miniatures she had collected for her sandplay studio (Figure 3).

Figure 3.   Mermaid (photograph courtesy of the author).

The past-president of ISST, Ruth Ammann (1991), also emphasised the symbolism of miniatures: "A sandplay therapist needs the same training as a Jungian analyst. Especially important are profound knowledge of and experience in the dynamics of psychic processes and symbolism" (p. xvii).

Space layout in the sand tray

Joel Ryce-Menuhin (1992) and Ruth Ammann (1991, p. 48) discussed the connotation of each of the regions of sandplay, which is how the conscious levels (conscious, individual unconscious, collective unconscious) project on to each region of the sand tray.

Ryce-Menuhin believed that there were three levels of psychic contents that were projected into the sand tray: conscious, personal unconscious, and collective unconscious. She wrote, "in my search for the hidden forms the psyche utilizes in sandplay, these diagrams express a form present 950 times out of 1000 in a random sampling from my adult patients' archives of sandplay photographs" (p. 94) (Figure 4).

From the perspective of the client and based on clinical experiences, Ruth Ammann believed that the sand tray could be divided into four regions, with each region usually presenting an implicit theme (Cai & Shen, 2005) (Figure 5).

Sandplay themes

The client presents the internal world through creating a visible "sand tray world". The research of Mitchell and Friedman (2003) found that almost

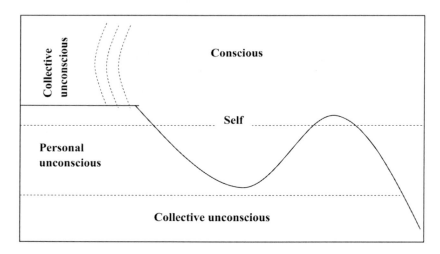

Figure 4.   According to Joel Ryce-Menuhin, revised by Cai.

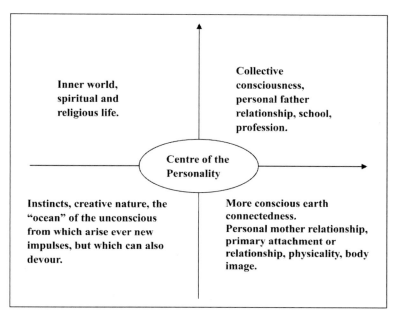

Figure 5.
Regions of the sand tray according to Ruth Ammann, revised by Cai.

every sand tray world has its own themes. They proposed the concept "sandplay themes". The sandplay theme is a visible image or a series of visible images that is presented in the sand tray world created by the client. Sandplay themes exist in almost all sand tray worlds. Each sand tray world can contain several themes. They can be divided into two classes:

1. *Themes of wounding.* These themes often appear in cases in which there are maltreatments, injuries, failures, or death of family members at an early age (Figure 6).

2. *Themes of healing.* These themes often appear in cases that are healthy and people who have enjoyed good early environments; they also frequently appear in the latter stages of sandplay therapy (Figure 7). Based on his own research and experience, Dr Shen Heyong (2004) brought up the concept of "themes of transformation" (p. 84). This concept bridged the "themes of wounding" and "themes of healing", which conveyed the dynamic trend of a series of sandplay. So, Dr Shen has developed the theory of sandplay themes. In the practice of sandplay, we found that the analysis of sandplay themes could be easily understood and applied (Cai & Shen, 2005).

Figure 6.   "Themes of wounding": buried (photograph courtesy of the author).

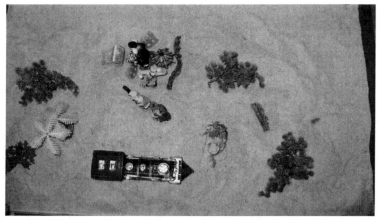

Figure 7.   "Themes of healing": journey (photograph courtesy of the author).

THE CORE ELEMENT OF SANDPLAY THERAPY: "ANALYTIC ATMOSPHERE"

Related clinical experiences

On 12 May 2008, a devastating earthquake hit Sichuan, China. On 18 May, as the member of first group of our team, I arrived at the earthquake area to help the survivors. The following picture is one of the group sand-play work on the sloping lawn in Beichuan High School (Chang Hong Training Centre) (Figure 8).

Through reflection on this process, I formed the impression that the group members, including myself, were all immersed in the work of sandplay. I

Figure 8.
Beichuan High School (Photo taken by the author 22/5/2008, 17:23).

hardly noticed where I was and how fast time passed. Between the morning when I went from Deyang Work Station to Beichuan High School Work Station, hunger and other somatic needs receded. While we were working an aftershock occurred, but the chaotic motion and noises outside did not seem to affect our work. I felt that our work seemed to be bounded by an intangible space. The group members and I have jointly built this safe atmosphere, thereby the internal beautiful spiritual garden could emerge, and was held in this containing atmosphere. Because of restraints on transport at that time, we were only able to bring with us two sand trays. My sandplay group did not have the container of a real sand tray, but the atmosphere that was formed by our work acted in the role of supporting and holding. This was not a real container, but a symbolic one. In the daily clinical practices, I had already experienced the important function of the analytic atmosphere, but this process especially made me firmly believe in its core status.

As to the core element in sandplay therapy, there are different opinions. Based on my clinical practice and theoretical study, I believe that "analytic atmosphere" (Dieckmann, 1991, p. 148) is the core element of sandplay therapy. Unlike miniatures, sand trays, sand, and water, the analytic atmosphere is intangible, but this inherent atmosphere is like a metaphorical space, in which the sandplay process unfolds naturally. It has a decisive influence that cannot be replaced by any external factor.

This intangible analytic atmosphere can be felt just like an archetypal field, similar to the magnetic field in physics, which is not an entity, but can exert a real influence. If we transform this analytic atmosphere into an image, it could be thought of as similar to an image in the alchemy process: Soror Mystica. In alchemy, Soror Mystica accompanied the alchemist. She usually appeared as a young female, who was the Yin factor on the path to explore the mystery of life. It is also the archetype of enlightenment, which inspires the artists, musicians, and writers to create great works.

What Soror Mystica brings is such an atmosphere, which in sandplay processes we could call the analytic atmosphere. If a sand tray is a visible "container", then the analytic atmosphere is a symbolic container. It provides containment, holding, safety, and protection. When unconscious contents need to be expressed, the analytic atmosphere contains them safely.

CREATING ANALYTIC ATMOSPHERE IN SANDPLAY

If the analytic atmosphere is so important, then how can we create it? I think there are two aspects that we should consider.

He has it in himself before he tries to give it to others

Analysts intend to create the analytic atmosphere, but before doing so, the analyst must have in-depth feelings about the analytic atmosphere, because it is linked less with rational logic and more with affected experience. As in *Chuang Tzu*,[1]

> The Perfect Man of ancient times made sure that he had it in himself before he tried to give it to others. When you're not even sure what you've got in yourself, how do you have time to bother about what some tyrant is doing?

Thus, the doctrine "he has it in himself before he tries to give it to others" might be the edification that we should attend to carefully. Then, in the process of training, the right path might be the combination of theory and skill, as well as individual analysis and supervision.

Analytic attitude

In my opinion, the function of analytic attitude in creating analytic atmosphere could be elaborated in three aspects: "respect", "sincerity" and "love".

Respect

Confucius said,[2] "When going out into the world, behave always as if you were at an audience before the Emperor; in dealing with the people, act as if you were at worship before God". This reflects the need for respect. In the sandplay process, we do not only confront consciousness, which we know to some extent. More importantly, we confront unconsciousness, which we do not know much about. Respect reflects an attitude aimed at this unknown territory. Probably a more sensible attitude is for us to revere the unknown unconscious, just as Confucius said,[3] "To know what it is that you know, and to know what it is that you do not know—that is understanding".

Sincerity

Sincerity is the way of Heaven. The attainment of sincerity is the way of men. He who possesses sincerity is he who, without an effort, hits what is right, and apprehends, without the exercise of thought;—he is the sage who naturally and easily embodies the right way. He who attains sincerity is he who chooses what is good, and firmly holds it fast.[4]

Sincerity can move mountains in a god-like manner. To be sincere enables one to attain the Golden Mean. "When we have intelligence resulting from sincerity, this condition is to be ascribed to nature; given sincerity, and there shall be intelligence."[5] Sincerity is the spiritual mirror that helps us reflect our nature. We should be sincere not only to clients, but also to ourselves.

Love

We believe that love is an important healing factor indicated through clinical practice (Cai & Shen, 2010). Because of love, we can feel in our hearts; we can stand in another's shoes and be benevolent; we can patiently accompany; we can better show compassion and activate the possibility of our client's internal transformation. The Chinese character meaning "love" clearly indicates, graphically, its intrinsic qualities: protection, holding, and trust.

THE PRACTICE OF SANDPLAY THERAPY

Tsang said, "Whether I have not failed to practice what I profess in my teaching"(*sic*)[6] or "Whether I may have not mastered and practiced the instructions of my teacher"(*sic*)[7], which Li Zehou (2007) interpreted as "You must practice the theory and method before you teach others". If not, you will mislead and cause harm. This cautions us that we, as sandplay analysts, should first practise ourselves what we would share with others. The sense that "whether I may have not mastered and practiced the instructions of my teacher", prompts us to practise earnestly.

My understanding of the idea of analytic atmosphere in sandplay therapy is inspired by my sandplay practice in the earthquake zone. Our analytical psychology team has been working there for several years, since 18 May 2008. We tried our best to create the analytic atmosphere. The Garden of the Heart–Soul work station transferred from the initial tent to temporary housing, and later transferred to a newly built, beautiful building. The new environment provided an important space for sandplay work, but I believe that the analytic atmosphere that was created by us from the beginning has had a more far-reaching influence.

ACKNOWLEDGEMENT

I am grateful to Professor Shen Heyong and Gao Lan, whose encouragement and advice have made this work possible.

NOTES

1. *The Complete Works of Chuang Tzu* (Chapter 4), translated by Burton Watson.
2. *The Discourses and Sayings of Confucius* (Chapter 12), translated by Gu Hongming.
3. *The Discourses and Sayings of Confucius* (Chapter 2), translated by Gu Hongming.
4. *The Doctrine of the Mean* (Chapter 20), translated by James Legge.
5. *The Doctrine of the Mean* (Chapter 21), translated by James Legge.
6. *The Discourses and Sayings of Confucius* (Chapter 1) translated by Gu Hongming.
7. *Confucian Analects* (Chapter 1), translated by James Legge.

REFERENCES

Ammann, R. (1991). *Healing and Transformation in Sandplay*, W.-D. P. Rainer (Trans.). Chicago, IL: Open Court.

Cai, C. H., &, Shen, H. Y. (2005). The sandplay collection and the themes of sandplay. *Science of Social Psychology, 20*(78): 47–51.

Cai, C. H., & Shen, H. Y. (2010). "Garden of the Heart–Soul" in the earthquake area of China: creativity and transformation. *Jung Journal: Culture & Psyche, 4*(2): 5–15.

Dieckmann, H. (1991). *Methods in Analytical Psychology: An Introduction*, B. Matthews (Trans.). Wilmette, IL: Chiron.

Jung, C. G. (1975). The transcendent function. *C. W., 8.* Princeton, MA: Princeton University Press.

Kalff, D. (1980). *Sandplay: A Psychotheraputic Approach to the Psyche.* Santa Monica, CA: Sigo Press.

Kalff, M. (2007). Twenty-one points to be considered in the interpretation of a sandplay. *Journal of Sandplay Therapy, 16*(1): 51–71.

Li Zehou (2007). *Reading the Analects Today.* Tianjin: Tianjin Social Science Academy.

Mitchell, R. R., & Friedman, H. S. (2003). *Sandplay Themes Expressed in the Healing Process. The Sandplay Journey.* Guangzhou, China. Encounter Psyche: Conference of Sandplay Therapy.

Ryce-Menuhin, J. (1992). *Jungian Sandplay: The Wonderful Therapy.* London: Routledge.

Shen, H. Y. (2004). *Sandplay: Theory and Practice.* Guangzhou: Guangdong High Education Press.

'Xie Yi Painting as a Culture of Therapy': Part 1 – Introduction

Richard Wu

Abstract

A brief description of the ancient practice of Xie-Yi painting in China is offered as an introduction to a more complete contribution to follow in the next issue of the journal. Xie-Yi painting includes the concepts of "evocative space–dialogue", metaphor, analogical representation, rhythm, play, integration, and images of authentic selves. The author describes these elements and relates them to corresponding functions of modern analytic psychotherapy.

Key words: Xie-Yi painting, Chinese painting, Chinese culture, evocative space–dialogue, metaphor, analogical representation, play, authentic self.

HISTORY

Over the past 900 years, China has endured the ravages of wars, rule under suppressive autocracies, and nomadic conquerors. The written word was harshly censored while widespread traumas and dispossession prevailed. Successive generations of Wen Ren, or scholar-gentlemen, thus retreated to self-cultivation and, to evade political persecution, collectively fostered Xie Yi, or *writing–mind painting*, a culture of therapy expressing Daoist philosophy through imbued metaphors. Xie Yi, in essence, provides an evocative visual journey that joins the artist and viewer from trauma, fragmentation to the coherent widening of one's inner scene. This ultimately arrives at the Daoist ideal of integration with nature, where the individual returns to being elemental and authentic.

XI-YI AND PSYCHOTHERAPY

Many models of western psychotherapy feature the therapeutic dialogue, in which therapist and patient also jointly create metaphors and embark on non-linear, unfolding visualisation of the inner world. In the process, the patient arrives at integration or wholeness, where he discovers his authentic self. Psychotherapy, thus, shares more in common with Xie Yi than most medical and psychological disciplines constructed on linear propositions and evidence-based verification.

Understanding the compatibility between Xie Yi and psychotherapy will be instrumental in developing cultural-fit models of therapy in China, as Xie Yi has over the millennium become the dominant Chinese classical art tradition with deep-rooted influence on Chinese culture, language, and psyche. At the global level, with the twenty-first century marked by increasing fragmentation, departure from the authentic self and the natural environment, a joint model of Xie Yi and psychotherapy has the potential to provide a cross-cultural, cross-modal alliance with a common purpose and path. Xie Yi is, after all, "dialogue in painting", and psychotherapy a form of "painting in words".

An article planned for the next issue of this periodical will explore the compatibility between Xie Yi and psychotherapy with an account of several historical Xie Yi masters' life traumas, accompanied by illustrations of their paintings which embody personal transformations. Examples of compatible elements between Xie Yi and psychotherapy contained in this forthcoming article will include the following.

Evocative space-dialogue

Brush ends, mind continues (笔断意连): Xie Yi painting is characterised by brief and incomplete depictions of subjects, which invite the viewer to reflect and wander in the space beyond. This resonates with the way psychotherapeutic dialogue follows the "shape" of the stream of consciousness, which William James described as "perchings and flights of a bird" (1890, p. 243). Lev Vygotsky similarly observed inner speech as "fluttering between words and thoughts" (1962, pp. 138–139).

Metaphors

Embedded meaning (寓意): As Xie Yi evolved over the centuries, elements of nature, such as mountains, waterways, bamboo, and orchids were adopted as metaphors that denote specific emotions and virtues. Painting of these shared metaphors forges connectedness with nature as well as with artists of the past. Xie Yi then forms a visual language that communicates one's inner world to others through metaphor. In a parallel way, the importance of metaphors in psychotherapy is commonly recognised and described for example by Russell Meares, who wrote, "empathic representation makes metaphorically visible that which is only partially glimpsed in the penumbra of consciousness" (1992, p. 181).

Analogical representation

Between likeness and unlikeness (似与不似之间): Xie Yi depicts metaphors in a semi-abstract manner, which tangibly represents one's abstract inner world while still allowing space for further elaboration. This parallels Donald Winnicott's notion of an "intermediate area of between inner and outer realities" (1981, p. 75).

Rhythm

Energy and tone (气韵): The Xie Yi artist seeks attunement with nature by painting brush strokes that capture common rhythms between his inner world and what he sees in nature. Attunement with nature is also frequently mentioned in psychoanalytic psychotherapeutic literature, including Carl Jung's writing on synchronicity and Abraham Maslow's descriptions of self-actualisation (Maslow, 1968, p. 97). Resonance of rhythm in the dialogue between patient and therapist is also central in forging therapeutic fit, as Russell Meares described well in his notion of "coupling and amplification" (1992).

Play

Play of ink (墨戏): Since its inception in the Song Dynasty, Xie Yi painting has been referred to as a "play of ink". Beginning with not-knowing, or half-knowing, the artist embarks on a process of observation and elaboration, responding both to his inner world and what is already painted, in the manner Winnicott described in "creative and spontaneous play of the true self" (1965, p. 141).

Integration

At one with Nature (天人合一): As the artist continues his ink play over time, his painting invariably becomes more succinct, thereby reaching greater freedom. This is seen in a painting by Bada Shanren (Figure 1), toward the end of his life. As a result of years of practice and reflection, the Xie Yi artist achieves increasingly divergent integration and, ultimately, the Daoist state of being "at one with nature". This process of unfolding is also referred to by Kohut as "creative, enlarging formation of self-structure" (1978), and reaching what Howard Gruber described as an "image of wide scope" (1978).

Authentic self

Returning to elemental and true (返朴归真): As the artist's vision widens, he is then freed from trauma, entrapment and contempt that often initiated his painting journey. He therefore returns to a childlike innocence of being elemental and true. The artist Zheng Xie thus inscribed in his painting (Figure 2), *trimming the excess and keeping the lean, when painting like a novice, the art has truly matured* (Wang, 2008, p. 175). This again resonates with Winnicott's notion of a true self in the process of being creative and real.

Figure 1.   Autumn Forest pavilion, by Bada Shenren (detail),
reproduced by permission of Shanghai Museum.

Figure 2.   Bamboo and Rock, by Zheng Xie,
reproduced with the permission of Shanghai Museum.

REFERENCES

Gruber, H. (1978). Darwin's 'tree of nature' and other images of wide scope. In: J. Wechsler (Ed.), *On Aesthetics in Science* (pp. 121–142). Cambridge, MA: MIT Press.

James, W. D. (1890). *Principles of Psychology Volume I*. New York: Holt.

Kohut, H. (1978). The disorders of self and their treatment: an outline. *International Journal of Psychoanalysis, 59*: 413–425.

Maslow, A. (1968). *Toward a Psychology of Being*. New York: Van Nostrand.

Meares, R. (1992). *The Metaphor of Play*. London: Routledge.

Vygotsky, L. (1962). *Thought and Language*, E. Hanfmann & G. Vakar (Eds. & Trans.). Cambridge, MA: MIT Press.

Wang, J. C. (2008). *Biography of Zheng Ban Qiao*. Tianjing: BaiHua Arts.

Winnicott, D. W. (1965). Ego distortions in terms of true and false self. In: *The Maturational Processes and the Facilitating Environment*. London: Hogarth Press.

Winnicott, D. W. (1981). *Playing and Reality*. London: Penguin.

Individual Development of Psychotherapists' and Practitioners' Motivation

Shi Qijia

Abstract

This autobiographical sketch by a leading Chinese psychiatrist and psychotherapist describes the development of the author's career and the growth of his interest in psychoanalysis, as well as some of the personal rewards in his career as a psychoanalytical psychotherapist.

Key words: autobiography, psychoanalysis in China, career.

I began my career as a neurologist. Having received a Masters in 1987 and graduating as a Doctor in 1992, I worked in a hospital until 1996. Everything was about neurology and neuroscience. Neurology is a field with clear diagnoses, ineffective treatment, and a high degree of relapse in the diseases it treats. The diseases are interesting: epilepsy, periodic paralysis, transient ischaemic attack, multiple sclerosis. Arriving at a diagnosis, the challenge of the basic technique, is especially interesting. In the teaching rounds, these questions were favourite puzzles for doctors. A whole neurological examination takes about two hours, longer if you are teaching. As a neurologist, two kinds of diseases impressed me: the first had a clear diagnosis, ineffective treatment, early onset, and a course with progressive deterioration, for instance, multiple sclerosis. This disease occurs in young and middle-aged patients, with variable symptoms including numbness, weakness of limbs, and disorders of vision or sphincter control. The effect of hormone therapy is good and treatment possibilities are increasing, but relapse is frequent. Two relapses affecting different locations indicates that the next relapse is likely to be more serious. The cause of multiple sclerosis is still unknown. When I met this kind of patient, especially young patients, they frequently asked, "When can I leave the hospital, doc?" I felt guilty, powerless, and filled with regret. When treatment was more effective, I felt more worried, because I did not know when the next relapse would come. Family members trusted me, but I did not think I deserved their trust, because I felt powerless, just as they did. A similar situation applied to stroke victims. The patients had dysphonia and paralysis, or other disturbances of their limbs. Family members had to take care of them for long periods of time, contributing to the patients' feelings of helplessness and hopelessness. Today, the psychological aspect of these diseases has become part of the field of psychosomatic medicine.

Another neurological disease appeared in the outpatient department where patients came because of headache, dizziness, and numbness or weakness of the limbs. There were no positive findings identified through physical examination. This disease was characterised by a pattern in which the patient came to see the doctor repeatedly, seeking out different hospitals to see different doctors. Nurses in outpatient departments also were familiar with these patients, calling them "doctor killers", or "troubled patients". In China, tense doctor–patient relationships began with this kind of patient. One year, as a deputy director of an outpatient department, I had to go to court three times because patients accused the hospital and the doctors of malpractice. Later, this kind of patient caused the medical system more difficulty when they declared "Three No Do" principles: no autopsy, no court, and no cremation. In this period, tensions increased to a crucial level between doctors and patients because patients could arbitrarily humiliate, attack, and even ruin or kill doctors.

When Freud was a neurologist in his early years, he also met this kind of patient, although perhaps he did not encounter so many of their family members. I remember a thirty-two-year-old patient diagnosed with a glioma. After apparently successful treatment, he suddenly developed epilepsy. On examination, we found that his tumour had returned and spread. His family contacted me and said, "We will sell our house. Please use the most expensive medicine. Please help him. He is the pillar of our family!"

I escaped from neurology. I felt exhausted by feeling powerless and helpless more often than I had the feeling of accomplishment from curing patients. With more than twenty patients a day in the outpatient department (this number would now be more like forty a day), I was continually uncomfortable. I no longer knew what to say to my patients. I could not establish deeper relationships with them and perhaps that was a principal underlying reason for my abandoning neurology and choosing to become a psychotherapist.

As I look for other reasons for turning to psychotherapy as a career development, it occurs to me that my family background is relevant. My father was a ship's captain, and so was frequently not at home. My mother was a teacher in middle school, and was strict with us children. In the 1970s, there was an attitude of suspicion that pervaded many neighbourhoods, which were then characterised by passionate paranoia and constant preaching. Some books that described emotional relationships, such as *The Dream of the Red Mansion*, had to be read secretly. We felt the pangs of love in the break-up between Paul and Tonya in the novel *How the Steel Was Tempered*. We read handwritten copies of detective novels such as *A Pair of Embroidered Shoes*, or the cheap, erotic novel *A Girl's Heart*. When I saw the official revolutionary operas, I longed to see dramatisations of love relationships. However all of them—*Tiemei in Red Lantern, Qingsao in Shajiabang*, and *Kexiang in Dujuanshan*—disappointed me. An old man who had worked in the Revolutionary Committee told young persons that female committee members who were hoping to catch adulterers in the act have a "hot heart for adultery".

Where was depression? Where was anyone's interest or fantasy? I remember that when I was ten years old, when I could not sleep at night, the moonlight shone through my window and reflected on the floor. I opened my eyes wide and imagined that an extraterrestrial being abducted me, and that I then returned to earth with some kind of superhuman powers to save the suffering people in the Third World and our Taiwanese compatriots.

Looking back, I have to appreciate this depressive streak that inspired my interest in literature and the plight of humanity. The man who tries to commit arson might someday become a firefighter; the man who tries to kill might become a surgeon; the woman who lacks milk becomes a cook. Persons who could not fulfil their childhood wishes might later find fulfilment through their work. I think this is the second reason I have found fulfilment through learning to conduct and teach psychotherapy.

My first psychoanalysis was in Austria, in the beautiful city of Innsbruck, which has also twice held the Winter Olympic games. There, I focused on my job so much I did not even see the Games. The room in which I lived faced an airport. The noise from the planes brought my mind back to China. The outlook on the other side of my room was a snowy mountain more than 3,000 metres high. Although it was beautiful, I still felt depressed and lonely. In the therapy room, I could only lie on the couch, look at the ceiling and the red wall, or out of the window. The therapist moved his chair occasionally, making a small noise. I could smell the smoke of his cigar. His silence aggravated my loneliness. I tended to sleep for a very long time. Other colleagues went for a walk after work, but I would go back home and curl up, sleeping until ten o'clock at night; I would wake, eat something, and then go back to bed again.

In therapy, I remembered my parents, who were forthright, lively, and hospitable. There were always lots of friends in our home. When my father came home, friends liked to visit him, bringing fish from the Yangtze River. At that time, when I crossed the river by ferry, we would feel the deck shaking. When we gathered in the open air on the ferry's deck, people pointed to the fish, crying, "Porpoise, porpoise." Actually they were white-flag dolphin. There were lots of fish in the Yangtze.

My father was often absent, and when he came back, the communication with my mother was intense. There were quarrels and problems with neighbours. My mother was harsh to her children. I talked with my mother after I had grown up. She told me that it was hard for a mother who had to look after two children. She thought that if she was not strict, the children might become bad. If the children made a mistake and mother did not hit them, it was shameful in front of the neighbours! I really wanted to know if there were any other ways to communicate.

Noise came from the radio's speaker, mostly loud revolutionary songs and slogans. What impressed me was hearing *The Internationale* from the radio before we slept every night. It has a beautiful melody, even though it was sung excitedly, especially the last lines, which were repeated: "And the last fight, let us face, / The Internationale unites the human race!"

Most of my family were lively, used to noise, and they expressed intense emotion (my mother was impatient). So, when I was in Germany and Austria, what I felt most deeply from the study and self-experience of therapy was the loneliness. Loneliness enabled me to reach another aspect of humanity.

In psychotherapy, silence is always there. Clients often do not know what to say. They might be afraid to offend the therapist and so they choose silence. They may struggle with the therapist, and they find their minds dwelling on something they think is not relevant. An anxious or gregarious therapist who cannot endure a patient's deprecation or cannot endure loneliness will have great difficulty.

When I began to learn to conduct psychotherapy in Germany, I worked from nine o'clock in the morning until nine or ten at night. Patient after patient, round after round, seminar after seminar. Sometimes, I spoke not at all, just listened and thought. I learnt that if you have no capacity to endure loneliness, you cannot be a therapist. If you cannot listen and remain calm, you cannot be a good therapist.

Finally, I want to talk about speed. Our growth and experience are increasingly subject to a speedy process. If we have suffered trauma, this speed will be even greater as we attempt to vault over memories. And we will have incomplete memories, full of forgetfulness. There are many things which we hope to forget, but it is like a baby and its bath: if you spill the bathwater, the baby will also be spilled. Trauma can also bring growth, but only if we deal with the trauma so that we have more space to accept and express love. However, this process must be slow, and so psychother-apy is a slow experience. Psychoanalysis is the prime example of this process. I shall close by mentioning a case of psychoanalytic therapy.

A female patient came for psychotherapy when she was twenty-one years old. At first, she talked about her difficulty in concentrating, but then she talked about her trauma, which included sexual trauma. Her diagnosis at that time was borderline personality disorder. Her relationships were poor, her mood was unstable, and she often acted out. She ended therapy after six years when she decided to continue her studies, and we lost contact. Fourteen years after she began therapy, and eight since she left, she came to the outpatient department again to see me. She told me she was married, had a child, and had bought an apartment in Wuhan. She came to bring me up to date on her life and to thank me. Here is a part of a letter from her:

> 25th February 2014, I walked into the Wuhan Psychological Clinic. My heartbeat was strong, and I told myself that I have never given up on myself, I am almost recovered, and I have self-confidence for my future. We have not seen each other for eight years. Did you remember the patient who was me? Buddha says, five hundred times you must look back to find true love, so that we could feel each other at one sight now. I would like to take five million times to look back, to see your smile. It is because you gave me a new life, just because you never gave up on me. I stood outside the therapy room, the door opened slowly, and Professor Shi stood in front of me. I smiled and said, "Hello Professor Shi, how are you?" I remembered a song which goes, "I tramped over mountains, just for finding who I am missing". When I heard this song, I always thought about Professor Shi. I didn't know why, until now, what I always want, is the hug from Professor Shi, I hope he hugs me and tells me, "Welcome home!"

Luxun said that tragedy is destroying the beautiful things. Psychotherapy can lead you into the deep side of your soul, and help you to find the way back to your real home. But this process requires you to endure loneliness, frustration, and suspicion, requires that you tolerate negative moods, and requires you to keep the hope of beautiful humanity alive and to deliver this hope to your clients.

Psychotherapy after tragedy finds the clean and silent calm that can occur after extreme sadness. Then there is room for love.

Psychotherapy can help you learn to do that.

SPECIAL SECTION ON DISTANCE ANALYSIS AND PSYCHOTHERAPY

Editor's Introduction

This section's four papers deal with the use of teleanalysis, telepsychotherapy, and telesupervision. These modalities are clearly going to be of real importance in China, with its vast geographic spread and its paucity of well-trained psychodynamic therapists in these years in which psychotherapy is being popularised. The need is great, and the number of therapists small, with the added complication of a concentration of trained therapists in large cities.

The first two articles, by Lin Tao and Irmgard Dettbarn, respectively, examine the advantages and disadvantages of using Skype or similar platforms for distance analysis, and especially focus on the need to consider the psychodynamics of this new kind of setting for analysis. The third article, by Alexander-Guerra, describes the use of distance communication for supervision of psychotherapy, again a need when resources for well-trained supervisors exist largely outside China itself. The final article presents a radical innovation, and one that will elicit both interest and controversy. Li Zhen's development of a service specifically offering distance psychotherapy in China and beyond is innovative, takes advantage of the new technologies, and takes on the problem of quality control in a field in which this is a major concern.

We welcome responses to these four articles and hope to publish some of them in a future issue.

Teleanalysis:
Problems, Limitations and Opportunities*

Lin Tao

Abstract

This paper describes the use of teleanalysis for conducting distance psycho-analysis. The author considers its limitations when compared to in-person analysis, recommending a thoughtful approach when such technology must be employed in order to conduct analysis that would otherwise not be possible.

Key words: teleanalysis, transference, distance psychoanalysis.

INTRODUCTION

In one of the most famous Chinese mythological novels, *Journey to the West*, two omnipotent figures in the heavens, Thousand-Mile-Eye and Wind-Accompanying-Ear, have supernormal powers of receiving information from far away. With the development of technology services offering voice over Internet connections with web cameras, we can communicate in word and image with family and friends at a distance, our words synchronous with our facial expressions and body movements. Innumerable people now use the Internet to communicate with one another freely and inexpensively, as if erasing the boundaries and limitations of space and time. Technology has been changing our way of thinking, behaviour, and life in general. How does technology affect the psychoanalytic situation in particular? Does a secure connection on the Internet offer a "good enough" setting for psychoanalysis, with enough oxygen in the atmosphere for the survival of the analytic couple and the analytic process? Or does it indulge an omnipotent fantasy of the analyst as both Thousand-Mile-Eye and Wind-Accompanying-Ear?

Addressing these questions stirs controversy. Some analysts find technology expedient and effective in supporting analytic communication. Others doubt that psychoanalysis is possible when communication is through cyberspace. Psychoanalysis in person requires a secure setting, with attention to many aspects such as agreed fees and manner of payment, regular time, length and frequency of appointments, and a physical and psychological space for meeting that supports an analytic process including trans-

---

* Published simultaneously in *Psychoanalysis Online Two* (2015), J. S. Scharff (Ed.), Karnac Books, pp. 105–120. By permission the author, editor and publisher.

ference, countertransference, interpretation, and working through. These elements together carry the weight of the analytic effort. Does Internet transmission of sound and image, in contrast to physical co-presence, throw analysis off balance? Will the practice of teleanalysis lead to the final collapse of psychoanalysis, or will it lift psychoanalysis to a new point of balance in keeping with the goals of psychoanalysis?

We must assess the potential of Internet communication for supporting an effective analysis. We must not accept its use without careful examination and reflection on experience. In this chapter, I will explore the vulnerabilities, problems, and limitations of Internet communication in terms of its technical fragility and impact on analytic process, the virtual setting, and the analytic frame, and the loss of access to the dynamics of slow entry into, as well as away from, the analytic session. I will address the risks of misperception, fragility of communication, and insecurity of the analytic setting and space, and illustrate them from clinical experience with patients in psychoanalysis and psychoanalytic psychotherapy. All the patients described began analysis in person, and after the analyst(s) had relocated, they continued with the analyst(s) through Internet communication using computer-to-computer voice over Internet protocol with web cameras. I want to raise points of difficulty not to discredit the use of technology, but to contribute to the current vigorous discussions of whether it can be useful in the psychoanalytic situation. Finally, I describe the criteria for selecting a patient for teleanalysis and I discuss the appropriate analytic stance.

TECHNICAL FRAGILITY AND ITS INFLUENCE ON THE ANALYTIC PROCESS

Incomplete perception

In teleanalysis, since the patient and the analyst can communicate only by seeing and hearing each other, many important sources of information may be lost, including non-verbal and preverbal aspects. The patient will lose the chance to feel the atmosphere in the room offered by the analyst, which always has significant meaning to the patient. When I walk into my analyst's room for personal analysis, I will be impressed by the psychoanalytic smell and atmosphere in that room with my analyst physically inside that room. When I walk into a real space within which a person is there with me, and all the elements of real interaction are involved, I feel that it is a true, human relationship in which I can grow. I feel warm, safe, and held by the surrounding subtle atmosphere in that room. In comparison to that, I cannot imagine I will have the same feelings if, instead of walking into that analytic room, I open the computer at home or office, log into my software programme, and see on my screen, sent by a camera, a mobile picture of the face and part of the body of my analyst and his room.

Although we are hard put to describe the analytic atmosphere in the consulting room, we perceive it with our whole body and mind, our sensory organs, and our intuitions. We can see, hear, smell, touch, and perceive intuitively, so that we can develop full non-verbal and preverbal communication. Technology-assisted psychoanalysis (even though it includes a moving image as well as sound) inevitably loses some important aspects of communication and perception. For instance, the patient cannot smell, cannot feel the vivid atmosphere in the presence of the analyst in the same room, and cannot feel the warmth of the room in which he would have been together with the analyst, all of which is important for the patient's unconscious infantile need to feel the security, constancy, stability, and intimacy of the mother's womb and her embrace. An experience of the container is essential to the development of the infant part of the patient. The analysand in the transference experiences not only an object, but a total situation (Joseph, 1985; Klein, 1952). However, analysis that is not in person restricts the patient's experience of both the analyst and the situation, which, in different degrees, may make the patient feel the analyst and the analysis to be artificial, rigid, machine-like, cold, and distant. Since the setting prevents both sides from perceiving the other's information in full, the patient could be anxious that the analyst would miss some important information about her. For his part, the analyst faces the problem of incomplete perception. For instance, he loses the chance to observe the whole process of how the patient comes into the analytic room. He cannot smell and vividly feel the patient as a corporeal presence.

Example: the influence of restricted visual acuity on the analytic situation

Miss H, a university student in her twenties. In one session soon after shifting to teleanalysis, she asked her analyst, "Can you see my tears through the video?" She worried that her analyst would miss her sadness in the session. Although this worry could reflect distrust in her analyst's attunement, his interpreting that as a transference resistance circumvents acknowledging the reality underpinning her question about the format. The truth is that, due to the limitation of information transported by the Internet, it is indeed very difficult to see tears clearly, unless the patient wipes them off her face or her voice shows some hint of crying, thus leading the analyst to become aware of the tears. This example poses the question: how does the patient feel in the analysis when silently shedding tears lying on a couch beside a computer with a picture of the analyst who cannot see the expression of sad feelings and who speaks to the patient as if there were no tearful sadness? Because of the actual limitation of the view offered in the setting, the attentive and attuned analyst might not be able to connect fully with the patient at this moving and crucial moment.

On the other hand, perhaps the teleanalytic couple, lacking total sensory perception of co-presence, can gradually adapt to this situation of incomplete perception by withdrawing their mind energy from other channels of perception, such as acute vision and smell, to focus on hearing as the main channel for arriving at intuition. It is not difficult to find the evidence in nature, where animals privilege individual organs to perceive the world: when one organ develops, other organs are reduced in importance. In fact, any analyst and analysand who have to switch from working on screen to audio because of a poor connection will need to adapt.

After periods of in-person analysis, patients who must change to teleanalysis gradually settle down into the analytic process; although they tend to complain about the technology-assisted setting, their complaints can be understood not only as objective complaints, but as having unconscious meaning. Discussing the problems arising from using technology generates useful material to explore the unconscious mind. The analysand becomes able to focus on hearing as the way of sensing the analyst and analytic situation. On one occasion, Miss H said to her analyst, "I like to hear you, as your voice makes me feel warm and safe, and I feel embraced by your voice holding me."

Meanwhile, with the ongoing adaptation, listening and looking at the screen, the analyst can find himself able to be fully engaged in a real and deep connection. The relationship between the analyst and the patient cannot simply be called a screen relationship: it is a human relationship through the medium of the Internet. The more both of them enter into an analytic process, the more real and human the relationship becomes. It seems that the screen is like a barrier, and both parties have to gradually get over it, and then can get into a relational field. Otherwise, all they see and feel is simply a screen. Once accustomed to working on screen, the analyst thinks of his patients as real analysands, not just as talking images, and vice versa. It is a subtle mental state, by which the analyst seems to see through the screen, and his mind seems to be with his patient in the same space: he sees her and hears her and seems to be with her, even though they are not in the same physical space. At that moment, there seems to be nothing stopping his intuitive perception and attunement and nothing in the way of detecting her hidden feelings of anxiety or anger. In the subtle atmosphere of teleanalysis, the analytic couple can develop a real connection as they adapt to the new, external, virtual space, and in their minds create an internal space where both parties are emotionally present.

Interruption or loss of connection in teleanalysis

Internet transmission of sound and image operates through software and depends on adequate bandwidth, both of which are easily disturbed by unknown and uncontrollable forces related to the Internet. These unseen factors cause loss of vocal clarity, irritating intermittent metallic sounds, or even the complete interruption of connection. These irritations are fewer with improved Internet speed and quality of computers, but they do still happen from time to time. Distortion and sudden loss of analytic contact influence the analytic frame and process in different ways. Since we cannot know when and why it happens, we cannot predict the moment of disturbance, but if and when it happens, it seriously disturbs the emotional connection. Then, patient and analyst may both develop a conscious or latent anxiety about it happening again to interrupt their connection—particularly likely for the patient, who cannot see the analyst and may not realise the interruption has occurred.

Example: sudden loss of analytic contact because of unknown causes

Mrs K, an accountant in her forties, felt that her sense of security was much threatened, and the natural process of the analysis negatively influenced, when the analytic couple began teleanalysis. She often asked her analyst whether he was still there if he remained silent when she was talking or thinking, because she worried that their connection might have been disrupted without her noticing it and that her analyst might, therefore, have missed what she was talking about. For some time, she would still ask him whether he was there and whether he could hear her, so as to confirm the good Internet connection between them, before telling her analyst something particularly significant for her. The anticipatory anxiety related to potential technology problems restricted the patient's free association and sense of security in the analytic process. With the analyst's voice arriving through her earphones being the only evidence of his existence, the absence of his voice predicted the possibility of his *complete* absence, which aroused strong anxiety in the patient when she was in deep regression. The analyst sometimes had to answer her by saying "I am here", or "I can hear you" when she asked him for confirmation. The patient in teleanalysis might need the analyst to answer her so as to differentiate between fantasy and reality, but such a deliberate action on the part of the analyst can disturb his freely associative mind and even sacrifice his neutrality and abstinence. The analyst's silence is an essential part of his being there with the analysand, in keeping with his ideal of being a secure container ready to receive whatever she might convey verbally or non-verbally by means of a projective, communicative process (Bion, 1970). However, at these times the analyst's silence destroys the container, and breaking the silence also destroys the container.

In Chinese Taoism, the natural process is stressed, because there lies the real path to the truth. When we deliberately do something to complete some aim, we, at the same time and to some extent, disturb or even break the natural balance in the system. In psychoanalysis, when the analyst has to speak to counteract the patient's sense of insecurity due to the constraints of technology, he has to sacrifice part of his mind and his energy to think about which sound to make or what to say and when to make the intervention, which is distracting for him and complicates the already complex analytic process. The analyst who intends to confirm the stable connection and prove his presence may unwittingly convey affirmation or disapproval. Certainly, this response could be coloured by the patient's fantasy, but could also be triggered by the analyst's inappropriate timing of his response to the patient's expression of anxiety, even though it might have been the right timing for breaking the silence to prove the analyst's presence. It is hard for the analyst to satisfy both sides at once. What is more, sometimes the analysand may seduce the analyst to utter a sound to prove he is there, or answer the question, as if to make up for the limitations of the teleanalytic setting.

Once, when Mrs K asked her analyst whether he could still hear her, her analyst replied by uttering "Hmmm." If he kept quiet, she could easily think they had a problem with the connection, and would stand up to check it, and, indeed, the connection was, at times, broken. When she smiled and said, "I love to hear you say something," her analyst realised he had been manipulated by her at that moment, even though he did not deny the need to demonstrate his presence and confirm the connection. My point is that the Internet connection really makes the analytic process much more complex and brings about problematic processes that are hard to deal with. The uttering of non-specific sounds, or having to answer the analysand's question, in teleanalysis could be a fruitful topic for further research.

Having discussed some problems and limitations due to the technical fragility of the teleanalysis setting and its influence on the analytic process, I shall turn my attention to discussion of the space for the setting, because it is so different from that in analysis in person.

THE TELEANALYSIS SETTING AND THE ANALYTIC FRAME

Concerns about the analytic frame

Classical analysis conducted in person requires a reliable, confidential setting in which patients can reveal their primitive wishes and fears. It is the analyst's responsibility to provide this setting and to maintain a firm frame within which patients can safely express themselves. Bleger (1967) eloquently addresses the importance of the frame and its symbolic meaning.

We may say that a patient's frame is his most primitive fusion with the mother's body and that the psychoanalyst's frame must help to re-establish the original symbiosis in order to be able to change it. The disruption of the frame, as well as its ideal or normal maintenance, are technical and theoretical problems, but what really blocks off any possibility of a profound treatment is the disruption the analyst himself introduces or admits in the frame. The frame can only be analysed within the frame, or, in other words, the patient's most primitive dependence and psychological organisation can only be analysed within the analyst's frame, which should not be ambiguous, or changeable, or altered (Bleger, 1967, p. 518).

Bleger sees the frame as the receiver of the symbiosis. How is this replica of the intrapsychic inheritor of the infant–mother relationship to be received in the teleanalytic frame? The development of a person needs a space, from the mother's womb for the foetus to the mother's embrace for the baby after birth, to the family environment, the home, and beyond. All of these spaces function as a holding environment. The interaction between baby and mother occurs in a space that contains the baby and the mother's presence, a space that is the prerequisite for their relationship to develop and without which deep anxiety is the result. This deep anxiety is delivered into the analytic situation, where it needs to be addressed and understood. In a technology-supported space in which patient and analyst are physically in different rooms, both lose the common physical space that holds them and their relationship. The patient loses the ideal of the physical holding environment of the analytic room with the analyst physically in it. To such a patient, technology offers an inadequate setting, in which it might not be possible to create the necessary degree of security and confidence in the setting which is essential for moving on to interpretative elaboration (Carpelan, 1981; Meltzer, 1967).

Winnicott (1947) said,

> For the neurotic, the couch and warmth and comfort can be symbolical of the mother's love; for the psychotic it would be more true to say that these things are the analyst's physical expression of love. The couch is the analyst's lap or womb, and the warmth is the live warmth of the analyst's body. (p. 72)

In teleanalysis, no matter whether the patient is neurotic or psychotic, he or she can only see the analyst and parts of the analyst's space through the virtual space, which is like a window; the patient is outside the window and is not physically in the analyst's space, which can, to various degrees, result in the feelings of being excluded, of not being together, and of being separated.

Limitations of virtual space

When comparing teleanalysis with in-person analysis, the significance of the room chosen for analysis is one of the most important elements. Unlike in-person analysis, where patient and analyst inhabit the same room for the duration of the session, in teleanalysis patient and analyst are separated physically in different rooms, or, to be more precise, analyst and patient are not in the analyst's room. Instead, the patient is in a room selected without the analyst's input. The patient from the patient's room and the analyst from his consulting room enter a third space, the virtual space provided by the software through the Internet. When patient and analyst are connected, the mobile picture of the patient moving to lie down, and then lying on the couch in the room, appears in this virtual space, while the analyst appears as a head and shoulders against the backdrop of the consulting room. These three spaces in teleanalysis, compared to the one space in in-person analysis, complicate the work. (Here, I am talking about external space, not the internal space.)

With in-person analysis, the analyst offers the patient a reliable physical space, a room with a couch and other carefully selected furniture, books, and objects. That room, with its strong walls, floors, and ceilings made of cement and steel, is solid, symbolically experienced by the patient as the analyst's strong mind and embrace. Neither patient nor analyst need ever worry that this space will suddenly disappear due to unknown reasons. For teleanalysis, the two physical spaces and the one virtual space must be united so that they can form the required space for analysis. The survival of the three spaces for teleanalysis is totally dependent on the Internet, and this makes them inevitably less stable than that of in-person analysis.

Examples: the change from in-person analysis to teleanalysis

Even though the analytic relationship has been well established, after the analyst leaves, it will be as if the patient is connected to the analyst by a long and possibly unstable umbilical cord. The patient never, particularly at the beginning of teleanalysis, gives up the feeling that the analyst is far away from them, although they could, to some extent at some times, feel warm and moved in the analysis.

Miss Y, a twenty-year-old saleswoman in Internet technology, agreed to continue analysis before her analyst left for another city, but after the teleanalysis started, she firmly reduced her frequency from four sessions a week, refused to lie on the couch, and shortly afterwards, cancelled sessions with no warning, and finally dropped out. She told her analyst, "I feel you are like a picture projected on to the wall, when I want to reach you with my hands. I suddenly find it is an unreal image, and what I can touch is only the empty air." She could not tolerate the new teleanalysis setting after their separation. Mr M, a postgraduate in his thirties, once said to his analyst, "Your leaving is like a broken kite. And I am the kite. You lost interest in me. You will go away, leaving me alone, floating."

These patients' reactions to the analyst departing and switching to teleanalysis seem to indicate that teleanalysis might not have been strong enough to make them feel the analyst's presence and have a sense of their being together as securely as in-person analysis does. Even though the analyst could offer them regular teleanalysis sessions, the virtual space did not seem able to take the place of his previous analytic room. The patients felt, to some extent, distant and insecure. When patients regress deeply, they urgently need the analyst's physical presence. For instance, in one session, Mrs K suddenly regressed to physical expression of her anxiety and fear by rapid breathing and muscle tension, as well as a little trembling of her limbs. She said, "Where are you? I want to grasp you! I need to locate your exact position." In this case, where the physical space was replaced by a virtual one, the analyst's mental space for the patient was seemingly not enough to maintain her sense of security and warmth. Once teleanalysis was established and ongoing, anxieties appeared much less frequently. However, appearances may be deceptive. The anxieties might not have been dealt with once and for all, but might have gone underground, as the patient succumbs to the features of the virtual space so as to survive the analytic process. In that case, the frame of teleanalysis has led to a psychic retreat (Steiner, 1993) and loss of opportunity for the emergence of the true self. This is a real obstacle to psychoanalysis. In clinical practice, we need to look out for a gradual reduction of complaint about the virtual space of teleanalysis, in order to identify whether this implies adaptation or psychic retreat in need of analysis.

Misperception of information

As I have pointed out, in teleanalysis the patient on the couch can only perceive the analyst through sound. This limitation not only will result in incomplete perception, as I have discussed above, but also in misperceiving sounds that are heard. In one session, Mr M suddenly asked his analyst, "Is there someone else in your room when you are analysing me? I wonder because I heard footsteps in your room just now." This was not necessarily a paranoid transference, since he had no other clues to test his perceptions. The analyst noticed some knocking sounds outside the window, which he thought might have been misperceived by the patient as footsteps in the analyst's room. The analyst clarified what had happened and tried to explore whether there was some transference element in his doubts. Mr M did not express that sort of idea again about the analyst and his office security, but it is suspected that this paranoid anxiety had penetrated into the depth of the patient's mind and was lurking there silently.

At the beginning stage of teleanalysis, it was difficult for the analyst to choose how to respond to his patient at this moment. The analyst could be silent, or give an explanation of what really happened around him, or give an interpretation of the patient's fantasy based on the misperception, but none of these responses seemed good enough, because the analyst and the patient, at that moment, were not in the same real, objective world. They did not share a common physical reality. As a result, the analyst's response might be ineffective or even be experienced by the patient as a disguised comment, if the patient was in a paranoid state. It might be better not to interpret the patient's fantasy, as the analyst might do in in-person analysis, but to acknowledge the difficulties they both are facing. The analyst could say, "This is a difficult moment for both of us due to the constraints of the virtual setting. We are in different physical spaces, and have different perceptions of sound." In this way, the analyst would not deny the patient's perception of the sound, but leave open the possibility of exploring the element of fantasy that led him to attribute that sound to the presence of another person.

The journey to the analyst

Psychoanalysis requires of the patient motivation (suffering, curiosity, the wish to understand, and the willingness to be a patient), traits of personality and character, and capacities (Greenson, 1968). Here, I want to talk about another possible essential element that qualifies the patient for analysis, but I find it difficult to define, and so I will try to convey it by using a story.

There are some Chinese expressions related to Buddhism, such as: "Devote the pure mind to Buddha" (Yi Xin Xiang Fo), and "Your wishes will be realised if you are sincere" (Xin Cheng Ze Ling). Both expressions embody not only the disciple's sincerity, but also the ideal, sacred, reliable, and powerful figure of Buddha, who, the disciple believes, can bring good luck and change of destiny, all of which are actually in the mental attitude of the disciple. I am not trying to suggest that psychoanalysis is a religion, but I do think that the patient's sincerity and belief in psychoanalysis is important. In the famous Chinese mythological novel, *Journey to the West*, Ts Tang Seng set outs on the journey to the west to search for Buddhist scriptures with the help of his three assistants, one of whom is the Monkey Sun, Wukong. The Monkey Sun possesses numerous magic powers. However, although he is so powerful, the West Ru Lai (the most powerful Buddha) does not allow him to fly with Ts Tang Seng on his back, directly to the west. They must walk to the west, experiencing eighty-one dangerous difficulties, which is the precondition for seeking the Buddhist scriptures. It is not an overwhelming torture, but a way of testing and tempering the mind for sincerity and belief, without which Ts Tang Seng will not understand the truth of Buddhist scriptures. By analogy, in in-person analysis the analyst resides in the analytic room and the patient is on a journey to the analyst, and analyst and patient must believe that pains, conflicts, wishes, and fears should be expressed and experienced in order to achieve a final working through in the journey of psychoanalysis. Like Ts Tang Seng undergoing tests of his mental sincerity and faith, the patient on the journey to the analyst has in mind some essential elements to be confronted.

In this ritual procedure, sincerity and belief are interdependent and interactive. Of course, the patient may sometimes have resistance on the journey to the analyst, but the most important thing is that the patient has the chance to experience it and overcome it and continue the journey to the analyst. I suggest this makes the analysis deeper and the patient's mind for analysis much richer. The journey to the analyst is a subtle, overlooked but important part of psychoanalysis, which cannot be ignored. However, teleanalysis, born of modern technology, condenses this journey to just one click of the computer mouse. It is just as if the Monkey Sun directly flies to the west with Ts Tang Seng on his back, which the West Buddha will not allow them to do, because, although they could obtain the Buddhist scriptures by using this short cut, it is not considered the road to the truth of the Buddhist scriptures. To be able to find the analyst just by clicking the mouse is more like a magic game than making a real, serious connection. This mouse-clicking connection probably deprives the patient of elements of the journey that are important to experience. In my view, in teleanalysis something essential may be lost.

For those in in-person analysis, the journey to the analyst functions as a kind of buffer zone against too strong an intrusion of real life into the analytic session. So, the journey is like a path around a transitional zone protecting the analytic field from the direct interference of real life. In tele-analysis, this protection zone is lacking. By mouse clicking, patients can go directly in time and space from daily life to analytic field. Several minutes before the session, the patient could be having dinner, talking or quarrel-ling with someone, sleeping, watching television, or working, and then jumps into the analytic field through the Internet. This sudden "jumping into" has repercussions on the analytic state of mind in the patient.

Klein (1952) thought that external incidents and actions in daily life that might seem to refer only to external reality turn out to be meaningful in analysis because they connect to, and represent, accessible unconscious fantasies. Similarly, we might think that what is happening just before a teleanalytic session could have unconscious underpinnings useful for analysis. That is interesting, but I am focusing on something different. On the journey to the analyst's room, the patient's mind has been preparing for the coming session, consciously and unconsciously. The patient could bring any external event that happened outside the analytic room before the session and use it for in-person analysis. All the external events reported in the session can be considered as scenery on the way to the analysis. Upon analysis, we find that they have been seamlessly combined with unconscious fantasy that can then be analysed.

If you want to cook dinner, on the way home you buy anything you need for the meal. Similarly, as you head towards a traditional analytic session, you sort your thoughts and feelings to prepare your mind and open it to the analytic task. But attending a session of teleanalysis is a switch-on and switch-off event, as if you suddenly jumped into the kitchen from your place of work without any transition. Much is lost. For instance, tele-analysis patients can often present themselves in a similar way, no matter whether they are late or not. In in-person analysis, if the patient were late, the analyst would hear footsteps either hurrying or unconcerned, different ways of knocking at the door, of entering the room, with sweat on the face or not, out of breath or not. In short, the analyst can see the immediate impact of all these external experiences that are so real before the session. The patient cannot hide them. The instant arrival of the patient on the screen, always the same no matter what has happened, cannot reflect the patient's state of mind. The advantage of convenience and connection across a distance carries within it a disadvantage in terms of foreshortening the journey to the analyst and all that it brings into the session.

The ending of the session also contributes material for analysis. In in-person analysis, when the analyst says that it is time to finish, patient and analyst stand, the patient sees the analyst in person, walks to the door, possibly saying goodbye, crosses the waiting room, opens the door, and goes out to the street. During this process, the elements of reality are gradually re-established in mind, even though some residue of regression may still hover. We can consider the departure from the session as another journey, a transition to everyday life. The patient who suddenly gets a phone call on this journey may feel that the transition has been interrupted, strongly or mildly. The phone call, intrusive and sharp, drags the patient away too quickly from the natural transition back to reality. Teleanalysis condenses the journey away from the session to just one click of the computer mouse.

In in-person analysis, it is the analyst who is left in the analytic room, and it is the patient who leaves that room for the journey away from the session, meaning that regressions may be left there, protected in the safe space of that room with the analyst in it until the patient's return. This makes for a feeling of being "held", not only when the patient is in the session, but also outside it. By comparison, when patient and analyst close the connection, the patient's experience is of being the one left in the room, while the analyst is the one who is felt to be leaving. Facing the sudden loss of the analyst and being left alone in front of a machine, the patient might feel abandoned.

What happens externally will surely influence what happens internally. The holding environment in teleanalysis may be good enough in some respects, and better than nothing for those who cannot have in-person analysis, but it might lose out on the precious moments so rich with information just before and after sessions. In teleanalysis, the analytic couple replaces the physical entry and exit with a routine of beginning and ending the session.

In order to reduce the influence on analytic process by the problems discussed above, the analyst might like to establish with each analysand a rite of saying goodbye as a special setting for the ending of the session in teleanalysis. After letting the patient know it is the time for ending the session, the analyst waits for the patient to click off the connection. Concluding the session in this way leaves a fantasy that the analyst is still there in the virtual space, as he would be felt to be in in-person analysis.

However, there is another aspect of this problem: the patient may use the clicking on and clicking off to satisfy an omnipotent phantasy. Miss L, a business woman in her thirties, in psychoanalytic psychotherapy twice a week, insisted on her clicking on to start the session and her clicking off when the session was going to end. When the analyst addressed this phenomenon, she explained that her clicking on and off made her feel safe, as she had captured the analyst's image and stored it in her laptop. With a click, she could make the analyst appear on her laptop and she still had him in her laptop after the session ended. The analyst was like a little magic man magically stored in her laptop that made it seem as if she possessed him, rather than coming to him for help.

In summary, the journey to the analyst, as well as the journey away from the session, should be part of what Bleger (1967) called the frame of the analysis. The manner of clicking and its timing in relation to the beginning and ending of sessions is a complex feature of teleanalysis and cannot simply be compared to the knock at the door or closing of the door in in-person analysis.

Patients' power over the setting

Even if the Internet connection were perfect, the virtual setting would still have limitations. In in-person analysis, it is the analyst who offers the setting, the room, the couch, and the rules. It is the analyst who holds firm against any attack by the patient on the setting so as to create the necessary, safe analytic environment for the patient. However, the maintenance of the teleanalysis setting is done equally by analyst and patient. For instance, both of them have to provide a reliable computer, a fast-enough Internet connection, a good quality headset, microphone, and web camera, and a private room. The patient's power over the setting can subvert the analyst's power of maintaining it. For instance, the resistant patient can influence the setting and the analytic process by choosing a slow Internet speed that breaks up the screen image and interrupts the communication, or a poor quality microphone that distorts the analyst's perception of sound and interferes with the ability to make sense of what is said. These choices reduce the security, constancy, and consistency of the teleanalysis setting and attack the analyst's linking and thinking.

Example: Interruption in communication by the patient

In the middle of one session, Mrs K suddenly sat up and checked her computer. When the analyst commented on the sudden interruption, she explained to him that she had become unsure about whether the battery of her computer would last the whole session. Her unconscious had taken advantage of her power to influence the setting for reasons that they could explore. But even if she could understand her motivation for the attack on the setting, she had experienced, consciously or unconsciously, that she had the power to influence or even damage the working space. In another treatment, as the analyst began saying that it was time to finish the session, Mr M immediately took off his earphones and lay on the couch quietly, not getting up as usual. The only way the analyst could reach Mr M, through his voice, had been removed by Mr M, and so the analyst found himself put into a position where he was powerless to communicate with Mr M.

*   *   *

Carpelan (1981) held that the analyst, unless absolutely obligated, should not change the external frame of the analysis. Thus, he should not let himself be manipulated and controlled by the patient. To a degree quite different from in-person analysis, the patient in teleanalysis really can manipulate and control the setting, in a way beyond the analyst's ability to establish a firm frame. When this leads to an image of the analyst as weak and unreliable, the patient cannot develop the basic trust and necessary dependence in the transference. In in-person analysis, the patient would lose trust in the analyst who failed to maintain the setting under the patient's attack. This would strengthen the conviction that the analyst is an unreliable object who cannot meet the patient's fundamental need for security. If we imagine the patient's primitive infantile conflict as a monster imprisoned by defence, the monster will be let out only when it feels safe enough, only when the analytic environment is strong enough to bring the monster under control. How can patients dare to let out their imprisoned and threatening monsters if they might destroy the analyst, the analytic environment, and the objects in it? How can patients dare to let out their primitive unconscious infantile conflicts if their unconscious fantasy might destroy the analytic space and the analyst?

When connecting with the analyst on the Internet, an adolescent patient, Q, in twice-a-week therapy, usually moved his webcam to and fro, or let it turn over on his computer desk and then suddenly drop, making it seem as if the analyst had fallen and was lying on the ground looking up at him. The analyst associated to what one would see through a videographer's camcorder if he were shot and the camcorder were to fall on the ground in the battlefield. The analyst felt that the young man had a wish to make him dizzy or shoot him. In fact, in one session, he actually pretended to have a gun in his hand and directed it at the analyst. In later exploration, he acknowledged his wish to "kill" the analyst's analytic mind, which might be too threatening to him. Finally, he dropped out. One would wonder whether he felt he owned the power to really kill the analyst's mind and felt unsafe in the virtual setting.

This leads to a consideration of which patients are suitable for teleanalysis. We have to assess the developmental level of the patient, the capacity for object constancy, and the ability to distinguish between fantasy and reality. Borderline and psychotic patients might not be suitable if they are unable to make the distinction. Patients who act out their destructive wishes on the frame make it impossible to work in teleanalysis. Patients who do not want to try the novel frame, do not feel able to explore and work in the virtual environment, cannot bear the actual distance, or try but cannot get over their discomfort, are not going to get what they need from teleanalysis.

For teleanalysis to have a chance of being effective, patient and analyst must both fully and honestly acknowledge the problems and limitations of the frame, accept that it is the only choice open to them, and decide to work together within its limitations as best they can. Neither analysts who completely distrust teleanalysis nor those who boast of its value without acknowledging its problems may really help the patient in teleanalysis. Both members of the analytic couple need to have sincerity, a firm wish to survive the difficulty from the beginning, the hope of making a good enough connection, and the courage to travel together on the road to their common destination.

The patient's resistance: acting in

Teleanalysis can function as a kind of space where both members of the analytic couple are able to find each other. When the patient and the analyst are connected on the Internet, they come into the same virtual computer space, one in which they can see each other while they are in their own rooms. Then something interesting happens: patient and analyst are connected even though in separate rooms. The analyst observes how the patient is behaving on screen, which makes the patient appear small and far away, and presumably the same is true of the analyst's appearance to the patient. This weakness of the analyst's power over the frame encourages the patient towards acting in and acting out. The patient has the power to decide when and how to connect to the analyst, and he or she also has the potential to close the connection and so close the door on the analyst. Patients in their own rooms can wear whatever they want, even pyjamas. They can make tea beside the computer and drink it in the session without any explanation. They can change the position of the furniture, add or remove something from the room, and change the décor, all of which reduces the firmness of the frame.

Before his analysis changed to teleanalysis, Mr M had always wanted to wear slippers into the analytic room, take them off, and put his naked feet on the couch. He never actually did that, so there was enough time and space to explore the meaning of that impulse. However, when the frame was changed to teleanalysis, he really did put his naked feet playfully on the couch in his own room during sessions, without any interest in thinking about its the meaning.

At the beginning of one session, the analyst was surprised to find that Mr M did not lie on his couch, but on a mat on the floor. Mr M explained that it was a mat that he used for meditation, and on which he felt relaxed. The analyst was aware that Mr M had expressed anxiety and insecurity in recent sessions regarding something that was unclear but that would be fearful for him to talk about, if only he could figure out what it was. Lying on the mat, Mr M told the analyst that he felt relaxed, and he was able to say what the fearful "something" was. By exchanging the couch for the mat, he projected his anxiety into the discarded couch, and then he could tell the analyst the fearful "something". But he told the analyst only what the something was, not what he felt about it, or how he felt about telling it to the analyst. The analyst lost the most important and valuable element, the patient's feelings, combined with his thoughts and their inhibition in relation to the analyst, represented by the use of the couch.

Reflecting on Bion's (1970) container function, based on Klein's (1952) concept of psychoanalysis as a total situation, Carpelan (1989) writes,

> The internal object which by projective identification is transferred into the analyst is linked with various kinds of psychic phenomena, and it is the totality of all this which the analyst has to receive. Thus, the transferred becomes the contained. The analyst's task is then to find the meaning of the transferred and of the whole situation. (p. 148)

Mr M adjusted the setting to suit himself and meet his needs, and the analyst could do nothing but watch it happening. This left the analyst feeling that he could not engage with the total situation, because it had not *been* a total situation. There was a hole in it, through which important feelings leaked. Here, we again see how fragile the teleanalysis setting is. This kind of acting in is very different from that in in-person analysis, which is a more solid setting, while in teleanalysis the patient has more potential to damage the setting. Even if the analyst gave the patient some interpretation of the meaning of his moving from couch to relaxation mat, it would not be effective because the feelings have disappeared. As Joseph (1985) said, "Interpretations dealing only with the individual associations would touch only the more adult part of the personality" (p. 448). In that session, although the patient could tell the analyst about his anxiety, he gave a highly intellectual narrative. The analyst thought he was being perceived as a potentially critical but also significant figure, and that Mr M was afraid of exposing himself to the analyst, suspecting that this might result in the analyst's contempt and criticism, although, on the other hand, he also wanted to be dependent on the analyst and to trust him. These conflicts, related anxieties, fantasies, and defences associated with his attachment to the analyst might have been more contained in solid and stable in-person analytic space and, therefore, potentially easier to explore and analyse. The analyst was left wondering to what extent Mr M had left the couch altogether because of the limitation and problems of teleanalysis.

DISCUSSION

I have referred to early anxiety and insecurity that are conveyed by technical insecurities. I have shown that the process of analysis can be influenced. I have compared teleanalysis to in-person analysis, and shown how the problems and limitations of the virtual space could present obstacles to the required functioning of the analytic frame. In teleanalysis, the maintenance of the frame is not the sole purview of the analyst: the patient can disrupt or even damage the frame quite beyond the analyst's control. In my view the teleanalysis setting is, to some extent, not as safe, stable, constant, and consistent as that of in-person analysis. For instance, I think it is doubtful that the setting of teleanalysis can allow the patient to experience fantasy states of primitive fusion with the mother's body. As Bleger stresses, the frame which receives the infant–mother symbiosis and the patient's most primitive dependence and psychological organisation can only be analysed within the analyst's frame, which must therefore be neither ambiguous, nor changeable, nor altered. But, in teleanalysis, the patient can alter the frame. The problems, limitations, and fragility of the teleanalysis frame, which I have discussed in detail, may threaten or even damage the function of the frame as a stable projection screen for the patient's mental state. Despite these limitations, teleanalysis has been a boon for many patients who would not otherwise have access to psychoanalysis, but enthusiasm and gratitude should not block our critical assessment of what works and what does not. Applying technology in the conduct of analysis is still a new and controversial path in the psychoanalytic field, and there are still many facets which need to be explored in the light of theory and clinical experience. We need further research to address the various weaknesses.

By facing the problems and limitations of the frame in teleanalysis, compared to the in-person analytic frame, I do not aim to sentence teleanalysis to death, but to argue for an appropriate attitude towards teleanalysis. New technology poses many questions that psychoanalysts have not previously had to address. They could not have imagined psychoanalysis occurring when patient and analyst were not in the same physical space. If the analyst or the patient in an established, in-person psychoanalysis temporarily moves to another place, but can have access to the Internet, is it reasonable to maintain continuity of care or should that be considered an enactment, fulfilling the patient's infantile wishes or alleviating both parties' separation anxiety? As we seem to be attracted by the "convenience" or "better than nothing" aspect of teleanalysis, we must constantly dedicate our analytic minds to understanding all the questions raised by this new technology.

By exploring the advantages and problems and limitation of teleanalysis, we see that it has much in common with in-person analysis, but also has its own new aspects. Teleanalysis in the twenty-first century can provoke excitement, interest, curiosity, and enthusiasm, but, at the same time, doubt, a sense of betrayal, hatred of the unknown, and threat to the established protocol, as did Freud's introduction of psychoanalysis itself in the late nineteenth century. As in analytic work, the appropriate attitude towards teleanalysis should be non-judgemental and exploratory. We face the positive and the negative aspects equally without judging teleanalysis to be right or wrong. We approach it with trust and hope and a degree of constructive doubt, as we explore it, get to know it, and understand it. An extreme positive or negative preconception damages the open, exploratory analytic process to some extent. If the enthusiastic analyst denies the problems and limitations and their unconscious meaning for the analytic relationship, he will not be successful in telanalysis. If the sceptical analyst is too doubtful of teleanalysis, he will blame the frame and lose confidence in his analytic work. Appropriate levels of trust, curiosity, and doubt facilitate analytic exploration.

Another aspect requires attention. As Feldman (2009) said of in-person analysis,

> In addition to the inevitable and appropriate doubts about his understanding and his work, the analyst is subjected to conscious and unconscious pressures from the patient, the aim of which seems to be to fill him with uncertainty, confusion and doubt. (p. 217)

In teleanalysis, the pressures on the analyst are more complex. When the patient complains frequently about the teleanalysis situation, the patient's dissatisfaction amplifies any uncertainty, confusion, and doubt in the analyst. The analyst struggles with how much this complaint is coming from reality, and how much is coming from the patient's projection. When the patient complains that the analyst is distant, cold, and indifferent, the analyst wonders if he is being constrained by the virtual space or if the patient is using the problems of the frame to meet her unconscious needs. When the analyst accepts the patient's complaint and then analyses it, he can see how the patient "contributes to the creation and maintenance of internal objects whose qualities are ambiguous, and whose motives doubtful, with which the patient is engaged" (Feldman, 2009, p. 217).

SUMMARY

In this paper, I have discussed the limitations and problems of teleanalysis. I presented my reflections on clinical practice in this relatively new area of psychoanalysis, and illustrated my ideas with clinical examples. I concluded by arguing for a balanced, open-minded, profoundly analytic approach to teleanalysis.

REFERENCES

Bion, W. R. (1970). *Attention and Interpretation*. London: Tavistock.

Bleger, J. (1967). Psycho-analysis of the psycho-analytic frame. *International Journal of Psychoanalysis, 48*: 511–519.

Carpelan, H. (1981). On the importance of the setting in the psychoanalytic situation. *Scandinavian Psychoanalytic Review, 4*: 151–160.

Carpelan, H. (1989). Reflections on Bion's container function and its pathology. *Scandinavian Psychoanalytic Review, 12*: 145–161

Feldman, M. (2009). *Doubt, Conviction and the Analytic Process: Selected Papers of Michael Feldman*. Hove: Routledge.

Greenson, R. R. (1968). *The Technique and Practice of Psychoanalysis*. Madison, CT: International Universities Press.

Joseph, B. (1985).Transference: the total situation. *International Journal of Psychoanalysis, 66*: 447–454

Klein, M. (1952). The origins of transference. In: *Envy and Gratitude and Other Works* (pp. 49–56). London: Hogarth Press, 1980.

Meltzer, D. (1967). *The Psycho-analytical Process*. London: Heinemann.

Steiner, J. (1993). *Psychic Retreats: Pathological Organizations in Psychotic, Neurotic and Borderline Patients*. London: Routledge.

Winnicott, D. W. (1947). Hate in the countertransference. In: *Collected Papers* (pp. 194–203). London: Tavistock, 1958.

Skype as the Uncanny Third[*]

Irmgard Dettbarn

Skyper an acronym for *Sky peer-to-peer* was the original name given to new software designed to make free phone calls possible on the Internet in 2003. However, at this time, another domain with the same name already existed in cyberspace. So the "r" was simply deleted and *Skyper* became *Skype*. In Skype, described by *Peer to Peer Technic* as a peer-to-peer network,

> [R]esources and data can be simultaneously exchanged between two networked computers, however, both computers must be on an equal footing, as the name suggests. Using a microphone, the computer records the user's voice; it then converts this information into individual datagrams (or network packets) and sends it via the Internet Protocol (IP) to the respective receiving computer. Thus, the entire data exchange occurs via the Internet. The receiving computer puts the incoming datagrams back together and transforms the data back into language that is delivered via a loudspeaker. (www.voip-information.de/peer-to-peer.html)

In March 2011, it was reported that thirty million users, who were simultaneously online, could be reached through Skype. By now, a few million more are surely using Skype. In fact, today I was one of these Skypers. I spoke to two separate analysands via Skype, each call lasting fifty minutes. So I carried out two analytic sessions today. Or did I? If the unconscious knows neither space nor time, then the answer is "Yes". If, according to Sandler, whatever the analyst does is "analysis", then "Yes". If one reads the International Psychoanalytic Association's definition of psychoanalytical treatment, the answer remains unclear. The question arises whether transference and resistance can develop in such a setting, sufficient to enable a genuine psychoanalytical process.

From 2007 to 2010, I had the opportunity to live and work as an analyst in Asia, where I conducted in-person analysis with analysands who each had four sessions per week on average. Once back in Berlin, a question arose: would it be possible to continue the work as "shuttle" analysis with my returning to Asia only twice a year? A second question occurred to me: could Skype sessions bridge the time gap between my visits to Asia? Back

[*] This article has been published previously in *Psychoanalysis Online* (2013) edited by Jill Savege Scharff, Karnac Books, pp. 15–25. By permission of the author, editor and publisher. It is reprinted here because of the central role of the author in introducing formal psychoanalysis to China, and because of the importance of the subject to practice in China. (Editor's note.)

in the 1990s, extensive discussions on the use of the telephone in psychoanalysis could already be found in publications of the International
Psychoanalytic Association, and numerous other articles on "remote
therapies" have been written since then (see for instance, Carlino, 2011;
Lemma & Caparrotta, 2013; Fishkin et al., 2011; Scharff, 2012, 2013a,b;
and an article by Lin Tao in this issue). Personal discussions and conversations held among professionals have been quite controversial, often revealing very opposing viewpoints. On the one hand, some analysts have
completely rejected the idea. On the other hand, some have enthusiasti-
cally highlighted their finding that analysts could not distinguish between
the process notes of in-person sessions and those of analytic sessions conducted on the telephone or the Internet.

I use Skype of necessity, but I have mixed feelings towards Skype. Doubt
and fascination seem to go hand in hand, which has led me to think further
about my experiences with this new tool. My thoughts revolve around
what I have noticed and what has occurred to me when I am sitting (and
just after I have been sitting) in front of my laptop, talking with the
analysands who are thousands of miles away in another part of the world.
I am very interested in finding out more about the influence of Skype on
my analysands, on me, and on the analytic process itself. The two Skype
contacts that I had on the day when I first started writing this text could not
have been more different. The technical difficulty with Skype in each case
was sometimes experienced differently depending on whether the context
was a negative or a positive transference.

I bought my laptop specifically for Skype. It has particularly good
speakers and a built-in camera. Every now and again, when starting up
the computer, welcome messages from the software company pop up on
my screen informing me that there will be an update of this or that programme, and enquiring as to whether I want to download it now or later. I
am faced with many questions calling for decisions and, unprepared, I am
forced to answer them one way or the other, that is, with "yes", "no", or
"later". My intellectual resources are diverted to making unwelcome decisions when I want to be in a state of reverie preparing for an analytic session. Carr (2011) notes the same: "Links have to be constantly evaluated
and related decisions regarding the navigation made, while at the same
time we are bombarded by an enormous amount of fleeting sensory stimuli
. . . our brain is not only strained but also overwhelmed" (p. 18, translated
for this article).

Today, I am able to log on to Skype straightaway, without encountering
any difficulties. For me, in Berlin the first session is at 7 a.m., but for my
analysand the local time is 1 p.m. It is a beautiful sunny spring day in
Berlin. Eight thousand kilometres away, it is lunchtime, and I have no idea
if the analysand is looking out of the window at smog, sunshine, or rain. Is

it important to know this? Neither of us shares the same space or the same time-zone, and yet we are both in our own individual real time, both of us part of the media revolution.

On the screen, I can see all the names and photos or icons of the people whose addresses are stored in my Skype address book. I can also see who is available on Skype right now and who is not. Although I do not know where my Skype contacts actually are, I am still informed as to whether they are currently available, busy, or not online. So, every time I click on Skype or my Skype address book, I know who is online. Therefore, the Skype user can find out whether the other person is online or not, twenty-four hours a day. However, Skype also offers its subscribers the option of showing an "offline" message, when in fact they are still online, or they can activate a red icon requesting others not to disturb them. So, my experience of Skype has taught me that the information presented by the displayed icons does not always coincide with the facts. For example, the small green "cloud" beside my Skype address indicates that I am online, but the analysand's display might tell him something else. Thus, neither the analysand in Asia nor the analyst in Berlin can be sure if either of us is online at the time of our appointment. When the analysand clicks on my Skype address on his computer, it should cause my laptop to ring. But here I am, sitting in front of my laptop, and it fails to ring.

Depending on the different types of computers being used, several essential preliminary actions have to be made before contact can be established via Skype. Instructions have to be followed and this task remains in the foreground of the analyst's attention until it becomes automatic. It is interesting to know that when Skype was first invented, intensive attention was being given to the place of the therapy room and the couch in psychoanalytical literature (Guderian, 2004a,b).

With the great changes that have occurred in all aspects of life following the media revolution, the inevitability of being tied to traditional settings has been called into question. How significant will these new media opportunities become, how will they affect us and our society, and to what extent can they be put to use in psychoanalysis? In the 1950s, the media theorist McLuhan, author of the famous quote "The medium is the message" (McLuhan, quoted in Grampp, 2011, pp. 175–218) noted the close connection man makes to the tools he has made to extend his capability and ease his life. As Carr puts it, "We shape our tools and thereafter our tools shape us" (Carr, 2010, p. 323). As Kramer puts it,

> Whenever we use a tool to gain greater control over the external world, we change our relationship to this world . . . The medium is not simply the message but it really perpetuates the message of the mark of the medium . . . as the unconscious is in relation to what is accessible to the consciousness. (Krämer, 1998, p. 81)

But Carr warns, "If a carpenter takes a hammer in his hand, he can only do with this hand what the hammer allows him to do [with it]. The hand becomes a device to hammer in and pull out nails" (Carr, 2010, p. 323). So if, as analysts, we use technology, does this mean that we will find our analytic sensibility constrained by technology or that we will respond to technology with a creative, flexible adaptation of our technique in synchronisation with the changing society in which we live?

The impact of information technology is one of the biggest changes that humanity has encountered since the invention of the clock, which fragmented our time, and the arrival of the printing press, which extended our knowledge and memory storage and heralded the age of industrial manufacturing and mass production which brought wealth to many. As we participate in the realm of technology, we are also changing the relationship with ourselves. The media revolution, expressed on radio, telephone, television, and film, and now burgeoning with the rapid development of cyberspace, has become a part of our conscious and unconscious experience. So imagine how it feels for analysts who are used to in-person analytic settings to read the Cyberspace Independence Declaration at the World Economic Forum in Davos on February 8, 1996 from the Internet pioneer, John Perry Barlow:

> Governments of the Industrial World, you weary giants of flesh and steel, I come from Cyberspace, the new home of Mind. On behalf of the future, I ask you of the past to leave us alone. You are not welcome among us. You have no sovereignty where we gather. Our world is different, cyberspace transactions, relationships, and thought itself, arrayed like a standing wave in the web of our communications. Ours is a world that is both everywhere and nowhere, but it is not where bodies live. Our identities have no bodies, so, unlike you, we cannot obtain order by physical coercion. (Barlow, 1996)

When I contemplate a matter-free world of thinking, I recall Freud's description of "magic and sorcery, the omnipotence of thoughts . . . all the factors which turn something frightening into something uncanny" (Freud, 1919h, p. 243). Is that what technology is? The writer Arthur C. Clarke thought so: "Any sufficiently advanced technology is indistinguishable from magic" (Herbold, 2012, p. 25). Before I continue with the uncanny and magical aspects of the new strange world we occupy, I would like to consider the influence of Skype has on the setting and the analytic pair in psychoanalytic practice.

By eliminating the geographical distances created by locations spaced far apart, Skype can remove barriers to analysis for analysands who live in remote areas without access to analytic centres. However, Skype, with "its flickering screen" (Carr, 2011, p. 18, translated for this article) can be problematic and physically strenuous. At the same time, Skype connects the analytic pair by means of a machine. The vertical relationship (in the traditional setting) between analyst and analysand arises from the fact that the analysand actively seeks and then makes his way to the analyst. In turn, the analyst awaits the analysand and provides him with a safe room in which the analysand can enter a psychological space for work. With the advent of technology, this has all changed. Instead, a peer-to-peer communication is created. Both sit in front of the computer, both touching the keys. The similarity in the arrangements is that the analysand calls first.

Returning to an example, I am in my office waiting at the appointed hour for my analysand to call. The computer has yet to ring. In trusting the Skype icon, I assume that my analysand is present on his computer at the other end of the connection. I wonder why it does not ring. However, I know that the icons can sometimes be wrong or misleading! So I call him myself. Behold, the analysand had tried several times to reach me, but, according to his computer, I was not connected to Skype. The machine, a third party that suddenly determines the rules, becomes a part of our work. We are both affected by this; both of us are unprotected from the intrusion as we would be if the analysand who meets us in person has a road accident on his way to the analyst, or the analyst's next door neighbour begins to play the piano, or a handyman is drilling in the apartment above the practice. However, these disturbances come from a very understandable reality and we know what is to be done, whereas a malfunction in the computer is something that "very few of us would understand, even if the hidden codes were revealed to us" (Carr, 2011, p. 20, translated for this article). Unexplained computer malfunctions and broadband interferences that may interrupt and terminate the conversation at any given time, combined with the possibility that the person we are talking to may do so by happening to touch a key on the keyboard, leaves us questioning our reality.

This third party that not only participates in the Skype contact but also determines it to a degree is an inanimate object that is rapidly spreading itself throughout the world, especially among the younger generations, and revolutionising their way of being. It is becoming an "evocative object" (Turkle, 2007). Here is a report of an intense relationship with a person's laptop.

> My laptop computer is irreplaceable, and not just for all the usual reasons. It's practically a brain prosthesis. Besides, I love it. I would recognize the feel of its keyboard under my fingers in a darkened room . . . I carried it on my back all over England, Cuba, Canada, and the United States. When I use it in bed, I remember to keep the blankets from covering its vents so it doesn't overheat . . . It doesn't just belong to me; I also belong to it. . . . It just so happened that I had early romantic experiences with machines, and so computers make me think of love. (Newitz, 2007, p. 88)

When I read this text I am, of course, reminded of Winnicott's (1971) transitional object, and of Habermas's (1999) personal objects that accompany us in life. Newitz's descriptions of her relationship to her laptop provide an impressive and vivid example of Habermas's definition of personal objects. However, her text also reveals just how the object sets its own conditions; for example, when the author describes protecting it from over-heating! Writing before Skype was invented, Habermas (1999) defined these personal objects as follows:

> Personal objects mediate not only between man and nature and between man and culture, but also thirdly, between the individual and his fellow man, especially his significant other(s).
>
> A) Personal objects can remind us of a significant other and therefore the relationship with him or they can even represent him. Personal objects help to symbolically maintain the connection to another or others; they make him present, even when he is no longer there following separation or in situations of separation.
>
> B) Personal objects can also serve as a medium to connect with others by acting as a common object, organizing joint activities or by making communication over long distances possible, i.e. technology such as the telephone and car. (Habermas, 1999, p. 500)

The device that is programmed to use Skype, whether it is a computer, laptop, notebook, or iPad, fulfils these personal object functions. In its technical existence, it mediates between man and culture, and when used as a means of communication, it not only links the analyst to the analysand during sessions, but it can symbolically make and potentially maintain the connection eternally, as when a Skype participant looks to see if his analyst is online around the clock.

The beloved object has, as it were, become a living object, having settled somewhere between living and dead matter. Once again, I hear the ring of the magical and uncanny. The uncanny is that which exists between life and death and creates the impression of living. Why do we treat or deal with dead matter as if it were "alive"? In addition to psychological explanations, perhaps the neurosciences can be materialised, too. According to Mitchell (2009),

> Evolution has imbued our brains with a powerful social instinct . . . a set of processes for inferring what those around us are thinking and feeling . . . Recent neuroimaging studies indicate that three highly active brain regions—one in the prefrontal cortex, one in the parietal cortex, and one at the intersection of the parietal and temporal cortices—are specifically dedicated to the task of understanding the goings-on of other people's minds.

As we have entered the computer age, however, our talent for connecting with other minds has led to an unintended consequence!

Mitchell says, "Chronic overactivity of those brain regions implicated in social thought . . . can lead us to perceive minds where no minds exist, even in inanimate objects" (Mitchell, 2009, p. 213).

Inanimate objects may be thought to assume the functions of human abilities. The creepier they seem, the more we project vitality into the inanimate object, and the more perturbing it is to us. Just as the child with the help of the transitional object in imagination learns how to bear the absence of its mother, the adult tries to bring the mighty inanimate object to life, and, in doing so, hopes to evade the uncanny, the terrifying absence of life, and the imagined encounter with death.

> In addition, there is mounting evidence that our brain naturally imitates the spirit of those with whom we interact, whether real or imaginary. Such "neural mirroring or reflections" explain why we so quickly ascribe human characteristics to our computers and computer properties to ourselves. (Carr 2010, p. 213).

> Even as the larger system, into which our minds so readily meld, is lending us its powers, it is also imposing its limitations on us. (Carr, 2011, p. 19, translated for this article)

Let us return to the Skype session. The computer has given us the power to overcome a seemingly insurmountable distance for a short time, but its technical possibilities have limitations, such as presenting false information concerning the presence of the Skype user. The computer has created a relationship of equality, as previously described. It has also put us into the realm of disembodiment. Do our voices become disembodied on the computer? Are they ghostly voices? But who still believes in ghosts? Surely we have long since left this notion behind us. Or have we? Perhaps technology throws us back into an encounter with the uncanny "when infantile complexes which have been repressed are once more revived by some impression, or when primitive beliefs which have been surmounted seem once more to be confirmed" (Freud, 1919h, p. 249).

As the normally vibrant mark of our presence, does the voice lose its vitality in the absence of the body, or does it lead us into an emotional area between the living and the dead? A witness to history in the making impressively describes his feelings about the disembodied voices of the first talking machines:

> You can't believe it dear friend, what a strange sensation and impression it made on us; hearing a human voice and human speech for the first time ever which did not seem to come from a human mouth at all. We looked at each other in stunned silence, and afterwards we openly admitted that during those first few moments a secret little shiver had run down our spine. (Macho, 2006, p. 136)

In 1878, Edison enthused about the voice of a dog that he had recorded:

> One day, a dog came passing by and began barking in the hopper, and . . . this barking was reproduced in such fantastic quality. We have removed the roll well and now we can let him bark at any time. As far as I'm concerned this dog may die and go to dog-heaven . . . but we have him – everything that has a voice survives . . . This dead apparatus presented the dead voice as the overcoming of death. (Edison, 1878, quoted in Macho, 2006, p. 139)

"Since time immemorial, human beings have tried to use voices to humanize inanimate matter. Animals, plants, objects, dead people or abstract entities were given a voice, so as to provide them with human characteristics" (Macho, 2006, p. 139, translated for this article). The lifeless should be brought to life and technical inventions are supposed to refute the statement that all of us are mortal, "but no human being really grasps it, and our unconscious has as little use now as it ever had for the idea of its own mortality" (Freud, 1919h, p. 242). This is the deadly sinister side of technology, laptops, notebooks, or Skype.

Computer technology puts us at the mercy of an apparatus that we do not properly understand: it functions according to its own laws and, therefore, it can be controlled only to a limited extent. When the connection fails in a Skype session, this may be a minor obstacle for some people. However, for others it might mean the reactivation of a trauma, or it might even cause a trauma with associated feelings of powerlessness, helplessness, and vulnerability. Both analysand and analyst are equally exposed to this: maybe there is even the risk of a seductive symbiotic "joining of forces" against the uncanny third. In turn, this can prevent the working through of conflicts within the analytical process. The ensuing potential aggression and fear should not be underestimated. It can be a relief not to be left alone at the mercy of unpredictable technology. In terms of the analysand, this can also mean disillusionment, if he has attributed magical powers to the analyst. On the other hand, this traumatic situation can lend support to mutually complicated and negative feelings being experienced in the transference: if the analyst is experienced as a bad object, malfunctions or disruptions in Skype are interpreted as confirmation of the analyst's aggression towards the analysand. Since the technical problems with Skype cannot really be controlled, the field of magic and the uncanny is activated.

In another Skype session, a patient raised a very touching, but also troubling, issue. My eyes are closed as I listen to him. I often do this during in-person sessions to tune in to my analytic reverie. I realise that I am deeply moved by what he is telling me. When I open my eyes again and look at the Skype images on the screen, I see that the patient is crying. I do not doubt the sincerity of his or my own emotions for one moment: the closeness and proximity between him and me, which, with the help of technology in a virtual world, happened at this very moment, even though we are far apart. I am not only surprised, but positively impressed by the possibility of this experience of emotional presence in a Skype session.

A few hours later, it is now early afternoon in Berlin and late evening in another analysand's city. The connection is established without any initial difficulties, until a text bubble from Skype appears on the screen, announcing that it has found a fault and is trying to reconnect. Even so, the conversation continues. I endeavour to understand what the analysand is saying. But despite all my efforts, I often have to ask him to repeat or explain himself again, because our words are being lost somewhere in cyberspace. I cannot quite connect to what he is saying. Both of us are really annoyed. Alternately, we try to call each other again and again. The analysand asks me to stop asking him to repeat himself so often. He suggests that we should try to guess what each other has meant. I understood this as an attempt to install an illusionary symbiotic form of communication, rather than submit to the dictates of technology. Needless to say, this particular session took place with a negative transference in the background. The problems are piling up: the computer forces us to constantly focus on restoring the connection, and we are both upset at the lack of continuity. Should we stop or just switch to the telephone? But on this occasion the phone also fails to work properly. The analysand, who already would have preferred to do anything else other than have a session, is now full of anger. To me it seems very much like the uncanny third party has become his ally. Neither of us can change the situation. By the time the session comes to an end, both of us are angry. We are in a state of "double negative transference". "That's unfair," he says, "I was waiting the whole time when we weren't connected." I also think it is unfair: technology is simply unfair. When I found the term, "machine-loathing" (Ziemann, 2011, p. 116), I could only confirm that someone had found the right name for my current feelings.

With regard to the voice, silence is also a part of speaking. In the last session described, the troubled or malfunctioning technology made it impossible for any "sense-perceptible silence" to occur (Gehring, 2006, p. 91). In any case, Skype makes it difficult for any "silent understanding" to take place. If neither the analyst nor the analysand is speaking on Skype, we cannot tell whether the silence is due to a technical problem or if it is an active silence on the part of one of us. This can result in an unwanted "forced-to-speak" situation for both parties. A poor Internet connection can create distortions of the voice so that it repeats like an echo. In her article on the repeating voice, Gehring describes the story of the nymph, Echo, who needs to speak, but can no longer say anything other than repeat the words of others. "An echo loses its ability to remain silent, it loses all semantic scope (or space), sentences are also truncated and the echo is robbed of the dimension of listening" (Gehring, 2006, p. 106, translated for this article). Your voice cannot communicate any sense. It can neither really "live" nor "die". Skype guides us back into the uncanny space between life and death.

The next day, I have another Skype session, also of poor technical quality. So we change to the phone without difficulty. During this session there is a positive transference mood and any technical problems with Skype are irrelevant. Although the patient finds the change of media somewhat distracting, he is so intent on his thoughts and feelings that not even this change seems to cause any kind of disruption, even though, for this particular session, he was away from his usual location. This raises the question, what role does the room or space play? Gumbrecht addresses this as follows:

> [This is] the most difficult existential consequence of the electronic age . . . eliminating the spatial dimensions at various levels of our experience, our behaviour . . . Thereby, we encounter a fascinating paradox: with the help of electronics, globalisation has, on an unimaginable scale, expanded and strengthened our control over the space on earth and at the same time, it has almost completely excluded this space from our existence. (Gumbrecht, 2010, p. 42, translated for this article)

With the elimination of space and distance comes dislocation. According to Attali (1992), the highly mobile residents of the global village seem to live like nomads equipped with communication devices that he refers to as nomadic objects.

> To use these devices, they only need to be connected to global electronic information and trading networks, the oases of the new nomads . . . It does not matter where you come from; a number or name is enough to identify the nomads of the Millennium. [p. 26]. Like the objects of pagan antiquity, the nomadic object of the future will be an inanimate object; however, they will embody the life, spirit, and values of those who develop and use them. Basically, they are branches of our senses and our bodily functions. For example, computers supplement the human brain. (Attali, 1992, p. 107, translated for this article)

When Attali continues to develop his ideas about the future, he places future technical developments in the area of the horrific and the uncanny:

> One could imagine that man also becomes a nomadic object subsequent to this cultural mutation. . . . One day, you will be able to create an inventory of yourself or others; browse and rummage in the organ department store, consume other people as objects, and change into another body or spirit. (Attali, 1992, p. 116, translated for this article)

Now I would like to go back to the beginning of this text, to Skyper, the word that dropped its "r", so that it could enter the stage of the Internet. We can use Skype to overcome distances and hold real-time conversations with the intense quality of analytical sessions. Then again, a disrupted

Skype contact can remind us of Echo's punishment: that she is forced to speak the words of others again and again, however senseless this may be, her never-ending repeating voice preventing her from taking or giving any comfort or relief from silence.

Just as an echo must repeat itself and cannot be silent, the punishment's distinguishing feature is its immortality: it never ends. Using this metaphor, it seems Skype is becoming a punishing superego. In any case, a man-made machine superego cannot be merciful to the human ego. Do we submit because "the digital revolution is irreversible" (Schirrmacher, 2010, p. 1, translated for this article) and because we can no more hold back the impact of technology than we can dismiss the sun or the sky? Talking metaphorically of sky reminds me of another metaphor—the cloud, a name for repositories of data that are stored in geographically remote data centres that can be accessed via the Internet. Again, to the technology neophyte, it sounds uncanny.

Before communication satellites appeared on the scene, stars, angels, spirits, and the gods were to be found in the clouds. In *Clouds*, a comedy by Aristophanes (423 BC) a middle-aged Athenian tells Socrates that he wants to know the truth of the divine and communicate with the deities in the clouds. In the post-modern western world, we are caught between the clouds of Aristophanes and the clouds of the computer world. Although they are separated by more than 2,000 years, they still have one thing in common. They are there where "it often seems to be uncanny, when the line between fantasy and reality is blurred, when something real steps out in front of us, which we hitherto had considered fantastic" (Freud, 1919h, p. 244).

Skype, a representative of a man-made digital world that is based on the number line between 0 and 1, is programmed to decide automatically between right and wrong. In contrast, psychoanalysis addresses ambivalence and the constant inner conflict between right and wrong. The computer can only function when the user makes a clear decision: yes or no. This is in complete contrast to the unconscious, which does not differentiate between contradictions. Yet, a function so binary as Skype is asked to support the complexity of psychoanalytic process.

Unlike analysis, Skype guarantees a special identity for eternity. A Skype address is unique and never deleted. Even though there can be anonymity on a large scale, there is also eternal life. Does this give us some narcissistic gratification? Or does its virtual reality abandon us to a new kind of solitude? We can be reached on Skype at all times and everywhere, but we are not actually together, physically present in the same room.

We have lost not only the "r" in Skype, but also the bodily presence of analyst and analysand. This negative can also be a positive in some cases, in that it can eliminate the threat of physical aggression or potential sexual attacks.

> When two bodies come close to each other geographically, this reinforces the sexual (or aggressive) attraction, and simultaneously the visual perception of the overall shape of the other person begins to blur . . . Close spatial proximity implies emotional closeness. (Habermas, 1999, p 64, translated for this article)

The gain of reduced threat is countered by the loss of closeness. In analysis by Skype, is it "a dangerous illusion, if in a 'broad present' (now), we are robbed of our physical presence?" (Gumbrecht, 2010, p. 130, translated for this article). It seems that there is danger and opportunity whether the body is present or not. Extreme acts of physical violence, including sexual abuse and murder, are not a literal possibility as they are in traditional in-person analysis. Skype provides a particularly safe setting that might elimi-nate the stimulus for passionate declaration, or it might facilitate its expression because there is no possibility of actual violence.

Although we do not share a common physical space, now we can always be reached. Does this spare us the pain of separation? Gumbrecht suggests that "we have replaced the pain of loneliness caused by physical absence with the permanent semi-loneliness of unlimited availability" (2010, p. 130, translated for this article). Does this affect the process of mourning?

Technology as a tool reduces the workload and increases possibilities: it leads to experiences and facilitates processes that without devices would be not simply weakened, but would not exist at all. On the downside, the goal of media technology seems to be global reach rather than improved performance (Krämer, 1998). So much interaction across distance in real time is now possible, but what if, sitting at our computers and speaking to each other on Skype, "everything merges into one another, everything is fusion" (Gumbrecht, 2010, p. 130, translated for this article)? How do we differentiate and adapt the technology to our use without fooling our-selves? Turkle (2007) suggests, "As we begin to live with objects that challenge the boundaries between the born and created and between humans and everything else, we will need to tell ourselves different stories" (p. 326). Until then, does technology, the third uncanny party, remain a threat? Technology as a device or apparatus, however useful in some ways, creates artificial worlds. Can and do we want to use this newly created world for psychoanalysis?

REFERENCES

Aristophanes (423 BC). *Clouds.* http://records.viu.ca/~johnstoi/aristophanes/clouds.html

Attali, J. (1992). *Millenium.* Düsseldorf: Econ.

Barlow, J. P. (1996). Cyperspace Independence Declaration. www.eff.org/~barlow

Carlino, R. (2011). *Distance Psychoanalysis: The Theory and Practice of Using Communication Technology in the Clinic.* London: Karnac.

Carr, N. (2010). *The Shallows—What the Internet is Doing to Our Brains*. New York: W. W. Norton.

Carr, N. (2011). Wie das Internet unser denken verändert. *Du*, 815: 14–21.

Ellrich, L. (2011). Phänomenologie des Mediengebrauchs. In: A. Ziemann (Ed.), *Medienkulur und Gesellschaftsstruktur*. Wiesbaden, Germany: Springer Verlag.

Freud, S. (1919h). The 'uncanny'. *S. E., 17*: 217–256. London: Hogarth.

Gehring, P. (2006). Die Wiederholungs-Stimme. Über die Strafe der Echo [The repeating voice. On the punishment of Echo]. In: D. Kolesch & S. Kräme (Eds.), *Stimme* [Voice]. Frankfurt: Suhrkamp.

Grampp, S. (2011). *Marshall McLuhan*. Konstanz: UVK Verlagsgesellschaft.

Guderian, C. (2004a). *Die Couch in der Psychoanalyse*. Stuttgart: Kohlhammer.

Guderian, C. (2004b). *Magie der Couch*. Stuttgart: Kohlhammer.

Gumbrecht, H. (2010). *Unsere breite Gegenwart* [Our Broad Presence]. Berlin: Suhrkamp.

Habermas, T. (1999). *Geliebte Objekte* [Loved Objects]. Frankfurt: Suhrkamp.

Herbold, A. (2012). Bezaubernde Siri [Enchanting Siri]. *Der Tagesspiegel, 18*: 1.

Krämer, S. (1998). Das Medium als Spur und als Apparat [The media as trace and apparatus]. In: *Medien Computer Realität* [Media, Computer, Reality]. Frankfurt: Suhrkamp.

Lemma, A., & Caparrotta, L. (Eds.) (2013). *Psychoanalysis in the Technoculture Era*. London: Karnac.

Macho, T. (2006). Stimmen ohne Körper. Anmerkungen zur Technikgeschichte der Stimme (Voices without body. Comments on the technical history of voice). In: D. Kolesch & S. Krämer (Eds.), *Stimme* [Voice]. Frankfurt: Suhrkamp.

Mitchell, J. (2009). Quoted in: Carr, N. (2011). *The Shallows—What the Internet is Doing to Our Brains* (p. 213). New York: W. W. Norton.

Newitz, A. (2007). My laptop. In: S. Turkle (Ed.), *Evocative Objects* (pp. 88–91). Cambridge, MA: MIT Press.

Peer-to-Peer-Technik, VOIP DSL-Wlan-specials www.voip-information.de/peer-to-peer.php

Scharff, J. S. (2012). Clinical issues in analysis over the telephone and the Internet. *Int. J. Psycho-Anal., 93*: 81–95.

Scharff, J. S. (Ed.) (2013a). *Psychoanalysis Online*. London: Karnac.

Scharff, J. S. (2013b). Technology-assisted psychoanalysis. *J. Amer. Psychoanal. Assn., 61*: 49–509.

Schirrmacher, F. (2010). Preface. In: N. Carr, *Wer bin ich, wenn ich online bin . . . und was macht mein Gehirn solange? Wie das Internet unser Denken verändert* (German edition of *The Shallows*). Munich: Blessing.

Turkle, S. (Ed.) (2007). *Evocative Objects*. Cambridge, MA: MIT Press.

Winnicott, D. W. (1971). *Playing and Reality*. London: Tavistock.

Ziemann, A. (2011). *Medienkultur und Gesellschaftsstruktur* [Media-culture and the structure of society]. Wiesbaden: Springer.

Not So Lost in Translation:
Supervising Psychoanalytic Psychotherapy Candidates in China

Lycia Alexander-Guerra

Abstract

This paper describes a two-year supervision by Skype with a candidate in China enrolled in the China American Psychoanalytic Alliance's psychoanalytic psychotherapy training, and an analyst in the USA in which the young analyst in training struggles with her career choice. The candidate has a dream about her choices disguised as a car journey and also dreams about the supervision, evidence that a strong relationship with its transference–countertransference implications can exist even via Skype across 8,000 miles.

Key words: Skype, supervision, psychoanalytic psychotherapy, China.

Sharing the professional life we love, helping it flourish around the globe, and consolidating our own ideas about the work we do are among the many gifts we receive when we give our time to nurturing young professionals in China. It was intriguing to me that psychoanalysis was being disseminated in China. I thought how exotic "Freud" might seem to many parts of China, just as names like Beijing and Shanghai seemed exotic to me. I thought no matter how little I might know about psychoanalytic theories or an analytic attitude, I was sure to know more than a candidate who grew up in a culture where metapsychological constructs such as ego or oedipal complex were not so common to its lexicon. I was eager to share what I knew, partly because I love psychoanalysis and partly because I am already a teacher at my local psychoanalytic institute. I was excited to meet the young woman who had decided to dedicate herself to training in a culture where her interest would be pioneering. It had been decades since I had made the same decision to dedicate myself to training. I imagined my supervisee must be heroic, or, at the very least, highly motivated, for I might be available to her at 9.30 in the morning, but she saw me at 9.30 p.m. after a long day, and I was moved by her dedication.

Blossom, the supervisee, who was enrolled in the China American Psychoanalytic Alliance's psychoanalytic psychotherapy training (CAPA), and I met first by Skype and it took a number of meetings for my ear to become accustomed to her accent. I wondered how she was able to understand me, English being foreign to her. She would always have an English-to-Chinese dictionary on hand. I always made an effort to enunciate each word carefully. It was, sometimes, slow going, but in a peaceful and meandering way, like boating on a shady, spring-fed river on a hot summer's day. Frustration came from the Internet Skype connection, which too frequently dropped calls, lost video, or had whirring noises which obliterated our conversation. We soldiered on, calling back numerous times, sometimes giving up and confirming by email that we would meet again the following week. It was a privilege to be part of this neophyte's growth and development and we worked together for almost two years. When the sixty required supervisory sessions were up and she had to move on to a new supervisor, we took a half dozen more sessions for termination. There were tears on both our parts at our final goodbye.

At times, I was curious about customs in China as I tried to feel my way into the lives of Blossom's patients and discern how they might experience things in the context of their culture. It turns out, not surprisingly, that people are people all over the world. Patients in China, too, experienced misrecognition from their parents. They survived childhood sexual abuse. They were raised by grandparents and missed their parents. Poverty took a toll there as it does elsewhere in the world. More often, though, it seemed a male child was preferred, and Blossom found herself with mostly female patients, most of whom grappled explicitly with this fact. Two things, though, struck me as quite different. There seemed a greater pressure to conform, comply, and defer to parental wishes and to expectations of authority figures in general. And I think the "one child policy" put a peculiar demand on the child, certainly a greater burden to be everything the parents needed the child to be. I wondered if the Chinese only child ever fantasised what had become of the other unborn, unconceived children.

It is often difficult for candidates in China, as it is where I am, in the USA, to obtain psychoanalytic patients. Many work in clinics where the culture is once a week therapy, and then for only a few weeks. I was repeatedly encouraging to Blossom about the benefits of more frequent and more protracted therapy. Eventually, Blossom was able to secure a patient for twice a week therapy for the remaining time we worked together. I was uncertain if she did this as much to please me or if Blossom recognised the benefits of developing a deeper and more intimate relationship with her patient. Chinese supervisees can be very deferential. Some of my colleagues gave up on the endeavour, complaining that their candidates' English or knowledge base was too poor. I approached the endeavour with less memory and desire and watched with delight what was unfolding between us. Baby steps seemed perfectly appropriate to me.

Early in supervision, Blossom used the time to ask lots of questions and request recommendations for papers, but as Blossom found her psychoanalytic footing, she put forth her own formulations about what she thought was going on intrapsychically and interpersonally with her patient. I became more and more impressed with her facility of mind. She had some ideas from her classes, of course, but most classes were about traditional theories, and so I moved her along gently with interjections of a more contemporary bent, the latter, I think, easier to integrate into clinical practice. She made use of classes and what I gave, and this spoke of both her intelligence and her wish to please.

Blossom and I got to know each other. What had drawn us to psychoanalysis? How might she and I make use of our time together? How did she conceive that people benefit from treatment? Blossom was quick to offer her understanding of therapy: that patients, in the presence of the therapist, might better become aware of themselves and their feelings. Blossom hoped to help them face things in their minds and hearts that were difficult to face. We discussed particular topics such as ambivalence and empathy. I told her empathy is about understanding the good sense of bad behaviour, and precedes any expectation of the patient to change her/his behaviour. Sometimes, Blossom would read papers she had asked me to recommend and we would discuss them. She expressed disappointment that many of her patients did not stay in treatment as long as she had hoped. She wondered how to manage the angry and disappointed feelings in her patients who were dissatisfied with their treatments. In other words, Blossom was becoming a therapist, struggling with all the same issues as any western therapist beginning to learn how to be with patients.

As supervisor, there was always an opportunity for me to say something taken as smart, for Blossom had so little theory yet on which to rely, compare, and contrast. This can be very confidence boosting for the supervisor. The medical school model is "See one. Do one. Teach one". Nothing helps us grapple more with our theories and attitudes than having to teach them. Thus, I highly recommend to all the supervising of a younger colleague. We started off slowly; I would ask Blossom's associations to the case material she presented. I asked her how she explained her patient's behaviour. We brainstormed aloud together. I and she knew too little about her patient yet. So we speculated. I asked Blossom what she thought her patient thought of her, and what their respective agendas for the work together might be. I asked her how the two of them planned to negotiate when they had differing agendas.

Blossom was always pleased to have a dream to present. She had been learning to think about what feelings (affects) were present in dreams. She was eager to have me interpret, like a magician, dreams of her patients. I would remind her of the context in which the dreamer presented the dream to Blossom. Was there something in their previous session or in their relationship that was hinted at in the dream?

A couple of months into our work together, Blossom began a long-term treatment with a young woman whose father, emotionally distant all her life, had died while the patient was away at college and while the mother was visiting the patient. The patient's father had died all alone. The patient felt guilty and sad. In treatment, the patient had a dream about her father:

> He is in front of me, his back to me so that I could not see the expression on his face, but I knew he was very sick. I tried to touch his back with my finger and his back bent completely in a right angle. I took him in my arms, as if he was a baby, and took him to the hospital.

Blossom had not known what to say about the dream to her patient, so she asked the patient if there was more to the dream. The patient added that both her boyfriend's brother and mother were intrusive. The patient felt her boyfriend had turned his back on her when he did not help her with the difficult relations with his brother and mother.

Blossom wished to discuss the dream with me. We started at the surface and we worked our way to speculating deeper. At the surface was the loss through death of the patient's father, about which she felt guilty and sad. The patient's boyfriend had figuratively turned his back on her and the father in the dream literally had his back to her. Her father's emotional distance in the patient's life could be described, too, as his having figuratively turned his back on the patient. The patient felt guilty about her father dying alone. In the dream, her touch with her finger bends him ninety degrees, occasioning both the need to seek additional care at the hospital and an opportunity for the patient to care for and help him as she had been unable to do at the time of his death. Perhaps the patient worries that she had in waking life injured her father in some way, but how? Perhaps she had been resentful of his emotional distance and had unconsciously wished to hurt him as she had been hurt by his lack of attention. Blossom would have to be alert over time to these speculated ideas and themes as she worked with this patient.

With her long-term patient, we watched together as themes were threaded throughout the sessions. One theme was the patient's struggle to respect her own perspective: could the patient use her own judgement or would she need permission and agreement from her mother, her boyfriend's parents or her boyfriend in order to feel safe and have happiness? This very theme also wove through the patient's relationship with Blossom, and Blossom's relationship with me. Blossom mused on the Oedipus complex: could one leave one's parents free of guilt? Blossom enquired whether I thought her own projection was at work in her relationship with her patient. I was pleased to see Blossom trying on different ideas from her classes, though, in truth, I had very little idea what she was actually being taught in her classes.

Blossom was eager to learn more. Even when her patient was on vacation for a week or two, Blossom wanted to continue to meet in supervision to discuss ideas, such as how and why patients change, how do participants know when termination is appropriate, and, perhaps most pointedly, does Blossom discuss her countertransference feelings with her own therapist or with the supervisor? (Blossom was worried because she had had a dream about the patient on two separate nights.) Supervision, just as in the treatment situation, includes, I think, creating together a safe space to discuss one's fears and fantasies. The medium is the message in supervision, too. The supervisor must, as must the therapist, create a reliable and accepting space that invites in all possible content. So I welcomed whatever Blossom brought to me

A couple of months into the supervision, Blossom also had a dream, which contained content about me, the supervisor, about which she was ashamed.

I was driving the car and I see two roads. I don't know which way to go so I park the car near the side of the road. One road leads to the highway but the highway is so high it is not on the earth, the other road is on earth but there are no signs to indicate directions, so I don't know which way to go. The sky began to darken. If I drive on the highway and miss the road [exit], it will go to another province and how will I get back home? I want to m[t]ake the road so the car can drive safely. I see a little house [like a toll house] near the car where I can ask for information about the road. I go into the house and I see people there asking about the road. Two people say they are busy but I see a woman who is free and I ask her for directions. She shows me a map and indicates the way. I am very surprised because there is a long river and I am very far away [from destination]. I ask "How can I get to here? How can I get back?"

Then it is time for supervision. I felt that you were already on the Internet but I could not reach you by Skype. First. I have the wrong computer. Then I can't reach you on mine. When I finally get on Skype, the time was over and you had already left. I receive an email from you with many sentences, in English, and with many pictures like a word map [rebus pictogram]. It seems like homework you have given me, as if you've asked me to translate sentences. I continue to look and it looks like a letter you've written me. In this letter you are saying goodbye, telling me that you are to commit suicide. I felt very surprised, shocked. It was painful. I felt very sorry for missing our time together.

Then there is a beautiful cloth, very white with a beautiful picture. There is another cloth with multi-coloured pictures. I touch it and it is painful. It is not you, but another woman [who committed suicide].

Blossom then laughs and says it was just a dream, but the moment she had awoken, she had thought of two women who committed suicide. She is sure I know them very well because one is Virginia Wolfe and the other is the American poet Sylvia Plath. Later, Blossom said, when she received an email from me, in real life, she was very glad I was alive.

I think the dream spoke of Blossom's anxieties about which road to take professionally. How does she reach her goal to become a psychoanalyst? Then there were her traditional Freudian courses and my attempts to inter-weave contemporary ideas. There is psychoanalysis and there is coun-selling. Which one was too lofty, not down to earth, too far reaching? The woman who gives her a map could be me, her supervisor. Blossom asks her in the dream how to get to her destination. The dream then shifts to supervision with me, which she misses. It is an anxiety dream. Does Blossom worry that if she does not comply with CAPA programmes and my demands that I will be disappointed, hurt or even destroyed if she does not continue with CAPA? (She had also received an email from Elise Snyder, President of CAPA, just before having received mine.)

I keep my thoughts to myself. Blossom then tells me her associations.

In the past I didn't have the courage to do long-term psychotherapy. Now I finally found a case, she wants to do long-term therapy, so I wor-ried about that. I don't know if I want to be a professional counsellor. This is my worry. One is the highway, to go ahead. The other is nearer to my friends and colleagues, so I don't know what to do in the future. So I [am] surprised that I did not understand before that this dream is about my career. Before I began to study with CAPA I did not decide if I want to do this for my professional career. I feel responsible with [for] my patient and have to continue because she asked for long term. If I begin, I have to do my best without leaving her. So I [am] very worried about that. Before I go to sleep I thought about writing [to] you with my worry.

I note here that Blossom had had a dream previously, about her patient, which had included a threat—the bakery manager and the vendor/delivery man had been fighting (with gunfire) in the bakery, so that she and her patient had to leave the bakery together and escape. Blossom thought the bakery was psychoanalysis, specifically her personal therapy from which she wished to escape. She had wanted a different analyst but that analyst was in a far away city and the wait was too long. She had had to settle for one about whom she was uncertain but who lived in her city. She had mused that maybe I could change my role from her supervisor to her therapist. Then the manager, Elise Snyder—presumed to make all the rules—and the delivery man, Blossom's therapist—or her supervisor (me)—would be at odds.

Blossom was able to continue to see her long-term patient, continue her training, and grow and bloom throughout the two years I supervised her. She did have a few more dreams about her patient, including feeling she could "do nothing except listen" and so felt "useless." She also wondered at times if she even had any effect on her patient. Over the course of Blossom's work with her patient, Blossom was courageously candid about times when her understanding and empathy flagged, about her wish for the patient to hurry up and get better, and about her desire sometimes, such as when the patient did not improve or cancelled sessions, to transfer her patient to a different therapist. We discussed enactments, and managing the therapist's helplessness and sense of incompetence. Blossom could recognise that her patient's new struggles with her boyfriend indicated a forward movement for the patient, a finding of her own voice. Blossom, too, was finding a voice and I was gratified to be part of that.

One example of Blossom finding her voice occurred in the tenth month of our supervision when she had to present her case before her co-workers and to the psychiatrist in charge of the clinic. The psychiatrist was somewhat famous, was more experienced, and was very aware of his authority. None the less, Blossom was able to joke with the psychiatrist about his criticisms, which she thought indicated he misunderstood the case and, to her delight and surprise, the psychiatrist changed his tone and encouraged her to be herself with her patient. Blossom, likewise, reported she was able to be more openly questioning and critical about information presented in her classes, and thus felt more engaged with her training.

When it came time to say goodbye, Blossom reported that her patient, also reaching termination, had said to Blossom, "What else do we need to do? Nothing, so I leave my case material [their experience together] to you as a gift. The only thing I can do for you is to give my private material to you as a gift." I acknowledged that it had been a gift to me to work with her in supervision. Blossom noted that she, too, had received gifts, from me, that would last, as what one gains from therapy lasts after treatment ends.

DISCUSSION

Supervision using Skype over 8,000 miles can, none the less, engender an intensity of transference (and countertransference). The supervisee Blossom experienced some of the same wishes that I have noted in face to face supervision, for example, the wish that the supervisor, more collegial, more didactic, less opaque, might replace the supervisee's analyst or therapist. Has there been a blurring with Blossom and me between supervision and therapy? This is an interesting question that I hope readers will take up. While mother and father may agree on many ways to raise a child, the child usually can distinguish her parents and distinguish who provides what. It has been my teaching methodology to utilise the medium as the message. If I hope, for example, that the supervisee will, with her own patients, welcome in all content and affect, then my doing so as well with the supervisee is a procedural lesson that practises what we preach. While I might encourage the supervisee to *also* discuss her dreams about me—and anything else that emerges in supervision—with her own therapist, this encouragement is not to say she should *only* discuss these things in her personal treatment and not with me. Welcoming in the supervisee's ideas about her dream of me, the supervisor, allowed her to further explore her wavering commitment to the profession. Her feelings about me would also have been welcomed in, but she, and I, left this to her personal treatment for additional exploration.

Psychotherapy in China:
Historical Context and the Future

Li Zhen and Li Hongya

Abstract

For the past twenty years, rapid growth of psychotherapy in China has been unregulated and without an overview of quality. This paper describes that history and an effort by a start-up company to provide high quality psychotherapy to Chinese patients inside China and around the world, vetting therapists in terms of their training and their capacity to deliver quality service.

Keywords: psychotherapy in China; distance therapy; quality control; training.

INTRODUCTION

For the past twenty years, China has seen rapid, even wild, growth in the field of psychotherapy. Such growth, while a welcome development, brought almost as many problems as it tried to solve. As both a therapist and an entrepreneur, I am actively taking part in this movement. This article provides a brief historical context of psychotherapy in China, and shares my view on how the field will develop.

PSYCHOTHERAPY IN CHINA

Until quite recently, psychotherapy was an afterthought in the country's underdeveloped mental healthcare infrastructure. It was not until around 2000 that the Ministry of Labour started issuing a psychotherapist certi-fication. As a minimum requirement for someone to start practising psychotherapy, the certification was easy to obtain. One had only to attend lectures part-time for a couple of months, and pass a final examination that includes written and oral elements.

The introduction of the certification spurred a large number of night schools to prepare people for the final exam. Many were drawn to these schools with the hope of better employment opportunities. As expected, the number of certifications issued skyrocketed in the past decade. By the end of 2014, it was estimated that 500,000 certificates had been issued. Of the numerous certificate holders, though, few had the necessary training and experience to actually practise as a therapist.

Before the government certification programme, though, there were some good, if quite limited in scale, programmes in China engaged in the training and continued education of psychotherapists. One of the earliest and most established programmes is the German–China Academy for Psychotherapy (DCAP). Starting in the mid 1990s, the organisers of this programme invited experts from Germany and carried out three-year, systemic training programmes in Beijing and Shanghai. It would set precedents of later programmes, all of which were jointly run with European or American professional organisations. These half a dozen programmes have distinguished themselves with their selectivity and rigour. Collectively, they are graduating a considerable number of well-trained psychotherapists a year.

Compared to the hundreds of thousands of certificate-holding therapists, though, these graduates remain a small and non-representative segment of the professional force, which, as a whole, was in a poor position to provide care to the estimated tens of millions in need of it.

LIMITED AND UNSATISFYING CHOICES

For someone in China seeking psychotherapy, the options are limited and unsatisfying. They come down to:

- hospitals;
- referrals from relatives and friends;
- Internet search;
- traditional agencies.

Each has its own problems. The psychiatry departments in Chinese hospitals are primarily places for dispensing prescriptions. Psychotherapy or counselling services, if available at all, were often understaffed. Most people do not have friends or relatives knowledgeable of psychotherapy, and an Internet search more often than not turns up information that is inaccurate and out of date.

Traditional agencies offer a comparatively better option. They can provide some valuable services to therapists, such as administrative support and, sometimes, supervision. In exchange they take a cut of over 50% or more from therapy fee. Despite their high commission, the agencies have done little innovation. They have not taken advantage of technology advances and social media. The better trained therapists are leaving such agencies to start their own independent private practice, even if it means having to spend considerable time on administrative tasks and attracting clients.

For those who needed it the most, information and service remains out of reach. Psychotherapy in China has experienced some twenty years of rapid growth, and is now in need of a trusted, transparent marketplace.

Even with the better programmes, such as the aforementioned DCAP, the limited number of their graduates and indecipherable professional credentials means that people looking for help often end up with the best marketers instead of the most qualified.

PERSPECTIVE FROM A PRACTITIONER

From 2008 to 2014, I was a lecturer and counsellor at a university in Beijing. In my spare time, I had a private practice, seeing clients from outside my university. Seeing that the Chinese public could well use some good information on mental health and psychotherapy, I started a blog in 2012. My blog soon attracted tens of thousands of followers, and I was getting frequent speaker invitations.

More people started requesting my service as a therapist. The stories were often similar: a troubled client was unhappy with what she was getting at the hospital, or agency therapist. She saw my article on social media or by recommendation from a friend, and thought that finally there was a therapist who made sense.

These anecdotes confirmed that my contribution was providing a needed public service, so when I was invited to do an open course on one of the largest online media platforms in China, I accepted without hesitation. My video series on depression was viewed hundreds of thousands of times, and I was bombarded with thousands of requests for help. Some of the emails were heart wrenching. Thanks to the Internet, my content reached beyond the metropolitan centres of Beijing and Shanghai. Many of emails were from people from small towns, suffering from psychological issues, and with nowhere else to turn for help.

I tapped into my network to refer clients to my colleagues, but it was quickly becoming obvious that it was an unsustainable solution. I had stumbled upon a big, unserved, and urgent demand that could only be properly satisfied by a dedicated service platform.

BUILDING A PLATFORM

Seeing that demand for service was fast outpacing what I or even my network of professionals, could provide, in early 2014, with backing from investors, including Tim Draper and China's Zhen Fund, I founded MyTherapist with the goal of creating a trusted platform to connect therapists with patients. We took the following steps to provide a trustworthy service platform.

1. Signing up only the most qualified therapists. We conduct a careful screening and selection process to admit therapists, taking pains to

verify information. We took a conservative approach, admitting only alumni from established programmes, and with more than 1,000 session hours, as well as ongoing supervision. Because information is hard to verify, we place particular emphasis on references and recommendations. We ask that each newly admitted therapist supply two references from the pool of therapists already on our platform.

2. Developing tools for therapists and clients. With our backend tools, therapists can easily manage clients, session schedules, and payment. Clients can readily browse therapists, scheduling sessions, access articles and educational videos, or take assessment tests. All of these services are accessible from our website and mobile apps. Automation simplifies administrative tasks for both therapists and clients, streamlining recurring sessions, reminders, and billing.

3. Creating content for social media. We have a wealth of in-house produced content, which we use to promote awareness of mental health and psychotherapy. Our outreach spans a portfolio of an online video collection, an Internet radio station, an online e-publication, as well as popular social media accounts. Our content collectively reaches hundreds of thousands of viewers, and it is often the first step to developing our relationship with them.

4. Providing professional support for therapists. We created web and app-based tools to enable therapists to form online communities. We connect them with supervisors and resources for their continued training.

5. Keeping a database of therapy and supervision hours. In the past, there was no record of such data. Agencies, professional organisations, and clients had to rely on therapists' self-reporting. With our online scheduling system, we now can keep track of the number of hours of therapy and supervision. In addition, we have created a system that allows clients to provide feedback upon completion of therapy.

We launched our service in early June 2014, and had paying customers right away. The service has been growing steadily since. As of April 2015, our platform has seen many thousands of sessions booked with 150 of the best trained Chinese-speaking therapists both in China and around the world. Our clients, too, have a global profile, covering metropolitan cities to rural China, and from Chinese communities in Europe and the USA.

PSYCHOTHERAPY, CHINA, AND THE INTERNET AGE

Psychotherapy has a history of adapting to the times and reinventing itself. The Internet Age brought with it unique challenges and opportunities, and I could think of no better place than China to fully realise the potential of technology on psychotherapy. Because of its underdeveloped state, China could leap over generations of development and take advantage of the latest technology. Many of the innovations we are seeing only made sense in a context of building a system from scratch.

The Internet and, increasingly, the mobile Internet pose a different set of possibilities and challenges. The Internet is how people consume information and services, and inevitably it will affect how people learn about and choose psychotherapy, and mental healthcare services in general. Importing psychotherapy, with its rich tradition and well known professional set-ups, to a new medium poses a challenge. For example, we are constantly debating how much information about our therapists it is proper to reveal to potential clients, or even how payments should be processed, and if it would affect the dynamics between therapist and client. We are fortunate to have a rich network of therapists and advisers, whom we frequently turn to for advice.

As more therapists come online, I could see the establishment of a comprehensive database of the best-trained Chinese psychotherapists. We are particularly excited that such a database will be instrumental in creating industry standards for China, as well as opening up opportunities for research, such as evidence based psychotherapy. My hope is that what is happening in China will not only bring relief to the millions in need of psychotherapy, but will also offer insights and practices that the rest of the world will find valuable and inspiring.

BOOK REVIEWS

Introduction

José Saporta

I am honoured to participate in this inaugural issue of the *Journal of Psychoanalysis and Psychotherapy in China*. The goal of the book review section is to review a wide range of books relevant to psychoanalysis and psychotherapy in China. We hope also to include books about social forces and contemporary life China in order to better understand the cultural context that western psychoanalytic therapists enter and which impacts on Chinese patients and our Chinese colleagues. We will also include reports and reviews of conferences and even reviews of films relevant to China.

Our first book review section accomplishes many of these goals. I feel fortunate to have such distinguished reviewers. Dr Alf Gerlach, a psycho-analyst and social science PhD with extensive experience in training therapists in China, reviews a book from the social sciences, by Professor Shi-xu of the Centre for Contemporary Chinese Discourse studies, that is relevant to the interaction of western and Chinese cultures. Dr Almatea Usuelli is a careful student of the philosopher and Sinologist, Francois Jullien, and is the translator of Jullien's book on psychoanalysis and Chinese thought into Italian. Dr Usuelli reviews Christopher Bollas's book on psychoanalysis and Chinese thought and includes some dialogue with Jullien's similar ideas. From the USA, Dr Caroline Sehon reviews a book about contemporary life in China by Evan Osnos, a writer and reporter for the *New Yorker* in China and a long-time observer of life and politics in China. From China, Professor Yuan Qi reviews the collection of papers, *Psychoanalysis in China*, edited by David Scharff and Svere Varvin. Yuan Qi is a literature professor in China who has published a book about Shakespeare and Freud. Finally, Xing Xiaochun, a psychotherapist in China, reviews an international conference on Fairbairn and object relations theory.

I invite our readers and colleagues to submit reviews of books, conferences, and even films which they find interesting and potentially relevant to the development of psychoanalysis and psychotherapy in China.

Psychoanalysis and Psychotherapy in China, Volume 1, 2015: pp. 163–179.

China on the Mind,
by Christopher Bollas, Routledge, 2013, 158 pp.

Reviewed by Almatea Kluzer Usuelli

"Exporting" psychoanalysis to China is a controversial undertaking: some think it is impossible, considering cultural differences; others believe that it is possible and promising. Among the supporters of this undertaking—in addition to people who ignore or understate cultural differences—are those who stress the interesting analogy between psychoanalytical practice and Chinese thought. Psychoanalysis could even provide a meeting point between the east and the west. In his book, *China on the Mind,* Christopher Bollas argues for a fruitful meeting of psychoanalysis and Chinese thought. He goes as far as claiming that through the study of Chinese thought "I was also learning things about psychoanalysis that I had never understood".

Before beginning my analysis of Bollas's book, I would like to point to the fruitful convergence of ideas forwarded by Bollas, a psychoanalyst whose ideas stem from clinical work, and those elaborated by Francois Jullien. Jullien is not a psychoanalyst, but is a philosopher and a sinologist, and his arguments about psychoanalysis and Chinese thought are based on Freud's text. His essays "Cinq concepts proposés à la psychanalyse" refers to themes which—although underdeveloped in Freudian theory, as it is based on western thought—are, none the less, present and active in clinical work, and furthermore, represent openings to Chinese thought.

The similarities and differences in the approaches to these themes by these two authors makes their convergence and the analogies they present all the more interesting.

The first part of Bollas's book, entitled "Preconceptions", examines some of the main texts which form the basis of much of Chinese (and, therefore, Korean, Japanese, etc.) culture, and which the author calls "mother texts": the *Book of Changes* (*I Ching*), *Confucius Analects, The Book of Songs* (*Shi Jing*) and the *Book of Rites* (*Li Chi*). These ancient texts have a millenary history and have developed through the work of myriad commentators. Read through Bollas's eyes, these books become surprisingly familiar to us as psychoanalysts.

"Indeed, the hexagram (of I Ching)", the author states, "objectifies unconscious thought . . . So that anyone turning to the hexagram is contacting a culturally founded part of the human mind. This is rather like considering a dream: another mental event derived from the chance events of a single day". And again, "From a psychoanalytical perspective, to play I Ching is to enact the transient nature of our common lives". Moreover, the play allows the self the illusion of mastering what cannot be controlled.

The I Ching stress the value of the random nature of a moment, isolating it from the chain of cause and effect. The stress on the moment, the emphasis on the intense fleeting experience, is a characteristic trait of Asian thought, which favours that aspect in which fate and the single occurrence are harmoniously intertwined. In the western mind, fate fights against the single occurrence, which tragically opposes it.

Bollas goes on to examine the *Book of Songs*, another fundamental text, which "set(s) a thought form for the Eastern mind". Bollas considers poetry as "a home for the self", capable of communicating hidden meanings which elude censure. Unlike western epic poetry, Chinese poetry does not tell a story, it has no narrative content. Listening to poetry, for the Chinese, is thinking unthought known experiences, a dream-like experience which connects the individual self with the collective thought. The special role of poetry in Chinese culture is determined by the special way it is written: every sinogram is a world-thought that is open to meanings that branch off one another. Bollas notes that this special form of Chinese poetry, which presents itself—so to say—on its own, without the narrating voice of an author, bestows to it "another" reality, "strikingly similar to Freud's theory of unconscious thinking". Examining literature and noting the pre-eminence of the poetic form over the narrative form, Bollas comes "to the startling conclusion that the Eastern mind seems to have privileged unconscious thinking over conscious thought".

Similarly, Jullien writes, in the work previously mentioned, that the salient feature of Chinese poetry is its allusiveness, a concept Jullien develops extensively, and that allusiveness is also a characteristic of the analytical discourse, both in the patient's free associations and in the analyst's "unsaturated" words.

In his analysis of the *Book of Rites*, "literary boot camp for character formation", Bollas wonders to what extent this training and the adapting that it entails ends up by taking away spontaneity and naturalness from the true self, risking the encouragement of a false self. The dilemma between the individual and the collective seems to be resolved by means of a form of harmonious split. Bollas's ideas here build on Winnicott's notions of the false self as a form of protection for the true self.

In the second part his book ("Realisations"), Bollas sets out his personal reading of Dao (the Way), with a view to clarifying how Lao Tsu conceptualises the self which forms within the maternal order.

Indistinctness of beginnings, the true self in its pure state, the favouring of being over doing, the importance of the pre-verbal world, mother as a transforming object, silence as communication, would be "mystical moments" of psychoanalysis—all of which point to Dao in a way that Bollas calls "spiritual integration", which is realised through the personal idiom, or, rather, the expression of the unthought known.

While in the pre-oedipal period, the maternal order transmits modes of being to the newborn, Confucius addresses the oedipal self in order to bring it to Dao, the Way. His teachings, repeated over generations, have become axioms for humanity. This teaching underlines the value of the Rites as a means for structuring the self: the ritual becomes a kind of "environment mother" which contains and supports the self. Lao Tsu is concerned with the true self, Confucius with a presumed false self. These two philosophies combine the private and the social.

Here, the true self in the clinical setting, for Bollas, assumes an almost mystical character: in order to bring forward the true self, Bollas proposes, following Winnicott and Masud Khan, a vertiginous regression, all the way back to the formless, preferring silence to free associations, a proposition which would revolutionise psychoanalysis as a talking cure. This point raises a series of questions fundamental for psychoanalytic practice and theory. It seems to me that the emphasis that Bollas places on silence could be misunderstood. According to him, Winnicott did not do a lot of inter-pretations, but was a silent analyst—meditative, dreaming, and, thus, approaching the model of a Zen master.

Others, however, describe a very active analyst in Winnicott. Guntrip, for example, in describing his analysis with Winnicott, portrays an analyst ready to give deep and exhaustive interpretations as early as during the first session. It is true that Guntrip had come out of analysis with Fairbairn and that he was particularly active in the search for a solution to his own con-flicts. It is also true that the rhythm of sessions in the new analysis with Winnicott was two sessions a month for six years. But we still cannot fail to be surprised and awed by Winnicott's ability to enter so quickly into the heart of the problem and illuminate the scene with his interpretations.

The discrepancy between Bollas's Winnicott and Guntrip's makes us think of the "creative use of the object"—the creative use of the analyst by the patient—or, in other words, Winnicott's ability to be in tune with the patient's idiom.

The issue of silence also makes us think of the role of free associations. In Chapter 8, "Cultivation", Bollas describes the technique which Winnicott employs to overcome the false self and enter into contact with the true self. The point is not to interfere with the patient and to suspend the request for free associations, thus provoking "a state of formlessness". This highlights the rejection of the verbal aspect of the classic psychoana-lytic tradition. However, the search for the true self in its pure state should, in my opinion, be understood as a trend that the analyst is trying to encour-age, rather than a possible realisation. Furthermore, the false self has, in fact, a protective role in relation to the true self and it is active in negotia-tions with the external world—something that Bollas underlines in connec-tion with Confucius's teaching—and, as such, it cannot be eliminated.

Bollas likens the analysand's speech to a form of "meditative praxis"; "aimlessly, thoughtlessly, as in a dream . . . And in doing so he unknowingly speaks unconscious ideas . . . The theory of free association states that the unconscious speaks, not in the worded but in the spaces between units of utterance. . . . In the awareness of the voice of the absent, Freud's theory finds a remarkable link to the Eastern view of meaning within silence".

Here, too, Bollas's ideas about the analyst's and the analysand's speech resonate with Jullien's similar analysis of the fundamental rule of psycho-analysis, which forces the patient to "talk without saying". In the chapter dedicated to allusiveness, Jullien reminds us that Freud used to say to his patients to "tell" (*erzaehlen*) what "passes through his head" (*durch den Kopf geht*), without trying to "say" anything. This rule undermines the status of the subject, the famous subject of Cartesian "cogito". The thought that passes through the mind is a process that goes through the "I", which is removed from its role of a subject. The rule of free association forces the patient to give up logos—and reasoning—in order to start the treatment. Just like the Daoist word, the words of free associations (and we know how difficult it is to make it free!) is not meant to "say" something, but to let through; it is an allusion, and it is in its intervals, its silences, in what is not said that it is listened to.

The third part of *China on the Mind*—"Conceptualisations"—deals with the topic of group dynamics and individual psychology. This is an extremely interesting topic that raises numerous questions. "While the father plays a crucial role in the child's mental life", Bollas writes, "his destruction by the group . . . is important for any modern self's capacity to live within the real". According to the author, the group, by breaking the oedipal configuration, makes the self capable of living in the real, thereby promoting an evolutional stage in the life of the subject. This statement causes some confusion, though, in that Bollas writes a few lines later that in the group, the oedipal self becomes blinded by psychotic hatred.

But where, Bollas asks, does psychoanalysis place group dynamics that are not influenced by the system of paternal (oedipal) thought, but by "horizontal thought", which reveals the dark dimension and destructive-ness of human experience. This statement left me more confused. It seems to me problematic to maintain that group dynamics should elude the oedipal structure to access the real: perhaps it would be more appropriate to say that the destructive dimension which emerges in groups is inherent to regression to schizo-paranoid functioning, and not to a "horizontal thought system", a term which refers only to an absence of hierarchy and not to a regression of thought.

Bollas maintains that, while the west has based its sense of the self on the negative hallucination of the group and the illusion of safety (Winnicott), the east has opened the door to the coexistence of the individual and the collective. Chinese thought has, in fact, invested itself in the harmonising of the life of the individual self and that of the group. That was Confucius's lesson, passed on through generations. The aim of the extreme hierarchical formalisation of behaviour is the limitation of destructiveness which permeates life in groups. This suggests an early awareness in Chinese thought of the psychotic component and destructiveness of the group.

Western thought, on the other hand, has not displayed a similar concern. Stress has been placed on individual freedom and the autonomy of the subject, leaving in the shadow the obscure life of the group, with its potential destructiveness, without trying to establish a harmonious integration between forms of the self and life in community.

On the theoretical level, these ideas are very interesting and they may be interpreted, as the author suggests, as a remaking of the aims of psychoanalysis. Even the lightly suggested criticism of the western-style democratic system is worthy of the reader's attention. However, the appreciation of Mao's thought (action?) and his attempt to combine western Marxist ideology with Confucian tradition is not convincing. There have been numerous projects to create an ideal society in the west, too, but when they moved from the idea to realisation, all the attempts ended up in massacres and deaths. Mao was certainly no exception. Bollas's writing here is certainly fascinating, due to the wealth of cultural references and the vastness of the topics that he takes up. But it is precisely this vastness that risks becoming too diluted and not sufficiently supported with arguments when he moves away from psychoanalysis and touches on the topics related to sociology and politics.

Returning to the question of the relationship between individual life and life of the group, I believe that this is a crucial issue for psychoanalysis, with clear social consequences; the comparison of the two cultures can certainly help us by opening up new perspectives.

Psychoanalysis has clearly favoured the study of the development of the individual becoming the subject. In the oedipal phase, the "other" is implicated in an ambivalent and conflictual way. This conflict is, for psychoanalysis, at the heart of psychic life. In the regression produced by the group dynamics, the conflict becomes radicalised and reactivates primitive schizo-paranoid dynamics.

Is it right to ascribe these dynamics to the "Chinese mind"? It seems to me that the Oedipus myth, based on patricide, incest, and, at least, conflict prevailing over the paternal figure, ill fits the interpretation of a psychology which attributes major value to harmony and which has maintained, over a several millennia, a rigid hierarchical structure in a society which seems to us immobile. Certainly, we could imagine a formidable repression (or removal or split) of conflictual aggressiveness achieved through millenary rites engrained by Confucius's teaching. But it could also be that the "Chinese mind" has followed a different path of development.

In any event, the encounter with China offers us an extraordinary occasion to rethink our psychoanalysis. The reading of this book in fact raises many questions about our discipline, and this is without a doubt one of its merits.

In conclusion, the central point of the book is the analysis of the two cultures, seen as representative of two different sets of order, one western and paternal and the other eastern and maternal. Paternal order, developed by Freud, is the order of the word, interpretation, and oedipal organisation; the maternal order refers to preverbal development, being rather than doing, and implicit knowledge. These two orders, or mentalities, represent two different possibilities of thinking which can enrich one another through contact. Psychoanalysis, born of the Freudian paternal order, later extended by Winnicott, Kahn, Bion, and others to encompass the maternal order, would, according to Bollas, be capable of achieving a synthesis and building a bridge between western and Chinese cultures.

A Cultural Approach to Discourse,
by Shi-xu, Palgrave Macmillan, 2005, 233 pp.

Reviewed by Alf Gerlach

The book *A Cultural Approach to Discourse,* is published by the author as one of several works dealing with cultural representations of our world and the people living in it and with discourse as linguistic communication in social, cultural, political and historical contexts. Shi-xu has a personal background that allows him to write about these themes not only from a theoretical point of view, but also from direct experience in his exchange with western universities. He has been Research Fellow at the University of Amsterdam, Lecturer at the National University of Singapore, and Reader at the University of Ulster. Today he is professor at Zhejiang University in Hangzhou, where he is Director of the Institute of Discourse and Cultural Studies. He is founding Editor-in-Chief of *The Journal of Multicultural Discourses* (Routledge, UK) and author of several books in this field.

Shi-xu develops his cultural approach to discourse as an interrelated research system, as new ways of thinking and speaking which are motivated by explicit cultural politics. His aim is to overcome a totalising theory of discourse by stressing a cultural, post-colonial perspective. He prefers, rather than methods defined as universal, political–ethnographic studies that are designed to undermine culturally repressive discourses.

In the first two chapters, he outlines the theoretical framework of his new approach, discussing especially the relation between discourse and reality and between discourse and culture. He argues against the notion of linguistic communication as a mirror of reality and underlines "the capacity of language to create, maintain and transform reality" (p. 7). Here discourse "is conceived of as construction of meaning—representing and acting upon reality—through linguistic means in concrete situations" (p. 3). He criticises the situation that from his point of view research often does not pay enough attention to context, including that of the researcher, and to the role that language itself has in the constitution of knowledge and facts.

Shi-xu understands discourse as always, in any given moment, "infiltrated by culture". So he criticises universalism in discourse studies and argues and proposes an in-between cultural strategy. In Chapter 3, he discusses this way, to generate knowledge from in between cultures, as his new methodology. He offers that this methodology must be "deconstructive", subverting discourses of cultural imperialism and repression. As deconstructive strategies, he includes "Identify and characterize discourses of cultural imperialism", "Investigate and confront cultural imperialism in diverse modes and settings", "Uncover and undermine 'common sense'", "Expose and contradict hidden meanings, silences and inequalities". He then formulates "transformative" strategies, formulating and warranting new discourses of cultural cohesion and progress. Such transformative strategies are "Investigate and reclaim the voices and identities of the subaltern", "Create conditions and need for intercultural communication", "Create and advocate discourses of cultural cohesion and prosperity", "Cultivate the willpower to speak for cultural cohesion and progress". He proposes to experiment with these new designs of research and argumentation in scientific discourses.

After the first three chapters about theory and methodology Shi-xu turns to practical studies. Chapter 4 concerns the western popular discourses of its cultural "others", as often observed in western colonialist discourse, with handling stereotypes as its central strategy. Shi-xu explores mass-mediated western data, for example, Dutch travel literature on China or western media reports on the Hong Kong transition. He detects a discourse of contradiction as an apparatus of pleasure and prejudice with respect to cultural-other places that are constructed in the media. He expresses very clearly the dangerous results of such colonialist discourse:

> . . . the contradiction of the cultural Other is also strategically oriented to anxiety, discovery, surprise, puzzlement and such like. That is, the contradiction renders the unknown Other absurd, primitive or untrustworthy . . . It becomes only a short step then to the conclusion that the Other needs to be taught, corrected, governed, disciplined and, if it refuses, to be destroyed. (p. 107)

In Chapter 5, Shi-xu applies a non-western discourse in order to give the cultural "Other" a voice in the western discourse. He uses the example of the return of Hong Kong to China to show the difference between the notions of self, identity, and boundary in the western media and, in contrast, the concern with relationship-building in the Chinese media. As western readers, we are confronted with new, complex, and unfamiliar discourses that confront us with our own culture-bound discourse. Chapter 6 uses the method of a cultural approach to discourse for a deeper understanding of "troubled" communities, using media discourses in Northern Ireland over the past 100 years as example. Changes in collective identity become visible, from the discourse of a militant nationalism to a discourse of neighbours and even partners. Shi-xu underlines that the concept of identity is constructed through different symbolic modes, verbal and visual, and that it is a constituent element of discourse. It is often used for power struggle in social and cultural life, it can be created, claimed, denied, redescribed, or monopolised for control or resistance.

Finally, in Chapter 7, Shi-xu expresses his hope that cultural approach to discourse has a power to transform the ordinary as well as the academic world. He identifies the neglect of power and domination as fundamental theoretical and practical problems that can only be overcome by new communicative norms, new socially accepted ways of speaking.

In his arguments, Shi-xu stresses the importance of the culture that the researcher is bound to. He also speaks, together with Habermas (1972), about the human interests linked with all activities, including the social sciences, so that it is never possible to separate value from fact (p. 82). Although he underlines that "linguistic communication is characterized by human motivation and meaning creation" (p. 17), he does not refer to unconscious aspects of culture that may be common to all people living in a given culture. If we broaden his approach with the psychoanalytic concept of the unconscious, we could argue that all scientists and researchers are restricted by unconscious fears giving rise to professional defence strategies. In his book, *From Anxiety to Method in the Behavioural Sciences*, Devereux (1967) showed, with many examples of various sciences, that the relationship between observer and object is always influenced by the observer's countertransference. Methodology is then often used as sublimation or defence of unconscious anxieties. In his view, a continuous analysis of the countertransference must accompany all interpretations of scientific data. This would include the culture-bound prejudices expressed in communication Si-xu is dealing with.

In his new approach to forms of discourse, Shi-xu is also close to some psychoanalytic ideas about group identity and about tensions between groups that think and feel in a narcissistic, unidirectional way about their own group and the "Other". The subject of large-group identity has repeatedly been raised and elaborated upon in psychoanalytical discourse by Vamik Volkan (1999, 2002, 2004). Having developed this term, he has, above all, applied it to the examination of international relationships between nation states, communities of states, and ethnic groups, as Shi-xu proposes for his "in-between-cultural" stance (p. 43). In so doing, Volkan's interest focuses on the extent to which differing large-group identities affect international relationships, how they can lead to obstacles in bringing parties closer together who have hitherto been hostile to one another, and how targeted intervention can render these obstacles conscious and at least diminish the conceptions and fears unconsciously associated with them. In his argumentation, Volkan makes use of certain core concepts, which, in his opinion, most definitely relate to the subject of large-group identity and can be important in better understanding the associated phenomena. In his view, externalised images common to any one group act like a shared reservoir, a cultural reinforcement for non-integrated images of self and object. They transmit a deep feeling of belonging to one's own group, as opposed to a group-related need for enemies, a search for suitable targets that can be externalised, at the same time maintaining a principle of non-alikeness to another group. Psychoanalysts will, in particular, concentrate on the fears that can arise from an encounter with the alien—in this case to be understood as the supporting medium of one's own varying large-group identity. It is these fears that underlie the various psychosocial defence formations (Mentzos, 1976) and which can be understood as those aspects of the large-group identity such as described by Volkan. They do not develop from their very innermost, but from the outset are interwoven in a communicative context, in the encounter and confrontation with the Other, who does not seem to "be one of us".

Another perspective to bring into dialogue with Shi-xu's ideas about culture and discourse may be some ideas from ethno-psychoanalysis. Devereux (1978) expressed the idea that ethno-psychological work—and, let me add, any intercultural encounter—is rendered easier if we differentiate between an ethnic and an idiosyncratic unconscious. The ethnic unconscious is determined by processes of repression, typical for a culture, which start with the traumata typical for a certain ethnic group and affecting each individual member of this culture: "Each culture allows certain fantasies, drives and other psychic manifestations to access and remain at a conscious level and requires others to be repressed. This is why all members of one and the same culture have a number of unconscious conflicts in common" (Devereux, 1974, p. 11, translated from the German for this edition). By contrast, the idiosyncratic unconscious can only be understood in the light of the personal fate of the individual in his own culture. Both forms of the unconscious relate in complementarity to one another; just like individual sociological and psychoanalytical insights, they cannot substitute one another and neither can either of them be diminished to just one. It depends on the observer and his own particular interest as to which level can be rendered visible. However, the insights then acquired over varying paths of approach do form a "complementarist unit". For the insights gained by means of psychoanalysis, on the one hand, and those won from ethnological observation on the other, Devereux formulated as follows: "If all psychoanalysts were to compile a full list of all drives, wishes and fantasies that can be detected in the clinical sphere, they would, item for item, cover the list of all known cultural beliefs and modes of action as compiled by the ethnologist" (Devereux, 1978, p. 78, translated for this edition).

The ethnic unconscious is also expressed in the linguistic character of a particular culture, that is, in the manner in which contents can be presented in what kind of language and which affective modulations are attributed to what contents.

The formulation of Mentzos (1976) relating to the unconscious aim of culture-specific institutions is also equally applicable to language, as cultural and symbolic tradition: it is a matter of "institutionally anchored patterns of action and relations satisfying regressive libidinous needs, securing protection and modes of defence against unreal, fantasised, and infantile fears, depression, and feelings of shame and guilt that are not really founded" (p. 91, translated for this edition). The language of a particular society with its own categorisation of classes, circles, and regions provides each individual of this society with the possibilities of satisfying or suppressing libidinous desires in harmony with others of that society, or also to form like modes of defence.

The fact that a psychically important universal phenomenon does not emerge at a conscious, culture-related level calls for an analysis of the psychodynamic processes, above all of the fears responsible for the repression of this phenomenon in the respective culture. This is true for aspects of the respectively strange culture and for the repressed libidinous aspects of one's own culture that thus only become conscious and, hence, can appear "strange", so as to then trigger fear.

Our own attitudes are determined by a process of enculturation in a language and culture that, for each one of us, is linked with the universal narcissistic fantasy to the effect that "the true nature of one's own language and culture is the best, even the only possible one, in order to cope with and understand the complexity of life" (Cogoy, 2001, p. 356, translated for this edition). This is why we need to be incorporated so much into a large-group identity, which—as Volkan says—is to protect and preserve, by insisting on the non-likeness with the Other and keeping hold of the psychological boundary in respect of the Other. In this direction, Shi-xu's book is an important step to overcome such narcissistic fantasies and to open new possibilities in the encounter between western and eastern concepts, between psychoanalysis and cultural studies and between different approaches in psychoanalysis itself (Saporta, 2014).

REFERENCES

Cogoy, R. (2001). Fremdheit und interkulturelle Kommunikation in der Psychotherapie. *Psyche, 55*(S): 339–357.

Devereux, G. (1967). *From Anxiety to Method in the Behavioural Sciences.* Den Haag-Paris: Mouton.

Devereux, G. (1974). *Normal und anormal. Aufsätze zur allgemeinen Ethnopsychiatrie.* Frankfurt: Suhrkamp.

Devereux, G. (1978). *Ethnopsychoanalyse. Die komplementaristische Methode in den Wissenschaften vom Menschen.* Frankfurt: Suhrkamp.

Habermas, J. (1972). *Knowledge and Human Interests.* Cambridge: Polity Press.

Mentzos, S. (1976). *Interpersonale und institutionalisierte Abwehr.* Frankfurt: Fischer.

Saporta, J. (2014). Psychoanalysis meets China: transformative dialogue or monologue of the western voice. In: D. Scharff & S. Varvin (Eds.), *Psychoanalysis in China* (pp. 73–86). London: Karnac.

Volkan, V. (1999). *Das Versagen der Diplomatie. Zur Psychoanalyse nationaler, ethnischer und religiöser Konflikte.* Gießen: Psychosozial.

Volkan, V. (2002). Religiöser Fundamentalismus und Gewalt. In: A.-M. Schlösser & A. Gerlach (Eds.), *Gewalt und Zivilisation* (pp. 165–181). Gießen: Psychosozial.

Volkan, V. (2004). *Blind Trust: Large Groups and Their Leaders in Times of Crisis and Terror.* Charlottesville, VA: Pitchstone.

Psychoanalysis in China,
edited by David E. Scharff and Sverre Varvin, Karnac, 2014, pp. 329.

Reviewed by Yuan Qi

It has been over 100 years since the publication of *The Interpretation of Dreams* by Freud, which we may consider the symbol of the birth of psychoanalysis. The argument about psychoanalysis never stopped in western educational circles in the last century, but even among Freud's strongest opponents, no one can ignore the revolution he brought about in exploring the depths of the psychic world. As Peter Gay, the editor of *The Freud Reader*, pointed out in the preface of the book: "Freud is inescapable. It may be a commonplace by now that we all speak Freud whether we know it or not, but the commonplace remains both true and important".

Psychoanalysis first emerged in the western world, but its influence has reached far beyond the west. Actually, some modern Chinese intellectuals in the early twentieth century briefly explored psychoanalysis. They include: Lu Xun, Guo Moruo, Pan Guangdan, Zhu Guangqian, and especially, Gao Juefu, who from quite a long time ago started to study and translate Freud's books. But for a long time the influence of psychoanalysis in China was limited to the worlds of literature and art. It was seldom used as a treatment for psychological illness. This did not change until the 1980s. With China becoming more open to the world, western culture has become more popular in China, and so has Freud. Many of Freud's works have been translated into Chinese. Since 1997, more therapists have been trained to become professional psychoanalytic clinicians, following a series of China–Germany, China–America, and China-Norway training programmes. These programmes have played a crucial role in moving psychoanalysis from the arts and literature to the clinic.

Psychoanalysis in China, edited by David Scharff and Sverre Varvin, is a collection of thirty papers by thirty-five experts in psychoanalysis from China and abroad, among whom the point at issue is the discussion of the development of psychoanalysis in China in recent years. The articles touch on the acceptance and practicality of psychoanalysis in China, and the differences between Chinese and western culture in relation to psycho-analysis. This rich book also explores some concrete psychological prob-lems faced by the individual and by families in the historical transfor-mation of contemporary China from the perspective of psychoanalysis, and it contains both the summary of training experiences in psychoanaly-sis in China and the case studies of psychological treatment. The papers are broad based and emphasise four main topics: "Chinese culture and his-tory relevant to mental health", "The development of psychoanalysis and psychotherapy in China", "Developing training in China", "Marriage and marital relationships in China and Taiwan".

Many of the foreign experts in this book, including David Scharff, Sverre Varvin, Mette Halskov Hansen, Antje Haag, and Tomas Plaenkers, have years of experience both in psychoanalytic teaching, training, consulting, and treatment in China and dealing with many cases of psychological problems following the huge societal changes in modern China. Thus, they have a good understanding of Chinese traditional culture and its historical status, and they also sense that there exist many mental problems caused by the rapid development in China. Their discussions mainly focus on the challenges facing psychoanalysis from cultural differences, especially the myriad problems that stem from implementing psychotherapy in Chinese culture. The incredible value these experts bring is that they do not teach psychotherapy as dogma, however, but through dialogue they try to under-stand Chinese culture, traditions, and the complications arising from the changes in society, and explore the possibility of acceptance and utilisa-tion of psychoanalysis in China. Thus, they lay a solid foundation for the deep communication between eastern and western cultures, despite facing up to great challenges stemming from Chinese traditional culture and all kinds of complicated psychological problems deeply rooted in Chinese individuals and families.

This book also includes contributions by experts from mainland China and Taiwan, such as Yang Yunping, Li Ming, Zhong Jie, Lin Tao, Shi Qijia, Gao Jun, Chen Jue, Xu Yong, and Xiao Zeping. Most of them are graduates from China–Germany, China–Norway, China–America programmes, and some have advanced psychotherapy degrees from overseas. They have a much deeper understanding in dealing with psychological problems in China and in regard to the acceptance and utilisation of psychotherapy in China due to their systematic training and years of experience in teaching, consulting, and psychotherapy, as well as their involvement in the changes to Chinese culture. Their contributions, in contrast to those of western experts, focus more on whether or not psychoanalysis applies in the Chinese context and how it can be of help in solving the psychological problems among Chinese. Whether they discuss psychoanalysis from the perspective of Chinese traditional culture, which is characterised by Confucianism, Daoism, Buddhism, and Yin–Yang philosophy, or from the application of psychotherapy in the individual and in families in present-day China, these papers try, directly or indirectly, to lessen the misunderstanding of psychoanalysis, answer questions related to it, and clear up confusions caused by the differences of culture. All in all, these papers concur that rather than traditional Chinese culture becoming an obstacle to the Chinese accepting psychotherapy, it can contribute to the understanding of psychoanalysis by the Chinese, and that the ideas and methods of psychoanalysis can help the Chinese deal with their psychological problems.

Chinese culture's openness to and acceptance of, western culture is actually rooted in Chinese culture. The first ancient poem collection in China, *The Book of Songs,* states that "stones from other hills may serve to polish the jade of this one". Lu Xiangshan, a philosopher of the Song period, once said, "One sage from the east coast cherishing his own brilliant mind meets the other sage from the west coast cherishing his own brilliant mind; different minds can melt into one". Although here the east coast and the west coast do not refer to the orient and the occident, respectively, the wisdom embodied in it is significant to modern people. Just as Qian Zhongshu sums up, "The orient and the occident: the same mind in metaphysics". Of course, valuing the same mind does not mean neglecting the differences between eastern and western culture. There is an allusion as well in China: "An orange tree planted in Huainan will bear fruit like its own; if it is planted in Huaibei it will not bear fruit like its own". It tells us that without consideration of the differences in the soil, the sweet orange tree from elsewhere might bear astringent fruit when planted in the local place. Thus, everything should be considered in the context of its circumstances.

No doubt, exploring psychoanalysis in China can deepen our understanding of the richness and complexity of human minds. The path to the greatest benefit is to respect the cultural differences and create a fair and harmonious space for dialogue. Both foreign and Chinese authors have agreed on this in the book. As the editors, Scharff and Varvin, conclude in the epilogue,

> Perhaps every traveler eventually comes to know that venturing in foreign lands is a way to know new things about one's homeland. We gradually begin to recognize that things taken as universal are really only one point of view, one way of living our lives. Foreign things that seem incomprehensibly strange at first begin to offer a logic of their own that just might make as much sense as our own way of seeing and doing.

Cherishing such a common view, we believe that the foreign orange tree of psychoanalysis can bear "sweet oranges" in the vast land of China.

ACKNOWLEDGEMENT

Thanks to Chen Qiushi and Xu Qinchao for the translation of this article.

The Age of Ambition: Chasing Fortune, Truth, and Faith in the New China, by Evan Osnos, Farrar, Straus and Giroux, 2014, pp. 403.

Reviewed by Caroline Sehon

China continues to experience growing pains when it comes to its philosophical and social systems. As the country undergoes a massive clash of forces between authoritarianism and individuality, the people, who are undergoing sweeping changes of personal and national identity, are inevitably affected. Evan Osnos, a Pulitzer Prize-winning investigative reporter with *The New Yorker*, illustrates these changes in a series of in-depth personal narratives that combine a scholarly treatise and a riveting travel essay. This work is the extraordinary culmination of Osnos' reporting for *The Chicago Tribune* while living in China between 2005 and 2013. Osnos relates his research, derived from hundreds of in-depth interviews, personal experiences, and documentary analyses (news publications, court reports, and websites), with a candour that transports the reader to the far reaches of China, to meet ordinary citizens, whom he calls "strivers". Like them, Osnos himself is an unstoppable force when it comes to searching out the truth behind the stories. In many ways, the book is fundamentally about the study of the mind.

As psychoanalysts, we study the unconscious motivations, the identifications with our primary objects and significant others, and the intergenerational transmission of links to understand the life choices of individuals, couples, and families. In the Acknowledgments, Osnos stated that his grandparents (who were not alive long enough to read his book) are "responsible for its inception". His paternal and maternal grandparents were refugees from the Second World War. He says "they started over", which brought to mind Osnos' fascination with the Chinese, who are also remaking their lives. He reflected, "Those experiences lingered in our household memory, and I grew up wondering about the unrecorded experiences of life under authoritarianism".

Structured in three parts, respectively labelled "Fortune", "Truth", and "Faith", Osnos helps us to understand how the "Chinese Dream" of rejuvenation (fuxing, 复兴) and power (quan, 权) has moved from the third voice to the first voice, from national power and solidarity to self-actualisation. One of Osnos' primary interests lies in studying China's relationship to risk. A poignant illustration is an unnamed physician who was terrorised during the Cultural Revolution—exiled to the western desert where his wife committed suicide—and who describes his personal mind-set following the ordeal. He said,

> To survive in China, you must reveal nothing to others. Or it could be used against you . . . That's why I've come to think the deepest part of the self is best left unclear. Like mist and clouds in a Chinese landscape painting, hide the private part behind your social persona. Let your public self be like rice in a dinner: bland and inconspicuous, taking on the flavors of its surroundings while giving off no flavor of its own.

Osnos accounts for the newfound opportunities—fortune, truth, and faith—available to the Chinese today that they were previously denied by poverty and politics. Having obtained all three, the current generation now yearns for more, especially more information. Osnos states, "New technology has stirred a fugitive political culture; things once secret are now known; people once alone are now connected".

On the one hand, as the Internet's introduction has opened up the world to the Chinese, their internal landscape of possibilities has mushroomed. On the other hand, the legacy of past oppressive regimes continues to exert a palpable force of self-censorship. In fact, Osnos notes that Confucius offered advice about duty and justice with only one reference to emotion, qing, in his teachings. The pursuit of self-awareness, the tenet of psychotherapy and psychoanalysis, is still in flux in China. Psychoanalysis bears the stamp of western Viennese culture of the nineteenth century. Rather than simply an imported product from western societies, the Chinese are conceiving their own models of psychoanalysis in concert with their evolving concepts of self and ideas, amid a changing social unconscious.

After reading *Age of Ambition*, the many interesting characters that Osnos brings to life now inhabit my mind, such as the dissident artist Ai Weiwei, Internet blogger/racing car driver Han Han, and the lowly street sweeper/Internet poet sensation, Qi Xiangfu. It can be tempting for westerners to project our own ideas about the Chinese self, but that does an injustice to their unknown uniqueness. Just as the political and socio-economic horizons in China continue to change radically at every moment, the psychoanalytic vistas will experience a metamorphosis that may bear little resemblance to the Western version of psychoanalysis. Osnos tried to "describe Chinese lives on their own terms". Perhaps analysts ought to follow Osnos' example. For these reasons and more, *The Age of Ambition* is an absolute must-read.

EVENT REVIEW

Presentations, Thoughts, and Reflections on the International Conference "Ronald Fairbairn and the Object Relations Tradition"

Xing Xiaochun

Abstract

To celebrate the publication of *Ronald Fairbairn and the Object Relations Tradition*, cross-continental contributors gathered at the international conference held at the Anna Freud Centre, London. The presentations of such contributors as Norka Malberg, Viviane Green, David and Jill Scharff, Anne Alvarez, Valerie Sinason, and Rubén M. Basili are extracted and introduced to a Chinese audience in order to better understand the legacy of Fairbairn and the current debates on the development of object relations theory, as well as how his conceptions can shed light on contemporary clinical work. Furthermore, the author's own reflections on Fairbairn's ideas and their acceptance in China are followed by a clinical vignette interpreted through the insight derived from the conference.

Key words: Fairbairn, object relations, conference, reflections.

OVERVIEW OF THE CONFERENCE

Ronald Fairbairn was the father of object relations theory, who first proposed that the infant's need to seek objects was central to development. The newly published book, *Ronald Fairbairn and the Object Relations Tradition* (Clarke & Scharff, 2014), one of the series of "Lines of Development: Evolution of Theory and Practice over the Decades", published by Karnac, formed the focus of the international conference "Ronald Fairbairn and the Object Relations Tradition". The conference was held in the Anna Freud Centre in London, 7–9 March 2014. The conference was co-sponsored by the Freud Museum, London, the International Psychotherapy Institute, and Essex University.

During this fruitful weekend, dozens of contributors—psychoanalysts and other clinicians from the UK, Europe, Latin and North America, Australia and other parts of the world—gathered together to review the legacy of Fairbairn and to share its extension, further development, and practical application in clinical work in particular and in society in general.

The presentations and discussions covered such areas as theory, history, clinical practice, and the broader application of Fairbairn's ideas in the fields of religion, philosophy, art, politics, and social issues.

PRESENTATIONS, WITH SHARING OF CLINICAL EXPERIENCE

From Friday night to Sunday afternoon, nearly two dozen contributors shared their ideas on the legacy of Fairbairn and the evolution of object relations theory along with interesting clinical cases, discussions, and debates. Here, I summarise several of the presentations which I attended. Some of the contributors are also involved in psychotherapy training in China, such as Viviane Green, and David and Jill Scharff.

Norka Malberg: On being recognized

Dr Norka Malberg trained at the Anna Freud Centre and is Associate Clinical Professor at the Yale Child Study Center and President of Section II of Division 39, American Psychological Association. She is also co-editor of the book *The Anna Freud Tradition* (Malberg & Rafael-Leff, 2012), in the same series of "Lines of Development: Evolution of Theory and Practice over the Decades".

Dr Malberg illustrated how Fairbairn's theories inform clinical work through her presentation of the case of Jeremy, a twelve-year-old boy adopted by lesbian parents. Jeremy had a history of early trauma prior to his adoption, in the form of abuse and neglect. He attended a special school for children with emotional disturbances. At eight years old, he would still leave faeces on his leg after going to the bathroom. He began four times a week psychoanalytic treatment with Dr Malberg when he was ten.

Jeremy's behaviour in the consulting room, such as hiding under the table or in the cupboard and crawling like a baby, was understood as a desperate attempt to repair his early experience of neglect. Such regression can allow a sort of psychological rebirth. He projected familiar exciting and rejecting objects on to the therapist. The therapist used her internal experience to further understand the libidinal and anti-libidinal objects that Jeremy remained attached to. By exploring Jeremy's fantasies and her own countertransference, Dr Malberg was able to recognise Jeremy's relational needs, resulting in psychological progress and some integration. Jeremy was better able to recognise his therapist as a real person, beyond being only the container of his projections.

Viviane Green: Internal objects: fantasy, experience, and history intersecting?

Dr Viviane Green is an adult and child and adolescent psychoanalytic psychotherapist in London, and a lecturer. She conducts training programmes in Beijing, China on mentalization in children and adolescents. Her paper integrated perspectives from attachment theory, mentalization, intersubjectivity, and neuroscience as a developmental perspective for the analytic exploration of internal objects and their relationships to fantasy, history, and experience. By describing a seven-year-old child's fantasy of dolphin babies living inside a prince's head, expressing both an oedipal scenario and the experience of the child's brain dysfunction, which was a kind of trauma, Dr Green illustrated a developmental view on different ways of internalising objects. Biology and fantasy contributed to the child's development and related unconscious meanings.

David Scharff: Internal objects and external experience

Chair of the Board of the International Psychotherapy Institute based at Washington, DC, Dr David Scharff also co-edited several books on Fairbairn, including: *From Instinct to Self: Selected Writings of W. R.D. Fairbairn* (Scharff & Birtles, 1995) and co-edited the book which formed the basis of this conference (Clarke & Scharff, 2014). He and his wife, Dr Jill Scharff, have been extensively involved in psychotherapy training in China.

Dr Scharff elaborated the central idea of Fairbairn's model of the self. During development, the child's experience of the outside world organises his or her internal world. Dr Scharff discussed the context within which Fairbairn developed his ideas—how Fairbairn expanded Freud's discovery of internalisation of objects. It is not the drives *per se* but the drives within relationships that organise development. Dr Scharff illustrated through diagrams Fairbairn's theory of the breakdown of the self, explicating the resultant parts of the self. Dr Scharff developed his own addition to Fairbairn's original diagram, which stimulated much interest and debate. He explained, by using this diagram, how, for some patients, love is impossible. For these persons, the possibility of love and being loved is under attack internally due to the dynamic of the anti-libidinal object (internal saboteur) attacking the exciting object. In general, Fairbairn's concept of self is a dynamic, open system, formed through the relationship between the self and its objects, influenced by the external world and influencing reciprocally the nature of external relationships. Attachment theory, neuroscience, and Bion's concept of containment also contribute to understanding the reciprocal shaping between the internal objects and external experience.

Jill Scharff: Fairbairn's clinical theory

Dr Jill Scharff is the Co-founder of International Psychotherapy Institute and Clinical Professor of Psychiatry, Georgetown University, as well as the co-editor (with David Scharff) of the book *The Legacy of Fairbairn and*

Sutherland: Therapeutic Application (Scharff & Scharff, 2005). She and Dr David Scharff conduct training programmes on couple therapy based on object relations theory in Beijing, China.

Dr Jill Scharff described the influence of Fairbairn's theory and the influence of the person of Fairbairn on her learning and current practice of individual, couple, and group psychotherapy. Speaking, as it were, to different parts of the self, psychotherapy can help people with the capacity to interact with the outer world and learn from experience. Dr Jill Scharff used clinical examples to elaborate Fairbairn's notion of the "internal saboteur", which persecutes the libidinal ego. The internal saboteur is a kind of representation of self-destructive actions, attacking the need for pleasure, satisfaction, self-confidence, and the capacity for love. The internal saboteur may also attack external objects. This was illustrated in a clinical case from a couple's therapy. Mora, a forty-two-year-old woman, suffered from depression and fragility. She imagined her husband's penis as a knife and she dissociated and blacked out during sexual intercourse. Her father had been violent and abusive and her mother acted as an exciting and rejecting object. Eric, her husband, had a mother who had been raped as a teenager. She gave Eric, who was the result of that rape, up for adoption. As a result, he found a traumatised woman, Mora, to attend to and love. The couple came to therapy with the images and expectations that Eric was to care for a mother and Mora needed a man unlike her father. After several months of couple therapy, they were able to better enjoy their sexual life. However, when approaching termination, they abruptly stopped their sexual therapy. From this transference, it can be seen that the internal saboteur attacked pleasure. The saboteur in the marriage came from Mora's violent father and Eric's rejecting biological mother. Projections of these internalised objects from the couple on to the therapist were heightened during termination.

Anne Alvarez:
Paranoid-schizoid position, or paranoid and schizoid position?

Anne Alvarez is a consultant child and adolescent psychotherapist, and author of *Live Company: Psychoanalytic Psychotherapy with Autistic, Borderline, Deprived and Abused Children* (Alvarez, 1992).

Dr Alvarez shared her experience of treating neglected, autistic, and deprived children. She presented the notion that an interesting or engaging object, rather than a bad object or a love object, is sometimes crucial for these patients. She elaborated a brilliant clinical moment for an autistic young adult, Robby, when she and Robby encountered each other at the front door. Robby, his eyes lighting up, said he wanted to be the shiny doorknob. The therapist adapted her technique to this encounter and felt connected to Robby through his eyes lighting up at the moment of their greeting.

Valerie Sinason: Abuse, trauma, and multiplicity

Working as a consultant psychotherapist at the Tavistock Clinic for twenty years, specialising in abuse and intellectual disability, Dr Valerie Sinason is the Director of the Clinic for Dissociative Studies. She edited the book *Attachment, Trauma and Multiplicity: Working with Dissociative Identity Disorder* (Sinason, 2011).

Dr Sinason used three clinical examples to illustrate Fairbairn's theories on trauma, dissociation, and the moral defence. The first example illustrated the moral defence. Mary, a ten-year-old with an intellectual disability, was referred for masturbating in the classroom. In the therapy sessions she would masturbate, offering her body to the therapist with a big smile, and calling herself, "Dirty Mary". Dr Sinason used a doll she called "Lucy" to further explore this with Mary. In the play with Lucy, the analytic pair took turns exchanging the roles of self and other. Mary treated Lucy, who was assigned to have, as Mary did, Down's syndrome, as her own girl. She said "No" to abusive behaviour towards Lucy and shocked Dr Sinason with the power of her response. Mary then stated, "I'm going to wash 'Dirty Lucy'", and she took the doll to the sink and gently washed her. It seems that Mary washed herself psychologically to embrace a "Clean, Happy Mary". Dr Sinason explained that children with intellectual disabilities have feelings and fantasies of their situation and origins. She argued that they have the emotional capacity for deep understanding. Fairbairn would say that Mary saw herself as bad in order to feel some control over having Down's syndrome. This was a vivid example of Fairbairn's idea and of clinical interaction.

Rubén M. Basili: Emptiness pathology

Dr Rubén Mario Basili is a training and supervising analyst of the Argentine Psychoanalytic Association (APA) and Founding Member and Coordinator of Espacio Fairbairn of APA.

Dr Basili presented his work on emptiness pathology as a pre-oedipal pathology in patients with borderline personality organisation. He pointed out that this form of psychopathology can be recognised and diagnosed in the transference and countertransference. Emptiness is used as a defence against separation–abandonment anxieties by keeping object loss unconscious. In the transference, the analyst is experienced as the part-object with a quality of emptiness—an empty breast/mother. He also quoted some words from his patients that described their feelings in intimate relations that felt empty. These patients feel empty to avoid feeling abandoned or becoming psychotic. When the fear or experience of abandonment becomes conscious, emptiness disappears. Emptiness is not only a defence, but also a claim, a transference that seeks help from the analyst to fill the patient. Dr Basili used his patient's words to illustrate the clinical importance of fantasies related to emptiness.

PERSONAL REFLECTIONS ON, AND CLINICAL APPLICATIONS OF, FAIRBAIRN'S THEORIES

Upon registering for the conference, I wanted to prepare myself to better understand the topics under discussion, especially relating to Fairbairn. I could find few resources in China—several articles by using key words that included Fairbairn, and half of a book dedicated to Fairbairn (Xu & Wang, 2010). On reflecting on what was the fruit I derived from this conference, and in reviewing my training experience, including Chinese–German Training Course in Psychoanalytic Psychotherapy, I realised that the legacy of Fairbairn is underestimated in China. Fairbairn's contribution has been less emphasised. This conference enlarged my view through presentations, discussions, debates, and talking with overseas colleagues so that my current clinical practice still draws on what I learnt about Fairbairn's ideas. I will present a brief vignette from China in which I applied Fairbairn's concept of internal saboteur and which also corresponds to Dr Basili's formulations on emptiness in order to show how what I learnt from the conference can match the clinical situation while working with a Chinese patient.

Case vignette

Miss Y was in her early thirties with borderline personality organisation, and also suffered from depression. Whenever a boyfriend proposed marriage, she would postpone the decision and suspend the relationship. Boyfriends would stop contacting her after many efforts to continue the relationship and often found someone else to marry. Miss Y would then feel abandoned. In a recent relationship, she went through the conventional ceremony of a feast, but not a formal, registered marriage. She then became pregnant and had an abortion.

Miss Y's sister, who is five years younger, was given up for adoption after birth, and came back to the family when she was a teenager. When the patient had a younger brother at the age of six, her father suffered severe illness. Her mother had to go away to earn a living, and Miss Y would see her only during Spring Festival each year. Miss Y was left to her grandparents and her sick father. Her father became violent and abusive towards her. In treatment, Miss Y would often mention her sense of emptiness. She said, "My whole inner part is filled with my mother, without anything from myself. I am empty." Whenever she felt threatened with abandonment by a boyfriend, she would suffer severe headaches and would fear becoming psychotic. She had a pervasive sense of emptiness during periods when she had no romantic partner. I understand her sense of emptiness to be a defence against the more painful feelings of separation–abandonment, as described by Dr Rubén Basili.

The internal saboteur for Miss Y was born of her violent, abusive father and her rejecting mother. She identified with her experience of a rejecting mother, and she would project this rejecting image on her boyfriends, and she enacted this by pushing them to leave her. In the third year of treatment, she was able to have some awareness of her wish to destroy our work when she complained of not making the progress she had expected. In the transference and countertransference, one can see the internal saboteur attacking the treatment.

Last, but not least, I was much impressed by the way Fairbairn's reach was expanded by this multi-disciplinary gathering of contributors, which also raised my awareness of how psychoanalysis can be influential in the wider society and in furthering our understanding of human nature. I hope that this kind of debate on contemporary and historical topics in psychoanalysis can be extended to China, where psychoanalytically orientated approaches are being increasingly accepted and embraced as helpful in meeting the urgent needs for mental health approaches in the context of pervasive rapid development and social change.

REFERENCES

Alvarez, A. (1992). *Live Company: Psychoanalytic Psychotherapy with Autistic, Borderline, Deprived and Abused Children.* London: Routledge.

Clarke, G., & Scharff, D. E. (Eds.) (2014). *Fairbairn and the Object Relations Tradition: Lines of Development—Evolution of Theory and Practice over the Decades.* London: Karnac.

Malberg, N. T., & Rafael-Leff, J. (2012). *The Anna Freud Tradition: Lines of Development—Evolution of Theory and Practice over the Decades.* London: Karnac.

Scharff, D. E., & Birtles, E. F. (1994). *From Instinct to Self: Selected Papers of W. R. D. Fairbairn.* Northvale, NJ: Jason Aronson.

Scharff, J. S., & Scharff, D. E. (2005). *The Legacy of Fairbairn and Sutherland: Psychotherapeutic Applications.* London: Routledge.

Sinason, V. (Ed.) (2011). *Attachment, Trauma, and Multiplicity: Working with Dissociative Identity Disorder.* New York: Routledge.

Xu, P. P., & Wang, Y. P. (2010). *The Object Relations Theory of Independent Group: Researches on Fairbairn and Balint.* Fuzhou: Fujian Education Press.

NOTES ON CONTRIBUTORS

Lycia Alexander-Guerra, MD, is a psychoanalyst in private practice in Tampa, Florida and the president of the independent contemporary training programme at the Tampa Bay Institute for Psychoanalytic Studies. She has volunteered for several years as an instructor and supervisor for the China–American Psychoanalytic Alliance. Email: lyciaa@gmail.com.

Cai Chenghou, PhD, is a Member, International Association for Analytical Psychology; Member, International Society for Sandplay Therapy; Clinical Psychologist, Chinese Psychological Society; Faculty, Guangdong University of Finance & Economics and The Research Center for Psychology of the Heart. Email: chcpsy@hotmail.com.

Irmgard Dettbarn, PhD, is a psychologist and has a private practice in psychoanalysis in Berlin. She is a member of the German Psychoanalytical Association and of the IPA, and has been Interim Training Analyst in Beijing since 2007. Former President of the Berliner Berufsverband Psychologischer Psychoanalytiker (BBPP), she has been a lecturer at Karl-Abraham-Institut-Berlin, a child and adult analyst in Zürich, a lecturer at the Université de Nancy in France, a clinical psychologist at the Shalvata Mental Health Center, Tel Aviv University, a lecturer at Kindergartenteacherseminar, Berlin, and a secondary school teacher in Berlin. Her special interest is in ethnopsychoanalysis, which she pursues in field studies in a nomad society, the Himba Tribe of Kaokoland, Namibia. Email: irmgard.dettbarn@googlemail.com.

Alf Gerlach, MD, is a sociologist and training analyst, Mainz (DPV) and Saarbruecken (DPG) psychoanalytic institutes, chair of the German Society for Psychoanalysis, Psychotherapy, Psychosomatics and Depth Psychology (DGPT) 2001–2003. He is President of the German–Chinese Academy for Psychotherapy, Member of the China Committee, International Psychoanalytic Association, and Head of the Psychoanalytic Psychotherapy Training Program, Shanghai Mental Health Center. Email: alf.gerlach@pulsaar.com.

Gao Jun, PhD, is assistant professor in the Department of Psychology, School of Social Development and Public Policy in Fudan University and a licensed psychotherapist of the Chinese Psychological Society. She has published thirty-one papers in peer-reviewed domestic and international journals, and has translated five books on psychology. Email: gaojun82@fudan.edu.cn.

Huang Hsuan-Ying is a post-doctoral fellow at the Australian Centre on China in the World, Australian National University. He received his PhD in medical anthropology from Harvard University. Prior to his career as an anthropologist, he received medical education and psychiatric residency training at National Taiwan University. He also received fellowship training in psychoanalytic psychotherapy at the Boston Psychoanalytic Institute. His research examines the rise of Western-style psychotherapy in urban China as both a popular movement and a mental health profession. Email: wozzeck.huang@gmail.com.

Almatea Kluzer Usuelli, MD, Psychiatrist and psychoanalyst, Member, Italian Psychoanalytical Society (Milan) and International Psychoanalytical Association. Italian translator of F. Jullien's book: *Cinque concetti proposti alla Psicoanalisi*, La Scuola, 2014. Articles: L'Idea platonica e la <malattia d'idealità> *Riv. Psicoanal.*, 2012,1. Commentary on Jullien's book: "L'invenzione dell'ideale e il destino dell'Europa ovvero <Platone letto dalla Cina>". Matteo Ricci and the meeting of Chinese and Western cultures, presented at IPASIA Congress, Beijing, 2010. Commentary on Winnicott Roundtable, 2008, in *Psychoanalytic Perspectives*, Vol. 5(2), "The significance of illusion in the work of Freud and Winnicott: a controversial issue", 1992, Vol. 19, *The International Review of Psycho-Analysis*. Email: almateausuelli@hotmail.com.

Li Hongya is Associate Professor of Psychology at Henan University of Urban Planning, where she is also the director of the university's mental health counselling centre. Ms Li has over fifteen years of experience as a psychotherapist, with research interests in the mental health of college students. Email care of: info@jiandanxinli.com.

Li Zhen is founder and CEO of MyTherapist. She also has a private psychotherapy practice based in Beijing. Prior to founding the company, she was a psychotherapist and lecturer at the Central University of Finance and Economics in Beijing, China. Ms Li has a Master's degree in Cognitive Neuropsychology from University College London. MyTherapist (in Chinese: 简单心理) www.jiandanxinli.com, is a venture-backed mobile Internet platform that connects psychotherapists and clients. Email: info@jiandanxinli.com.

Adrienne Margarian is a doctoral candidate at Deakin University with a keen interest the emergence of psychotherapy practices in China and Hong Kong. She is a trained Psychologist and Psychodynamic Psychotherapist with a private practice in Sydney, Australia. Email: alm11@bigpond.net.au.

Yuan Qi, PhD, is an associate professor at the School of Liberal Arts of Yangzhou University, and adjunct research fellow of SJTU Center for Life Writing, specialising in Western literary criticism and life writing studies. His recent book is *Dialogue with Freud and Shakespeare: Norman Holland's New Psychoanalytic Criticism* (Social Sciences Academic Press, 2014). Email: yuanqi69@163.com.

Shi Qijia, MD, is Clinical Professor of Neurology & Psychiatry, and Director of the Institute for Mental Health of Wuhan, at the Wuhan Mental Health Centre. He served as President of the Mental Health Association of Hubei Province and Chinese President of German–Chinese Academy for Psychotherapy. Email: qjshi-psy@163.com.

José Saporta is on the faculty of the Advanced Psychotherapy Training Program of the Boston Psychoanalytic Society and Institute and on the faculty of the Center for Psychodynamic Treatment and Research, Massachusetts General Hospital, Harvard Medical School. Email: jsaportajr@aol.com.

David E. Scharff, MD, is the Editor, *Psychoanalysis and Psychotherapy in China*; Co-Founder, former Director, and Chair of the Board, The International Psychotherapy Institute; Chair, The IPA's Working Group on Family and Couple Psychoanalysis; Director, Continuous Training Program in Couple and Family Psychoanalytic Therapy, Beijing; author and editor of more than 30 books, including most recently *Psychoanalysis in China* (with Sverre Varvin) and *Psychoanalytic Couple Therapy* (with Jill Scharff.) Email: davidscharff@theipi.org.

Jill Savege Scharff, MD, is Co-Founder and former Co-Director, the International Psychotherapy Institute (IPI); Founding Chair, the International Institute for Psychoanalytic Training at IPI; Clinical Professor, Georgetown University; Teaching Analyst, Washington Center for Psychoanalysis; Author and editor of many books, including recently, *Psychoanalytic Couple Therapy* (with David Scharff), and *Psychoanalysis Online* and *Psychoanalysis Online 2* both of which explore the impact of technology on development and the effectiveness of distance psychoanalysis and psychotherapy in the age of the internet. Email: jillscharff@theipi.org.

Caroline M. Sehon, MD, is Chair of the Washington DC Center of the International Psychotherapy Institute (IPI-Metro), a teaching analyst at the International Institute for Psychoanalytic Training at IPI, and a clinical associate professor of psychiatry, Georgetown University, DC. Dr Sehon maintains a private clinical and training practice in Bethesda, Maryland. Email: carolinesehon@gmail.com.

Lin Tao, MD, is the first qualified psychoanalyst of the IPA's training programme in China, a Direct Member of IPA, Member of the IPA China Committee, the IPA Working Group on Couple and Family Psychoanalysis, and member of the board of the China Psychoanalytic Association. In the UK, he is a qualified couple psychoanalytic psychotherapist and Member of the British Society of Couple Psychotherapists and Counsellors, a Member of the British Psychoanalytic Council, a visiting psychotherapist at the Tavistock Centre for Couple Relationships, and Guest Member of the British Psychoanalytical Society. Email: taolhl@126.com.

Marta Tibaldi is a Jungian analyst of the Associazione Italiana di Psicologia Analitica (AIPA) and of the international Association for Analytical Psychology (IAAP). She is a training analyst and supervisor in Rome, Hong Kong, and Taipei (Taiwan), a training supervisor of the C. G. Jung Institute, Zurich and the liaison person of the IAAP Developing Group in Hong Kong. Author of many articles and essays, she published *Oltre il cancro. Trasformare creativamente la malattia che temiamo di più* (Rome, Moretti & Vitali, 2010), and *Pratica dell'immaginazione attiva* (Rome, La Lepre, 2011), in translation in Mandarin. She is the author of the blog "C. G. Jung's analytical psychology between Italy and China" (http://martatibaldi.blogspot.com) Email: martatbld@gmail.com.

Richard Wu: Psychiatrist, FRANZCP, MBBS; Principal, Archway Practice, Sydney, Australia; Member of section of Psychotherapy, Royal Australian and New Zealand College of Psychiatrists; Member of Australian–Chinese Painters Association. Email: drwur1@gmail.com.

Xing Xiaochun, GM and psychodynamically orientated counsellor at Nanjing Caring Mind Counselling Centre, China and GM, translator and interpreter at Nanjing Archi-Translation Service Centre, China. Her recent translations include the book *Change in Psychotherapy: A Unifying Paradigm* by The Boston Change Process Study Group (2010). Email: jane_xing@126.com.

Xu Yong, MD, is Deputy Director of Department of Training and Education, Shanghai Mental Health Centre, Board Member of Psychoanalytic Committee of Chinese Mental Health Association, and Board Member of International Association of Group Psychotherapy and Group Processes. Email: suiyueran600@gmail.com.

LIST OF REVIEWERS

The Editorial Board wishes to thank those colleagues who have reviewed submissions for this issue. The quality of the issue has been enhanced by their thoughtful and generous reviews.

Patrizio Campanile
Irmgard Dettbarn
Lana Fishkin
Ralph Fishkin
Gao Jun
Alf Gerlach
Huang Hsuan-Ying
Li Ming
Lin Tao
Peter Loewenberg
Clara Nemas
Tomas Plaenkers
Jill Savege Scharff
Caroline Sehon
Warren Sibilla
Elise Snyder
Francis Thomson-Salo
Tong Jun
Sverre Varvin
Wang Qian
Janine Wanlass
Anders Zachrisson

INSTRUCTIONS TO CONTRIBUTORS

Procedure for submissions: Manuscripts should be typewritten, using double spacing. Submissions should be made electronically using Microsoft Word 97–2003 or later, and identified with the title of the file.

All contributions should be addressed to the Editor at davidscharff@theipi.org or descharff@gmail.com, and copied to angelamoorman@theipi.org. Direct subsequent correspondence to angelamoorman@theipi.org.

Submissions of full papers should be normally no more than 6,000–8,000 words in length, with exceptions by agreement with the editor. They should comprise two separate files, to assist in the editorial review process. One should include the paper, together with its title, a list of keywords, a list of references, and an abstract. The other should include a cover page for the paper with its title, the author's name and contact details, and a brief biographical summary of up to 150 words.

Languages: Contributions may be written in either English or Chinese. Authors may choose to use British English or American English, as the copy-editor will standardise the form. When contributions are submitted in Chinese, if accepted for publication, they will be translated into English at journal expense. All contributions will be published in both languages.

Abstracts: All papers must be accompanied by an abstract of up to 200 words in length. All submissions must have an abstract in English. Those submissions in Chinese should have abstracts both in Chinese and English. Footnotes and endnotes will only be accepted under exceptional circumstances. Please incorporate all footnotes into the body of the text, or omit them if they are extraneous.

References should be compiled using the format employed by Phoenix Publishing House. Further details can be found at www.firingthemind.com. (Go to "Journals" and then to "Psychoanalysis and Psychotherapy in China". Click on any icon listed and scroll down to the "Instructions to contributors" section.)

Author's Declaration: Authors are asked to complete and send with their manuscript an Author's Declaration confirming confidentiality, originality, and copyright. A copy of this Declaration can be downloaded from www.firingthemind.com in the same section as detailed above for References.

Confidentiality and consent: Contributors are expected to use all possible means of assuring the confidentiality of those about whom they write, such as by disguising significant aspects of the case material. Alternatively, authors should acquire their subjects' consent. In general terms, contributors are required to follow the procedure adopted in their own countries which govern the conduct of their work with human or animal subjects. If requiring further advice, authors are invited to discuss these matters with a member of the Journal's International Advisory Board in their country or with the Editor. If clinical material is included in your submission (which we encourage) please submit a brief note indicating to the Editor how confidentiality has been protected, or alternatively, that you have patients' permission to publish.

Originality: Papers submitted for publication should not have been published elsewhere or be currently submitted to other publications.

Peer Review: All papers will be subject to peer review. In order to preserve anonymity in the review process, authors should supply the Editor with two separate documents, as detailed above.

Copy Dates: While the Editor will welcome contributions at any time, authors should note that final copy dates for forthcoming issues will normally be on 1st June and 1st of December of each year.

Editorial Procedure: Contributors will receive a prompt acknowledgement of the receipt of their submissions. Following the process of peer review the Editor will decide either (i) to accept or reject or (ii) to accept, subject to modification. The Editor's decision will be final.

Editing and Publication: If accepted, manuscripts will be copy-edited and returned to the author for editorial enquiries and proofreading. Please be prepared to collaborate with deliberate speed in this process in order to ensure timely publication. The use of the management system "Scholar One"™ for manuscript tracking, editing, and production is planned and pending.